Bruised and Broken

Bruised and Broken

Understanding and Healing
Psychological Problems

Paul D. Meier, M.D.,
Frank B. Minirth, M.D.,
and
Donald E. Ratcliff

BAKER BOOK HOUSE
Grand Rapids, Michigan 49516

Library of Congress Cataloging-in-Publication Data

Meier, Paul D.
    Bruised and broken: understanding and healing psychological problems /
Paul D. Meier, Frank B. Minirth, and Donald E. Ratcliff.
        p. cm.
    Includes bibliographical references (p.   ) and index.
    ISBN 0-8010-6292-6
    1. Mental illness. 2. Psychotherapy—Religious aspects—Christianity. I. Minirth,
Frank B. II. Ratcliff. Donald. III. Title.
    RC460.M43 1992
    616.89—dc20   926988

Contents

Preface   7

1. What Is Abnormal?   11
2. What Causes Psychological Problems?   21
3. Depression and Extreme Moods   33
4. Problems with Stress and Adjustment   63
5. Anxiety Disorders   73
6. Psychosis   93
7. Physical Problems   105
8. Addictions and Impulse Control   117
9. Sexual Problems   133
10. Child and Adolescent Disorders   143
11. Personality Disorders   159
12. Healing and Preventing Problems   199

   Appendixes
      A: Personality Types in Marriage   227
      B: Medications Used in Therapy   235
   Bibliography   243
   Index   247

Preface

This world's getting bounced. All it is is animals, more than human creatures. No wonder God's having this world come to an end faster every day. But it was the same way when Christ was on this earth. And I'm gonna [do] the same thing for God [as] his holy son did. I don't have to be afraid [to] take my last breath. My home's above.

As I heard these words from the somewhat obese woman, I thought of how her comments sounded like those of some Old Testament prophets. Some of her theology I could certainly agree with. But I was not sitting in church, listening to a prophet giving a message from God. I was listening to a woman with schizophrenia in the ward of a state hospital.

How could it happen? At one time she lived a normal life; she was married with three children. Then one day something happened. The records do not tell what it was. Perhaps a parent died, a severe accident occurred, or chemicals interacted in the brain. The woman began to receive ideas and commands from strange voices. Because of her bizarre behavior she was admitted to this hospital where now—about thirty years later—she was telling me about the end of the world.

I visited her routinely and found that her moods varied from agitation and anger to extreme depression to joy and enthusiasm. What

7

did not change were the almost verbatim repetitions about the end of the world, the struggle between an evil spirit and God, and her role as a prophetess. Efforts to engage her in a discussion about anything else were fruitless.

This individual's problem, schizophrenia, is considered by many to be the most extreme psychological difficulty possible. She represents the "broken" person in the title of this book. A full interview with her is detailed in chapter 6. Other psychological problems are nearly as extreme, but most of us are more familiar with those who have less extreme problems, the "bruised."

Late one evening a friend of my wife knocked on our door. After her tears subsided she began to tell us of regular periods of deep depression when everything seemed hopeless and pointless. Her boss, a well-meaning Christian, had told her she just needed to pray more and purpose not to get depressed again. She began crying again. "Everything is so ugly, I've even thought about suicide."

With counseling and medication she soon improved. At last report her moods have remained relatively stable for several years, and her life is whole again. Healing came for her emotional bruises.

A local doctor (an internal specialist) recently commented that 80 percent of the patients who come through his office door report physical problems that really do not exist. Such difficulties are the products of an imagination—an imagination bruised by unhealthy experiences and relationships. This problem is considered in chapter 7, while difficulties with stress, anxiety, addiction, and sexuality are discussed in other chapters.

Bruised and broken. To some extent this describes everyone in a broken and bruised world. In this book, however, we will examine people who have emotional bruises and brokenness that require professional attention. Good Christian counselors who are skilled in both psychological techniques and spiritual insight have much to offer such individuals. This book is not intended to take the place of counseling, but rather it can supplement it, and also help the families and friends of those with psychological disturbances. The book may prove useful to pastors, students, and others who have a general interest in the dynamics of abnormality. Finally, it may help those who think they may have a problem to determine if they should seek professional help. It is our prayer that, by surveying the psychological problems people can have, many will be helped to overcome bruises and brokenness and better understand others.

Donald E. Ratcliff
Toccoa Falls (Ga.) College

For general information about Minirth-Meier Clinic office locations, counseling services, educational resources, and hospital programs, call (toll-free) 1-800-545-1819.

The national headquarters of the Minirth-Meier Clinic is at 2100 North Collins Boulevard, Richardson, Texas 75080. Telephone numbers are (214) 669-1733 and 1-800-229-3000.

Clinics are located in Austin, Belton, Fort Worth, Houston, Sherman, Longview, San Antonio, and Waco, Texas; Albuquerque, New Mexico; Wheaton, Illinois; Little Rock, Arkansas; Springfield, Missouri; Arlington, Virginia; Seattle, Washington; Denver, Colorado, and Gardena, Laguna Hills, Newport Beach, Orange, Palm Springs, Roseville, and Santa Anna in California.

1

What Is Abnormal?

Many people in modern society suffer from psychological problems. Researchers with the National Institute of Mental Health estimate that nearly one-third of all Americans will have some form of mental illness in their lifetimes, and nearly 15 percent suffer with a major mental problem at any given time (Regier, et al. 1988, 877–986).

We would like to think Christians are immune to psychological problems. With all the spiritual resources available to believers, why should they have mental problems? A number of answers will be considered in chapter 2. The fact is that Christians and nonbelievers alike experience a wide variety of psychological difficulties.

As we examine the multitude of potential mental problems, our emphasis will be to gain a Christian view of them. A Christian perspective of abnormality includes two aspects: obtaining a Christian understanding of the problem biblically and theologically, and seeing how a Christian framework can be used in overcoming or coping with the problem.

What are psychological problems?

Not everyone who has psychological problems is in a mental hospital; the large majority are able to live in the outside world. Most people consider themselves to have problems, and often these are psychological. When do these problems become severe enough to require the use of special counseling?

The American Psychiatric Association publishes a standard classification of mental problems, called the *Diagnostic and Statistical Manual of Mental Disorders* (Spitzer 1987), which is now in a revised third edition. While this is usually termed the *DSM III-R*, throughout this book we will use the shorter designation *DSM*. This new *DSM* divides mental problems into basic categories based upon symptoms, instead of by etiology (factors related to problem development) or by recommended approaches through therapy. Psychologists and psychiatrists from around the world have pooled their knowledge to develop the *DSM* system. Further, the system facilitates communication because its terminology is almost universally accepted. Christians can certainly use the *DSM* system, just as they have used other advances of modern science.

The *DSM* often emphasizes that psychological problems become disorders when they significantly interfere with one's occupational or social life. For example, a fear of heights is less of a problem for someone who works in sewers than for a high-rise building contractor. However, the *DSM* admits that there are no precise boundaries between disorders and normality. Two key aspects emphasized by the DSM are, first, that the pattern of behavior is clinically significant and, second, that it causes considerable distress to the individual or others. Obviously, both of these can be rather subjective judgments, made on the basis of the counselor's training and experience.

In classifying mental disorders, one must realize that psychological phenomena are considered disorders only when they have passed a point on an imaginary spectrum that places them clearly beyond normal limits. Every individual fits somewhere on those spectra: Most are not far enough along the line to be called "abnormal." We all have some anxiety. Most people have some obsessive-compulsive personality traits, but few would be classified as having a compulsive personality disorder. After the age of thirty we all lose thousands of brain cells every day; yet very few are classified as having an organic brain syndrome. The fact that a relatively fine line divides normality from abnormality should be kept in mind throughout this book.

Some psychologists and psychiatrists think that all such categories should be done away with. Some argue that labels are inherently destructive; others that emotional problems should be categorized only according to degree of irresponsibility. Certainly labels can be dangerous and should be used with extreme caution. To throw out all systems of classification would not be sensible, however, because we automatically organize information in our minds into categories. Eliminating one system would merely mean shifting to a different one. For example, to label people according to degrees of irresponsibility would produce a new system of classification.

Christian psychologist Gary Collins, in his book, *Fractured Personalities* (1972), states that three criteria are useful in assessing the behavior of an individual as abnormal. Abnormality may exist if: (1) behavior is at odds with the social expectations of the society in which the individual lives; (2) the individual experiences internal conflicts that lead to intense and prolonged feelings of insecurity, anxiety, or unhappiness, and (3) an individual is troubled by conscious or unconscious alienation from God (Collins 1972, 10–12).

Sometimes abnormal behavior is determined by the cultural norm or by comparison to other individuals within the culture. One may define abnormal behavior as *any behavior that is maladaptive or harmful to the individual or to society at large*. Sometimes abnormal behavior is traceable directly to biological factors, but beliefs may also cause trouble. The basic assumptions people make about God, themselves, and the world they live in contribute to their conscious and unconscious beliefs. Conflicting desires or erroneous views developed during childhood can lead individuals to experience stress and can affect their responses to such an extent that a psychological disorder is produced. Several kinds of emotional problems, including guilt, poor self-image, excessive grief, and depression, can grow from an inadequate belief system. Mental illness may result if a person's actions run counter to that individual's own beliefs. To a large degree, inner tension is due to an individual's failure to adjust properly to environmental pressures and stress, both past and present.

Specific categories of problems

The most recent *DSM* divides psychological problems into nineteen categories. Some of these categories include problems that are more medical than psychological, such as "rumination disorder of infancy" (persistent vomiting in babies). The emphasis upon medical aspects of problems reflects the fact that the *DSM* was developed primarily by psychiatrists, who are medical doctors with additional psychiatric training. The *DSM* also includes a number of problems that technically are not mental disorders, but which may require counseling. These include marital problems, parent-child problems, occupational problems, and uncomplicated grief from the death of a loved one.

Because some of the *DSM* categories are not psychological disorders, and also to simplify the organization of this book, we will consider psychological problems within nine general categories. These represent the spectrum of mental disturbances people may have, at least according to present understandings.

Depression and extreme moods

When the emotions change in a drastic manner, a mood disorder is likely. *Depression* is a major problem, perhaps the most common psychological disorder of all. Sometimes moods can change from extreme elation and high activity to lethargy and feelings of worthlessness. These major swings in one's feelings may also constitute a mood disorder. Depression and other mood disorders will be considered in chapter 3.

Stress and adjustment problems

Modern society is filled with stresses of all kinds. *Extreme stresses* can result in an inability to adjust to the everyday demands of life. This is most likely when a major catastrophe has occurred, such as an earthquake or traumatic war experiences. For some, the death of a parent or spouse can result in many years of maladjustment far beyond the normal time needed for grieving. These kinds of problems are described in chapter 4.

Anxiety disorders

Anxiety refers to unusual degrees of worry and apprehension. Perhaps the most common anxiety disorder is the phobia, an extreme illogical fear of some object, place, or person (or sometimes a group of people). Some experience episodes of extreme anxiety without any known cause. Intense anxiety may result in repeated and often unwelcome thoughts, called *obsessions*, or repeated actions, called *compulsions*. Multiple personality is also related to anxiety. Chapter 5 considers anxiety disorders in depth.

Psychosis

Some of the most extreme problems people have are called *psychotic disorders*. The loss of contact with reality reflected in schizophrenia characterizes all the psychotic disorders. Delusions (such irrational beliefs as thinking someone is trying to poison them) and hallucinations often characterize psychotic individuals. Psychosis is the focus of chapter 6.

Physical problems

Sometimes stresses and other psychological difficulties create such *physical problems* as ulcers and high blood pressure. While not all such physical problems are the result of psychological factors, some are. On the other hand, physical problems can also produce psychological difficulties. Some people suffer from brain or glandular problems with psychological consequences. These disorders will be considered in chapter 7. Physical symptoms that result from imagination rather than organic difficulties are covered in chapter 5.

Addiction

With the increased availability of drugs and alcohol in modern society, addiction and drug dependence are increasing problems. Addiction often involves the apparent inability to control the impulse to drink or take drugs. *Impulse control disorders* are considered in chapter 8.

Sexual problems

Many kinds of sexual difficulties are possible. These include *sexual dysfunctions*, such as lack of desire or premature ejaculation; and *paraphilias*, such as *voyeurism* (the "peeping Tom"), and *pedophilia* (child molesting). Chapter 9 surveys the sexual disorders.

Child and adolescent disorders

The largest single section of the *DSM* considers problems that characteristically begin prior to adulthood. Many of these continue to be a great concern throughout life, but they generally surface early. *Mental retardation, stuttering,* and *hyperactivity* are three disorders in this broad category, considered in chapter 10.

Personality disorders

Nearly any disorder is likely to affect the individual's personality. Some disorders, however, particularly originate in personality. These include extreme dependence upon others, avoidance of people, or consistent disregard for others' rights. The *personality disorders* can be considered extremes of more normal traits, so we discuss personality tendencies as well as the actual disorders in chapter 11.

Misconceptions about abnormality

Those who know little about psychological problems often hold seriously mistaken ideas. Even Christians reject or fear psychologically disturbed people, falling short of the example of Christ, who accepted those most rejected by others.

Collins identifies six common misconceptions about abnormality (1972, 78–82). One is the assumption that psychological problems result only from personal sin. But, as Collins notes, if this were true, every person who commits a specific sin should have a particular disorder. This is obviously not the case. Clearly there are many possible causes for psychological problems. Only one of those possibilities is guilt resulting from personal sin.

A second misconception is that abnormality is disgraceful. Collins notes that people with heart problems are much more likely to be accepted than those with mental disturbances. Occasionally families will attempt to conceal those with problems and feel shame if hospitalization becomes necessary. Employers, neighbors, and even church members may distance themselves from someone released from a mental hospital. This attitude is, fortunately, not as common as it once was. Most people come to realize that everyone faces stress and has a breaking point. Counseling and psychiatric hospitalization carry less stigma than in the past.

King Solomon said that "For lack of guidance a nation falls, but many advisors make victory sure" (Prov. 11:14). It is common to poke fun at the idea of "seeing a shrink." Such ridicule is often a product of naïveté and defensiveness. Guidance from a knowledgeable Christian pastor or professional counselor can help bring about victory over life's seemingly overwhelming stresses. To obtain and apply good Christian psychotherapy to one's life is synonymous with discipleship. God brings many people toward Christlikeness in their attitudes and behavior through loving and insightful friends, pastors, counselors, and psychiatrists. One should never be ashamed to obtain counseling when going through life's stresses.

A third misconception, says Collins, is that abnormality is always incomprehensible and weird. Mental hospitals are sometimes considered places where only "crazy" people reside. While some seriously disturbed people may be completely out of touch with reality, most are aware of what happens and are able to discuss their difficulties. Furthermore, normal people differ from the disturbed only by degree; everyone can get depressed, fearful, or have unusual thoughts. Those with mental disorders are simply more extreme in these respects.

Fourth, some believe that genius is similar to mental disability. While both of these are differences from normality and some highly intelligent people have psychological problems, research indicates that most gifted individuals have *less* mental disturbance than normal.

A fifth misconception cited by Collins is that there is no cure for mental illness. Prior to the 1950s some severe problems, such as schizophrenia, were "treated" by admission to an institution for life. Since that time, however, new medications and forms of therapy offer hope for even the most seriously disturbed. Many have been released from mental hospitals, significantly improved. While some kinds of problems resist treatment, most people who receive early and adequate treatment can be helped a great deal.

A sixth misconception is that the incidence of abnormality is increasing. More people now obtain counseling and hospital treatment for psychological problems, but that means people have changed their attitudes about abnormality, realizing it is better to get help than to hide problems. It is difficult to conclude whether abnormality is decreasing or increasing.

The history of abnormality

Psychological problems have existed throughout human history. Cain had antisocial personality traits, King Saul was paranoid, and King Nebuchadnezzar experienced a psychotic break with reality.

How did the earliest people treat mental disturbance? Archaeological evidence indicates that early people often chipped a hole in the skull of the afflicted, perhaps thinking that would allow evil spirits to escape. One of the earliest descriptions of mental disturbance is found in Deuteronomy 28:28, 34, in the context of punishment for disobedience to God: "The Lord will afflict you with madness, blindness, and confusion of mind. . . . The sights you see will drive you mad." Elsewhere in the Bible, mental disturbance is clearly not the result of sin, but this passage underscores the fact that sin *can* result in psychological problems.

Well over a thousand years before Christ the ancient Egyptians recognized that the brain was related to psychological problems, but while medications were sometimes suggested, most treatment used incantations to cure the mentally ill.

The Greeks took a more medical view of abnormality under the leadership of Hippocrates. This famous physician used clinical observation and recommended rest and tranquillity as potential sources of help. Unfortunately, Hippocrates had some rather serious misunderstandings of abnormality, thinking that bleeding a person might help and believing that hysteria in women was due to a "wandering uterus."

Christ was well aware of psychological problems, and he took time to heal those who were afflicted. Often these were supernatural healings, but some healings may have been psychological. Certainly he carefully listened to people and recognized underlying causes for outward disturbances. Jesus is a superb example for today's Christian counselors (McKenna 1977).

While superstition abounded during the Middle Ages, one must not overlook the positive role played by many of the clergy from A.D. 500 to 1500. Some monasteries served as respites for the mentally ill, who were given prayer and spiritual counsel. In the twelfth century the colony of Gheel in Belgium served as a treatment center for the insane. Treatment consisted of laying on hands, prayer, and kindness. This precursor to the modern halfway house had few restrictions except that alcohol was forbidden. Gheel continues today.

During the Middle Ages plagues claimed the lives of thousands. Some wondered if disease was God's punishment for sins. In an attempt to avoid death from plague the flagellant movement began. People whipped themselves to atone for their sins, an example of the pathological extremes to which people can go in an attempt to deal with the guilt that would have been more productively dealt with by the forgiveness of Christ.

From the 1400s to the 1700s many came to believe that mental problems resulted from demon possession. They theorized that torture could free an individual of demons, and that witchcraft caused abnormality. The pattern of torture and death revived in this century when Adolph Hitler emptied German institutions and filled gas chambers with the mentally ill. The euthanasia movement feeds on similar conceptions.

While conservative Christians regard demonic influence as real, they understand that death and torture lie completely opposite the biblical solution to the problem. Following the example of Christ, a demon possessed person needs to be delivered though the loving care and authority of God's servants. Yet it must be recognized that most psychological problems are *not* the result of demon possession. For a Christian perspective on demon possession, see Meier, et al. 1991, 259–61.

During the 1500s *asylums* for the mentally ill developed. These were often little more than prisons where those with severe problems were treated like animals. With little attention to cleanliness or proper treatment and no personal concern for residents, attendants used strait jackets, plunges into cold water, bleeding, inducing vomiting, and other forms of torture.

William Tuke, a Quaker, helped to bring people away from the superstitions of the Middle Ages. In 1796 he built a humanitarian institution for the insane in England called "Retreat at York." Much as at Gheel, he concentrated upon making the Retreat a quiet haven where guests were treated with dignity. He pioneered a sort of occupational therapy, teaching the value of work and learning skills. Those with psychological problems made agreements with those in charge to control themselves, the predecessor of psychological contracting.

Group discussions emphasized positive self-esteem; only violent or inconsiderate individuals were restrained. Many admitted to the Retreat greatly improved.

In the United States, *moral treatment* became a popular movement in the 1800s, largely borrowing ideas from Tuke. The doctor wielded absolute power, the forerunner of today's directive therapy. Those who submitted to treatment were honored; those who disobeyed were punished with solitary confinement, straitjackets, or less to eat. The idea of rewards and punishments continues in behavioral therapy. Those who led the moral treatment approach assumed that those with problems were normal people who had abnormal numbers of problems, an assumption many modern psychologists affirm. Seventy percent were discharged as recovered or improved in these early treatment programs.

Unfortunately, large, impersonal institutions became more popular in the late 1800s, and personal care less common. Overcrowded mental institutions lacked any concern for the individual residing there and became places where the unwanted were dumped and forgotten. Not until the 1960s and 1970s did the general population become aware of the deplorable conditions in many of these institutions, often through media exposés.

In the 1970s and 1980s a *deinstitutionalization* movement emptied the institutions by moving former residents into the community. Some halfway houses and group homes have not always been a great improvement over institutions. Some long-term mentally ill simply have been discharged to join the ranks of the homeless.

On the more positive side, community mental health clinics provide counseling and care for those with psychological problems. With the advent of modern psychoactive medications, many can now live a fairly normal life with only occasional visits to the clinic. A number of hospitals have developed wings or separate floors for those who need intensive treatment for their problems. More Christian mental hospitals now exist to offer spiritual and psychological help on an inpatient basis. We will return to the topic of hospitalization in chapter 12.

2

What Causes Psychological Problems?

People have psychological difficulties for many reasons. Each kind of psychological problem likely relates to a particular kind of situation. A fear of snakes, for example, is more likely if the individual has had painful or unpleasant experiences with the reptiles. Such experiences are extremely unlikely to produce schizophrenia.

It is a bit misleading to use the term *cause* to describe influences upon abnormal behavior. A cause-and-effect relationship tends to be considered an automatic process without exceptions. Human behavior is not that predictable. With certain kinds of backgrounds and past influences, we can say that a particular problem is *more likely* to develop, but not that it is inevitable. Often more people do *not* develop a given disorder from a supposed "cause." But because

21

there is a greater likelihood of psychological problems, the influence may be considered important. A given influence may contribute to any of several possible problems, depending upon the individual's personality, situation, and other factors. Sometimes cause simply cannot be determined. Human behavior is not the automatic result of past experiences but is a complex combination of influences, personality, and free will.

What tends to produce abnormal behavior?

While the specific influences related to individual psychological problems will be considered category by category in subsequent chapters, here we look at the more general influences. These influences fall into three categories: (1) the genetic background of the individual; (2) the past environment of the individual; (3) some kind of precipitating stress in the present situation.

Genetic factors

Publicity given to modern genetic research has produced some popular distortions. Some people blame everything on their "bad genes," including such sins as alcoholism and homosexuality. The genetic data have to be slanted considerably in order to grasp for such straws. Although our genetic makeup does have an enormous effect on our intellectual and emotional potential, our degree of wisdom and happiness as adults is *not* predetermined genetically. Consider people who suffer from depression, for example. Most human depression is the result of our own irresponsible handling of anger and guilt. Some individuals are irresponsible because they choose to be; others are irresponsible because they lack knowledge. One purpose of this book is to help readers grow in knowledge of how to handle their own emotions responsibly and how to put that knowledge to work.

Most human beings, however, hate to face up to their own responsibility, especially with regard to their emotional state. It is much easier to blame one's woes on bad parents, a poor mate, unfair treatment by the world, hypoglycemia, or—in today's world—"bad genes." Genes can predispose an individual toward all kinds of negative thought patterns and behaviors, but the genes do not magically force the person to give in to them. Some form of irresponsible action causes the problem.

From a Christian point of view, the genetic potential and predispositions of each individual lie within the plan of God. God allows each individual to have certain strengths and weaknesses as part of his plan ultimately to bring glory to himself. Psalm 139:13–14 and Isaiah 43:7 describe God's power and purpose in creating us. One can recognize that God chose not to make us perfect but instead made us so that we might trust the God of all wisdom, love, and justice to make the correct ultimate decisions. To be angry at God for not being more "humane" is arrogant and pompous. People who claim that God "makes mistakes" and who think that they are wiser and kinder than God are naïve. We see the pain of a moment, but God looks at the joys of an eternity. Sensitive human beings empathize with the pain of another's psychological problem. Since Christ suffered the painful death of the cross, God not only empathizes with emotional pain; he rejoices in the growth toward wholeness of any individual responsibly working his or her way out of difficulties.

Some of the genetic data on one type of mental disorder, depression, can be summarized:

1. Women clearly are more prone to depression than are men. Genetic factors may contribute to that predisposition, but sociocultural factors must also be considered.
2. Relatives of depressed individuals have a significantly higher incidence of depression than individuals in the general population. In fact, for all *mood disorders*, the risk among parents, siblings, and offspring exceeds that among the general population.
3. Studies of twins have influenced many scientists to suspect that a genetic predisposition toward depression exists in some individuals.
4. Manic-depressive illness is a relatively infrequent disorder which, in contrast to most depressions, is considered largely genetic. It is marked by severe swings of mood from elation

(usually with rapid, incessant speech) to severe depression with suicidal thoughts.

Obviously, even though people tend to overemphasize "bad genes" to avoid facing up to their own behavioral and emotional irresponsibilities as causes of their depression, we should be aware of genetic predispositions toward depression.

Heredity also may predispose toward a potential weakness in cases of schizophrenia. Schizophrenia occurs in only about 1 percent of the general population (Locke and Regier 1985, 1–6), but 28 percent of the children of parents who are schizophrenic become psychotic (Kringlen 1978, 9–24). Siblings and nonidentical twins of schizophrenics have a 9 percent concordance rate. In identical twins the concordance rate is 42 percent, whether the twins are raised together or apart (Gottesman and Shields 1972).

Early environmental factors

There is a wealth of data regarding the role of early environmental factors on mental health—and mental illness. For example, children raised by overly strict, harsh parents are more likely to have a problem with perfectionism and depression. Children raised with no discipline are more likely to lack a conscience. Children raised in a home with a faulty value system tend to adopt that value system themselves. Children raised in a church in which teaching stresses a conditional acceptance by God are likely to wrestle with doubts about their salvation and to feel insecure in their relation to God. Those from homes in which the parents divorced when the children were young tend toward depression, anxiety, and insecurity. Among children from homes in which the father and mother struggle for leadership, we expect to see more problems as the children become adults. A child from a home in which the father is overly passive and the mother overly dominant more likely shows delinquent or other problem behavior later in life. A child who does not receive enough love early in life is more prone to depression as an adult. If a little girl receives a lack of attention or inappropriate attention from her father, she is more likely to develop a histrionic personality.

Research into both genetic factors and early environmental factors produces statistical probabilities rather than absolute certainties. Undoubtedly early environmental factors contribute to mental disorders, but, again, those factors do not excuse irresponsible behavior. Through Christ, individuals can learn to overcome the most difficult early environmental factors.

Precipitating stresses

Genetic predisposition to a particular psychological problem, early environmental factors, or both combine with some present situation to initiate a disorder. The precipitating stress may be thought of as the "straw that breaks the camel's back." Often, when someone comes to a counselor for help, they describe the precipitating stress as the entire problem. Indeed it may very well appear to be the case to the troubled person. They were fairly normal before the crisis and developed problems afterward.

A wise counselor, however, realizes that only rarely does a single event alone create a psychological problem. Another influence sufficiently weakened the individual's ability to cope with the stressful situation, and thus a combination is responsible for the disorder. If the counselor only deals with the precipitating stress, the problem is likely to resurface, or another problem take its place, when a new stressful situation arises. Good mental health involves the ability to cope with new stressful situations without becoming disordered. Some kinds of problems indeed may be only surface-level, but most psychological difficulties involve deeper hidden aspects that relate to early environment or genetic influences.

The death of a parent or spouse may initiate a psychological disorder. People go through normal grieving in such situations but generally recover within a year or two. Delayed recovery or psychosis during the period of grief suggests abnormality that requires in-depth counseling. Normal grieving also may be helped by supportive counseling, but intense psychotherapy generally is not necessary. Other examples of precipitating stresses include losing a job, divorce, natural catastrophe, a physical or emotional attack or abuse, or an automobile accident. Any one of these, in combination with genetic or environmental influences, can cause a psychological problem.

Seldom are precipitating stresses the result of personal sin. (While one might conclude that the sin condition lies at the heart of all abnormality, and while the fall of humankind in the Garden of Eden has resulted in death and imperfection of all kinds, this is a far cry from blaming an individual's psychological problems on his or her sins). On the other hand, sin can at times contribute to precipitating stress. How many of its stresses did Israel bring on itself? Wise King David prayed, "Search me, O God, and know my heart; test me and know my anxious thoughts. See if there is any offensive way in me, and lead me in the way everlasting" (Ps. 139:23–24). God referred to his people who "have eyes but are blind" (Isa. 43:8). All human beings have blind spots. We are the primary source of our own unhappiness. When we grow in God's wisdom and gain insights into our own self-deceit, happiness results.

Other factors contribute to psychological problems, yet do not fit neatly into the three categories. For example, drug reactions or a serious fall can cause brain damage resulting in psychological problems. This might be considered either environmental influence or precipitating stress. Oxygen deprivation at birth might result in mental retardation. In most cases, however, some combination of genetic weakness or environmental difficulty combines with precipitating stress to produce the problem (see fig. 1).

We estimate that 85 percent of significant depressions are precipitated by life stresses, and acutely stressful situations precede most suicide attempts. A precipitating stress is thus more easily identified than genetic and early environmental factors. Spiritual factors may be difficult to identify, yet can be inherent in any of those causes. And in Christ spiritual factors can overcome any problem.

Why do Christians have problems?

More than two decades ago Gary Collins suggested six reasons why Christians develop psychological disorders (Collins 1969, 56–61).

1. Correcting sin

While not all mental problems result from sin, this can certainly be one reason for such difficulties. A Christian who deliberately sins,

figure 1
How Problems Develop

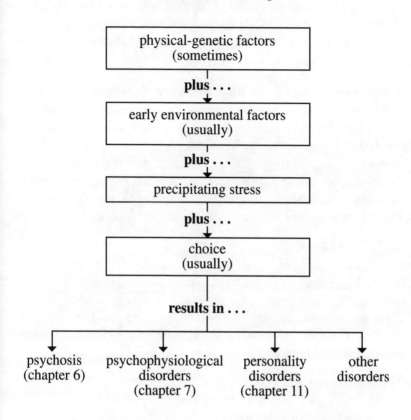

neglects the study of the Bible and prayer, or develops habits contrary to the Bible may require correction. God may correct by allowing psychological abnormalities. Rejecting or ignoring God, whether or not one is a Christian, is a serious mistake.

2. Developing virtue

Disorders show Christians their continuing dependence upon God or some other virtue such as humility or patience. Collins suggests that God may allow disorders so that others may grow spiritually by caring for the person with problems.

3. Following God rather than propriety

Abnormality may simply result from fellowship with God. Some of the things the Old Testament prophets did would be considered highly abnormal in today's society, but they chose to obey God rather than men. At Pentecost the disciples were thought to be drunk because of their unusual actions.

4. Standing apart from an abnormal culture

An entire culture can be mentally sick in some respects. One extreme example was the mass suicide in Guyana by followers of Jim Jones in November 1976. Genuine Christians do not blindly conform to their culture, but are prepared to stand apart from it at the risk of being labeled "abnormal." Collins cites Erich Fromm's comment that "the fact that millions of people share the same vices does not make these vices virtues."

5. Personal trauma

Christians experience early problems in the family or emotional trauma like everyone else. They have tremendous resources at their disposal, but this does not erase early influences. There may be a disproportionate number of Christians with mental illness because a disproportionate number of the mentally ill realize their needs and so are attracted to faith and its hope.

6. Organic causes

Christians are not immune from physical problems, such as brain tumors or brain injuries. Because we are Christians does not mean our bodies function any differently.

Other causes

Elsewhere (pp. 33–44, 73–91), Collins notes that religion can also be sick and so foster psychological problems. One thinks of extreme forms of Christianity which communicate a lack of acceptance by God in spite of genuine repentance.

A reason not mentioned by Collins involves the tendency of many Christians to be overly introspective, perhaps because of a continual emphasis upon the self. Occasional self-checks for sin and wrong motives can be healthy, but not preoccupation with the self. In contrast to excessive introspection, James 1:27 encourages a balance between the needs of others and self-analysis: "Religion that God our Father accepts as pure and faultless is this: to look after orphans and widows in their distress and to keep oneself from being polluted by the world."

There are no easy answers as to why Christians have certain psychological problems. We must be willing to admit we do not understand God's ways, because his plan is bigger than our understanding. Sometimes we must be content to suffer with those who suffer, as did Christ, rather than to hide behind theological jargon and pat answers. Ecclesiastes reminds us that, from our limited perspective, things sometimes look bleak and hopeless. We must trust God, affirming his will, yet realize we do not have all the answers for why God allows problems.

Making a diagnosis

Sometimes such influences are used in determining the specific *diagnosis* of a person's problem. The process of determining the person's problem results from a careful evaluation, called *assessment*, of behavior, feelings, thinking, and context. As noted above, one of the difficulties in making an adequate diagnosis is that the problem presented initially may not be the basic problem. Sometimes it is only the precipitating stress situation, overlooking relevant past influences. Some people will test a counselor with a minor problem to see how he or she deals with it before they reveal the main problem. This is unfortunate, because they delay and can misdirect a needed assessment.

A physical evaluation is one aspect of the assessment procedure. Physical problems can have psychological consequences. For example, brain tumors and other brain disorders can produce depression or other psychological disturbances. Glandular problems can likewise have psychological results. Physical examination and tests may help the psychologist or psychiatrist rule out a physical problem.

Psychological tests are sometimes used for assessment as well. Among the most common tools in this area, the personality profile, includes a large number of questions to answer. Often counselors do not give all of the test results to their clients because the results are only clues to what problems *may* exist, not a definite diagnosis. A client who hears all of the results may not realize that tests make mistakes and may unconsciously begin to develop some of the problems the test predicted.

Most counselors use an interview to evaluate the person in counseling. Counselors listen to what is described, noting the tone of voice and body language. Counselors sometimes ask questions about the family and past experiences to gain a better understanding of the person, as well as to look for likely psychological problems. Counselors observe whether the person opens up easily or defensively avoids discussing problems. Occasionally counselors provide the client with a problem checklist so that all potentially related difficulties can be quickly located.

To some extent the interview and other aspects of the assessment are influenced by the theories and techniques used by the counselor. Most counselors draw from a number of theories and related methods of counseling. Thus the evaluation is an attempt to find a pattern that fits one of the approaches, as well as finding a cluster of behaviors that becomes a diagnosis.

The disorder may defy precise diagnosis. There are seven levels of certainty:

1. *Diagnosis with no reservations.* The counselor feels certain of the problem, and feels no need to qualify his or her decision.
2. *Diagnosis followed by the phrase "provisional diagnosis."* This means there is some uncertainty, even though the counselor is fairly sure of the problem.
3. *Some other problem must be ruled out* to assure certainty. This often accompanies the second level of certainty, such as "Major depression, provisional diagnosis, R/O bipolar disorder."
4. *No diagnosis, but tendencies towards a particular problem.* This may mean counseling is needed to help the client deal with those inclinations, but the problems are not severe enough to warrant a diagnosis.
5. *Diagnosis deferred.* Problems warrant some diagnosis, but they cannot be clearly determined. Often this is a tempo-

rary designation while the counselor and/or others observe the client further.

6. *The problem is in remission.* There certainly has been a diagnosable problem in the past, but there are few or no current symptoms.

7. *No diagnosis nor other description given.* The person may have minor problems, but nothing diagnosable and not even any tendencies towards some problem area.

Three other adjectives are sometimes included in a diagnosis. A problem is considered *acute* when it is short-term (usually less than six months' duration) and more severe. In contrast, a problem is *chronic* when it lasts for a longer period of time. Usually chronic problems are less severe. Finally, a problem is *episodic* when it reoccurs now and then.

Several diagnoses may be made at one time. A person may have a personality disorder in combination with some other psychological problem. Sometimes the person will have both a medical and a psychological problem. These may or may not be related.

Finding problems that do not exist

This book is dangerous! One of the difficulties in studying abnormality is the tendency to see yourself as abnormal. Psychologists have sometimes called this problem *intern's syndrome*, because some medical students develop the symptoms of each problem they study!

The same danger exists, perhaps to a greater extent, when studying psychological problems. Normal people share characteristics with those who have psychological disorders; they just do not have them to the same degree. Some actions normal in private may be abnormal in public (such as disrobing). Those studying abnormal psychology often begin to doubt their own normality, and see themselves in several of the disorders.

Readers should carefully note all of the characteristics of a particular disorder, rather than just those aspects they see in themselves. It may help to talk to friends who can correct any misperceptions. Anyone with serious doubts about their normality should talk to a counselor about it; letting the nagging doubts fester may create additional problems.

Another warning regards the use of some of the names of disorders. It takes a great deal of skill to diagnose people, including several years of graduate study and a supervised internship while the student refines diagnostic skills. Saying "You have real depressive tendencies" can make things worse than they are or even create problems that did not exist in the first place. Misuse of a diagnostic term can seriously affect another person's morale. Only a qualified mental health professional should attempt to give a diagnosis. The whole notion of giving a diagnosis has been criticized because people are likely to see the worst in the person as a result. In one study (Langer and Abelson 1974), two groups of mental health professionals were shown identical videotapes of a man talking about past job experiences. One group was told he was giving a job interview, the other that he was a mental patient. Those who thought he was a job applicant tended to describe him as "attractive" and "innovative," while the group that thought he was a mental patient saw him as "defensive," "dependent," and "aggressive."

Terms used to designate the mentally ill also affect troubled people in undesirable ways. In the past the term *patient* was used of mentally disordered persons, which placed them in the role of a sick person unable to help themselves. They had to wait for the doctor to cure them. Today, the term *client* is used so the individual will take more responsibility in the treatment.

While some would like to do away with diagnostic labels because of their dangers, this is an overreaction. Specifying a disorder precisely can help determine the best treatment, at least for someone with severe problems. A cautious diagnosis can help the person better understand why they act and feel as they do, and may speed them toward proper therapy and recovery.

3

Depression and Extreme Moods

A mood is defined by the DSM as a "prolonged emotion that colors the whole psychic life." Two moods are emphasized in the mood disorders: depression and elation. Depression, the more common, can occur separately or it may alternate with elation (generally called a manic episode). The mood may be very intense over a period of a few weeks, or less intense but last for years. We also will examine some sleep disorders within this chapter, since sleep disturbance is often associated with mood disorders.

Major depression—Severe depression and loss of pleasure or interest in normal activities for at least two weeks. Can be a single episode or reoccur at intervals.

Dysthymia—Depression lasting for at least two years, but not as extreme as major depression.

Psychiatrists treat more cases of depression than any other emotional disturbance. With one out of twenty Americans medically diagnosed as suffering from depression, and many more persons having symptoms of depression but not seeking treatment, it is conservatively estimated that more than 20 million Americans suffer from this major health problem (Brown 1974, 117). When depression so affects a person's life that treatment is required, the individual may be described as *clinically depressed.*

About 20 percent of all women and 10 percent of all men in the United States have depressive episodes. About 6 percent of women and 3 percent of men will be hospitalized for a depressive episode.

Depression occurs more frequently in the higher socio-economic classes (Bagley 1973). Depression may be triggered by an outside event, in which case it is called *reactive depression*, but sometimes no obvious external cause can be found. Clinically depressed people often show severe physiological symptoms of insomnia, anorexia (loss of appetite), and fatigue. For an extended discussion of how depression affects individuals physically, emotionally, and spiritually, see Minirth and Meier (1978).

Symptoms of depression

Sad affect

Five major categories of clinically depressive symptoms have been identified, among them *sad affect*. The sad facial expression characteristic of a depressed person is seen in the reference to Cain's "face downcast" in Genesis 4:6. Depressed individuals may cry often, or at least feel like crying. Their eyes are downcast, the mouth droops, the forehead may be wrinkled. Their strained features make such individuals look tired, discouraged, and dejected. As depression worsens they may loose interest in their personal appearance and even appear untidy. They may exhibit what is termed *smiling depression*—depression that shows even when they smile.

Painful thinking

David exhibits *painful thinking* in Psalm 42:5–6—"Why are you downcast, O my soul? Why so disturbed within me? Put your hope in God, for I will yet praise him, my Savior and my God." Prone to pessimism and introspective in a self-critical way, depressed people tend to focus on past mistakes, often feeling guilty even when innocent. They worry excessively over past wrongs, both real and imagined. A negative self-concept causes them to blame themselves for all their problems. Deprived of emotional support, they may feel blue, sad, helpless, hopeless, worthless, empty, and lonely. Although they crave reassurance from others, depressed persons may be prevented by deep hostility from accepting it. Anticipating rejection, they feel rejected and unloved, often out of proportion to reality. Preoccupation with self impairs their attention-span, ability to concentrate, and memory. Anxiety and feeling perplexed make them operate at a low energy level and with a sense of futility about the future.

Often painful thinking centers around guilt. The effect of true guilt is described in Psalm 32:3: "When I keep silent, my bones wasted away through my groaning all day long." Frequently, however, depressed individuals feel guilty even when they are innocent. They may take unrealistic responsibility for events beyond their control usually to counteract an overwhelming sense of inadequacy. To take on a great burden of responsibility for so many events and acts seems to protect depressed individuals unconsciously from feelings of worthlessness.

Painful thinking causes a lack of motivation, a primary characteristic of depressed individuals. Such individuals lose interest in activities they once enjoyed. They avoid people and want to be alone. They lose their sense of humor, become indecisive, and eventually may even become suicidal.

Physical symptoms

During clinical depression, chemical changes in the nervous system lead to *physical changes.* Body movement usually decreases, and the quality of sleep declines. The depressed individual eats too much or too little, so weight changes significantly. Intestinal disturbances may persist, constipation being a more frequent complaint than diarrhea. A woman's menstrual cycle may become irregular or stop entirely for months. Sexual interest may decline or disappear. Headaches are a common complaint, as are dry mouth, rapid heartbeat, and heart palpitations. Depressed individuals sometimes become hypochondriacs as a result of these physical symptoms, preferring physical illness to admitting psychological conflicts.

Anxiety

Another major symptom of depression is *anxiety*, often accompanied by irritability. As depression increases, agitation, tension, and restlessness prevail. Holding in an excessive amount of anger causes most depression; the person fears even self-awareness of this repressed anger because it would lower his or her self-esteem to admit the truth. Most depressed persons develop considerable anxiety as their brains fight to avoid seeing their own anger, revenge motives, and other dark wishes. It is so much easier to believe a lie—that the anxiety symptoms are due to hypoglycemia or some imaginary illness.

Delusional thinking

Delusional thinking sometimes occurs in very severe depression. The delusions may be persecutory ("people are out to get me") or grandiose ("God has given me a special insight"). Auditory or visual hallucinations may be interpreted as coming from God.

Causes of depression

Anger lies at the root of nearly all depression. Long-forgotten early childhood experiences may cause the anger, but because the anger was not expressed at the time and because the source of the anger is now forgotten, it surfaces indirectly in depression.

Children often learn to repress their anger by imitating their parents. Sometimes the parents punish children when they share angry feelings, even when done appropriately. The Bible states, "In your anger do not sin" (Eph. 4:26), yet the same verse admonishes that we not let the sun set while we remain angry. When anger is expressed prior to bedtime, depression is unlikely to result.

Anger also may result from grudges held against others. Ephesians 4:31 reminds us that grudges are always a form of bitterness and malice. They hurt the one holding the grudge far more than anyone else. Keeping a record of hurts can eventually lead to depression. True or false guilt can be the source of the anger, making depression a form of self-punishment. We cannot pay for our sins through such punishment; Christ has already paid that price, and we should receive his forgiveness freely.

Depression sometimes becomes a powerful strategy of manipulating others to get one's way. Children may use depression to manipulate their parents; adults may use it to manipulate their mates, using depression to vent anger on others. To get even may relieve one's anger to a degree, but it makes others miserable. Living with a chronically depressed person can be punishing—which is frequently the depressed mate's unconscious intent.

Depression gains attention from others. If children are inappropriately rewarded for being depressed, such reinforcement encourages development of depression as a lifestyle. Depression can also be a conscience-pleaser. Because the anger is turned against self, the individual's conscience is appeased. Punishing oneself never imparts good mental health. Such disciplining for growth should be left to God.

Depression feeds on itself as one's thinking becomes progressively more painful. People who feel hopeless, helpless, worthless, and guilty become very self-critical and debasing. Cyclical in effect, inappropriate thinking results in irresponsible behavior, which increases depression, which stimulates more inappropriate thinking. Response to positive feedback from others is often necessary to break that cycle.

Masked depression, characterized by such physical complaints as headaches or body aches and pains that seem to have no physical basis, offers one face-saving *defense mechanism* (a method of reducing anxiety by unconsciously distorting reality) to cover up emotional conflicts. Individuals suffering from masked depression usually respond readily to medication.

Human beings resist change because change causes stress. Depressive individuals often continue familiar patterns that cause them great discomfort, even while continually complaining about those conditions. For example, a masochistic, depressive woman may divorce a sadistic husband, then marry another sadistic man. Her history may reveal that her parents were sadistic and that others treated her unfairly. Even though she did not like such treatment, it became a familiar pattern—one she tries to continue.

Who becomes depressed?

Some depression may be seen in any person at any age, but it most commonly occurs in compulsive personality types and in middle-life. When individuals realize that they will never obtain the goals they have set for themselves anger can cause clinical depression. In addition, many losses occur during middle-life. A woman's greatest fear may be loss of beauty, often associated with fear of losing her spouse or being alone. She may lose some of the attention her husband has previously given her just as her children begin leaving home. The sum of several such losses can become depression. Men facing depression in middle-life may express their sense of loss through "acting out" sexually, perhaps as an attempt to convince themselves of continuing youth. Feelings of depression may be expressed in increased alcohol use, drug use, weight gain, physical complaints, or progressively worsening interpersonal relationships.

When adults become depressed, they look and act depressed; when adolescents become depressed, however, they usually act out their depression. In place of a sad affect, an adolescent may appear belligerent, sarcastic, or hostile. Gripped by emotional depression, an otherwise moral teenager may begin to steal, lie, use drugs, or act out sexually. Often depression occurs after a loss, such as a death or divorce. The adolescent may be feeling a combination of the loss of childhood advantages (for example, relative security with slight responsibility) and the overall loss of identity accompanying physical, social, and sexual changes. Encouraged to talk out anger and hostile feelings, adolescents usually begin to improve and acting out ceases.

The elderly are also prone to depression. Increasing age often accentuates basic personality traits. Individuals who have been depressed all their lives become more depressed as they grow older. As inhibitions decrease because of loss of certain brain cells, increased guilt can be a problem. Loneliness following loss of a spouse often produces depression.

In young adults both normal and unhealthy forms of depression can develop after the birth of a baby. *Postpartum depression* can have psychological as well as biological factors. While the physical stress, fears, and hormonal interaction accompanying childbirth make having mixed feelings about the experience normal, a young mother may feel guilt that she is not more elated or finds herself resenting her infant. Perhaps she feels her husband does not show the support and appreciation she expected, or she may discover that the baby does not magically cure the problems in her marriage. The woman sees such feelings as inappropriate, represses resentment, and increases her normal postpartum feelings to an abnormal extreme. Discussing the ambivalent feelings with someone will usually ease postpartum depression, but antidepressant medication sometimes becomes necessary when repression has taken over.

Alcohol and drug abuse invites depression. Alcoholics find artificial self-esteem by drinking, but that mechanism is only temporary. Loss of self-esteem eventually gives way to increasing despair. In addition, alcohol is itself a depressant. The same problems that lead to drug abuse—pent-up anger, low self-esteem, and fear of responsibility—also lead to depression.

Biological factors in depression

In chapter 2 we noted that genes do not cause a person to drink alcohol or become a homosexual, but this is not to deny that such behaviors as drunkenness or the homosexual lifestyle are totally unrelated to genetic factors. At this writing research continues into genetic traits which we now understand only poorly. Whatever the level of genetic contribution to depression, that genetic makeup challenges us to grow in our responsibility to the God who makes us as we are. Although the relatives of depressed individuals seem to have a higher incidence of depression than the general population (see also pp. 23–24), that by itself does not establish a genetic basis for depression. In one study of twins, a much higher concordance rate (tendency) occurred among identical twins compared with the concordance rate in nonidentical twins (Kallmann 1958). The genetic sameness of identical twins may then be construed as evidence that genetic makeup does play a role, although cultural factors also must be considered. Another study showed that children of depressed adults who were adopted by families without significant depression were eight times more likely to be depressive, compared with adopted children from other natural parents (Wender, et al. 1986).

Depression also relates to changes in the body chemistry. Within the brain the lack of certain chemicals between the neurons is associated with feelings of depression. Medications such as Tofranil and Pamelor can help restore those needed chemicals. Once the neurons respond the way they should, depression declines.

Depression relates to the endocrine system as well. Depressed people generally experience a decreased sex drive because of the negative effect on the sex hormones. Medication to stimulate the thyroid gland or related glands may sometimes help depression.

Depression often accompanies a viral illness, even a relatively minor upper respiratory infection. On the other hand, depression can make a person more susceptible to infection. Fatigue commonly causes depression. In 1 Kings 19 the prophet Elijah, overextended both physically and emotionally, became depressed and lost his sense of patient thinking to the point that he wanted to die.

Women often feel anxious and depressed during their menstrual periods. Hormonal changes occurring during the menstrual cycle probably account for some of the emotional effects of menstruation, but, as with postpartum depression, psychological and cultural factors also influence the degree of emotional upset.

Precipitating life stresses

Psychiatrists estimate that 85 percent of significant depressions are precipitated by life stresses. Adjusting to a serious loss, such as death of a loved one or divorce, has already been mentioned. In the Book of Job, the central figure became very depressed as a result of devastating losses. Job lost his children, estate, health, and essentially everything he had. With the Lord's help Job was able to overcome his depression and become effective again.

It is important to separate grief reactions from clinical depression. However, grief inadequately expressed long enough can become depression. Generally grief for a loved one requires several months, during which time the person may go through episodes of denial (refusing to believe the death occurred), anger (towards medical personnel, family members, or even the deceased), guilt, crying and withdrawal, and times of reliving past experiences with the deceased. Ideally once these stages are worked through, genuine grief and resolution results.

Sometimes part or all of this grieving can take place prior to the death of the loved one, because he or she has been terminal for many months. As a result, grieving may be rather brief following death. It is most important that grief be expressed fully so that a zest for life and joy return.

Depression can be an *adjustment reaction*, in which a healthy person undergoing normal stress becomes depressed. The apostle Paul, in 2 Corinthians 4:8 describes such situational stresses: "We are hard pressed on every side, but not crushed; perplexed, but not in despair." Most people can deal with adjustment reactions, but too much stress in too short a period of time can overwhelm almost anyone. We will consider such overwhelming stress in greater detail in chapter 4.

A blow to one's self-image often precipitates depression. Such a blow can come from external circumstances that directly attack one's self-concept (for example, rejection by one's mate in divorce), or it can come from within.

False guilt can overcome people and turn them against themselves. When the conscience attacks the self in an unhealthy way, people eventually give in to depression. The Book of Galatians indicates that some Christians in Galatia were driven by an unhealthy guilt from within rather than being motivated by the love of Christ. True guilt, of course, can be a major source of depression. True guilt with remorse (a form of depression) should be the normal response when a person sins. Many godly persons have suffered from depression because of their sin and true guilt. David's depression over his sin, expressed in Psalm 32:3, was mentioned on page 35. If guilt is not resolved by confession to God, depression is to be expected. Christians continually need to claim God's promise to forgive sins (1 John 1:9), but Christians cannot willfully continue practicing sin without resultant depression.

Sometimes a wrong perspective becomes the precipitating stress. In a sense, one can consider all counseling to be a matter of changing perspective, of seeing the problem in a new light. Wrong perspectives and false values easily arise in a materialistic society. Psalm

73:1–3 records Asaph's depression as stemming from a faulty perspective. He envied the wicked for their prosperity, which brought oppression until he entered the Lord's sanctuary and realized their destiny (73:16–17).

Depression can also be an attack by Satan to render a Christian ineffective. Those who feel totally helpless and see no way out of their difficulties may have forgotten the provisions of Christ, both now and in the world to come. There are times when we must do combat with Satan, through the power of the Holy Spirit. Some dedicated Christians become depressed and discouraged because they attempt to live for God in their own strength (see Rom. 7:14–24). In contrast the apostle Paul exclaimed, "I can do everything through him who gives me strength" (Phil. 4:13).

One certain way to keep a right perspective is to honor God's priorities. God is, first of all, concerned that we get to know Him in a personal, intimate way (Phil. 3:10). Second, God wants us to meet the needs of our own families (1 Tim. 5:8). Third, God wants us to minister to others as we are most able to be effective. Scrambling those priorities can precipitate depression.

Precipitating stresses work with repressed anger to produce depression. Pent-up anger hides at the core of a genuine, clinical depression. Some precipitating stresses are brought on by unconscious, self-destructive attitudes, emotions, and behavior patterns, but life presents many other stresses. No precipitating stress need result in depression if handled responsibly.

Case histories

The following excerpts from case histories illustrate how some early environmental factors predispose adults to depression. One often sees a cycle of unmet dependency needs, hostility, fear of rejection, and avoidance of closeness to others.

Case 1

A young woman, very depressed, described her mother as a strict disciplinarian and moody. Whenever she would do something wrong, her mother would use the "silent treatment" for discipline. Both her mother and grandmother suffered from periodic depression. The client said she had a better relationship with her father but could not communicate with him. She described both parents as pessimistic, her mother as "a worrier."

Case 2

A middle-aged woman experienced depression and explosive episodes. The client's history revealed a very difficult early environment. During the first twelve years of her life she was in poor health and suffered from feelings of inadequacy. She had a low self-concept. She stated that she was not close to her mother and felt that her mother accepted her only on a performance basis. She resented the fact that her mother first began to accept her when she became good in sports during her teenage years. The client said that her mother loved her when she did what her mother wanted her to do, but when she did not, she encountered "suppressed rejection."

Case 3

A young woman in depression said that her mother was hostile and outspoken. The mother would slap the daughter when they argued. The mother was loving whenever the daughter complied with her wishes; otherwise the mother was cold and hostile. The client said her mother would make her feel guilty about various things, lowering the daughter's self-image with derogatory statements about her personal appearance. The client stated that her mother was harsh in discipline.

Case 4

A thirty-year-old man complaining of depression stated that, although his mother was overprotective in some ways, he did not feel she accepted him. In fact, his mother usually left him in the care of an aunt.

Case 5

A middle-aged woman complained of marital conflict. Although her depression centered on her marital conflict, some factors in her early environment contributed to the problem. She never really knew her father, since he had been dedicated to his business. Though her father was strict, her mother was more severe. The client described her mother as "totally strict and totally legalistic," not allowing the daughter to make decisions for herself. The mother researched the past of any boy her daughter dated; if minor fault was found, further dates with that boy were forbidden.

Case 6

A sixty-year-old woman's depression seemed to center around anxiety that she might not be a Christian. She feared this although she had been active in church for many years. Her history revealed that her mother had never accepted her, nor shown any affection. Now, years later, she thought the Lord could not accept her. During the course of therapy the client did improve. She said that she was especially helped by the Bible study on the concept of grace where she learned about the unmerited love of God.

Case 7

A middle-aged man complaining of depression, said that his father also had been subject to depression and had committed suicide when the client was five or six years of age. His mother also was described as "nervous and depressed." He stated that his mother would discipline him in anger.

Case 8

A young man with symptoms of depression gave a history of a passive father and a domineering mother. He stated that his mother was "bossy." He also said that his wife was domineering, just as his mother had been.

Case 9

A woman in her middle-thirties compared her own depression with that of both parents. She described her father as being sad and withdrawn and her mother as having been nervous and depressed. She stated that her mother had suffered severely from depression and had, in fact, committed suicide.

Case 10

A woman in her early-forties with depression described her mother as unloving, unconcerned, and indifferent. During the patient's early life, she had lived on a ranch with her family. She stated that because few people were around she had become a loner.

Case 11

A fifty-year-old man complained of anxiety and depression. He stated that he felt rejected by his strict mother, who never showed any affection. Before the client's first date, his mother had given his girl friend a lecture. He said that his mother was domineering and his father passive. His mother's overprotective domination continued after he married. The client said that he felt inferior and had a low self-image when he was young. He said he always wanted to win his mother's acceptance.

Manic-depression

Bipolar disorder—Alternating between hopelessness and severe depression at one mood swing and wildly optimistic manic episodes at the other.

Cyclothymia—Alternating depressive and hypomanic episodes that do not reach the extremes of the bipolar disorder.

Manic-depression is technically referred to as either the *bipolar disorder* or *cyclothymia*, depending upon the severity of the swings in mood. The bipolar disorder is the same as major depression during its depressive phase; thus many of the above comments apply. The major difference is the presence of one or more manic episodes in the person's lifetime.

People going through a manic episode have a lot of energy and may even appear to be high on amphetamines. They are very cheerful unless frustrated, at which time they can quickly become caustic and irritable. They often show ambition, enthusiasm and inflated self-esteem. Grandiosity or feelings of superiority cause some to engage in extravagant business deals too daring for the average person.

Characteristically the manic person talks rapidly and most of the time, frequently changing from one topic to another. During this phase they often become demanding and domineering, but may also be very sociable, even calling friends in the middle of the night because they do not sleep a great deal. They often involve themselves in many activities at the same time. Manic episodes generally begin prior to age thirty, while depression may begin at any age.

The *hypomanic episode* is similar to the manic episode but not so severe. Hypomanic individuals are often impulsive, intrusive, and lack good judgment. In their "high" mood they may show extreme self-confidence and be gregarious and creative. They are very talkative and may inappropriately laugh or joke. They have increased motor activity and often a decreased need for sleep. Unlike the manic, however, this individual remains in touch with reality.

Causes

Manic-depression, a relatively infrequent disorder, seems to be largely genetic in origin. Incidence in the general population is only 0.5 percent. But the concordance rate for parents of manic-depressive patients is 36 percent to 45 percent; siblings, 20 percent to 25 percent, and identical twins, from 66 percent to 96 percent (Slater 1944; Kallman 1958). Because the mood-swings often seem unrelated to environmental stresses, internal physical factors are considered to play an important role. This may account for the fact that lithium salts is one of the most successful treatments, particularly during the manic phase.

Cyclothymic disorders apparently develop because of conflict between a severe, punishing superego and powerful, primitive, unconscious impulses. Often an early childhood trauma, such as desertion, causes hostility, which is turned inward and later manifests itself in depression. Or depression may arise when a personality problem caused by an early childhood loss is reactivated by a similar conflict at the adult level. Diagnosis of a cyclothymic disorder is almost never applied to a child and only infrequently to adolescents.

Case history

Several years ago a young woman knocked on the door of one of the authors late at night. She was clearly depressed and suicidal. She said she became that way every few weeks and could no longer cope with her periods of despondency. Upon talking with her further it was discovered that some days she felt quite normal and other days she was quite busy and talkative.

The woman's employer, a Christian, repeatedly told her that a Christian should not have such changes in mood. Rather than suggesting psychological help, the employer recommended that she firmly resolve not to become depressed. The woman stated that she had tried but finally concluded that God had no use for her and would not help her.

Clearly the problem was manic-depression, either the bipolar or cyclothymic disorders. She was referred to a psychiatrist for medication, given lithium salts, and felt significantly improved within a short time.

Sleep disorders

Insomnia—Several times a week the individual has difficulty going to sleep, staying asleep, or feeling rested after sleeping. May be due to another disorder, a physical problem such as sleep apnea, or medication.

Hypersomnia—Excessive daytime sleep or sleepiness not caused by a lack of sleep at night.

Sleep-wake schedule disorder—The person's inner cycle of sleeping and waking does not match that of the environment, producing either insomnia or hypersomnia.

Dream anxiety disorder—Frightening dreams repeatedly awaken the person; awakened, the person immediately feels very alert.

Sleep terror disorders—The individual awakens from sleep with a scream, but no dream is recalled. The person shows little response to efforts to comfort him or her. Confusion and repetitive movements follow an episode for several minutes.

Sleepwalking disorder—Walking in one's sleep, usually during the first two or three hours after going to bed. While walking they are unresponsive to others and are difficult to wake up. They do not recall the event upon awakening.

Anxiety or depression usually causes sleep disturbance. More than 30 million Americans have sleep disorders. Severe sleep disorders should be treated, especially since individuals who sleep less than four hours a night have a decreased life expectancy. Among subtypes in this category are *temporary insomnia, persistent insomnia, temporary hypersomnia, persistent hypersomnia, sleep walking,* and *night terrors. Narcolepsy* is another subtype, characterized by exces-

sive daytime sleepiness, extreme susceptibility to sleep-inducing situations, and loss of muscle control or tone. *Sleep paralysis* (inability
to move while falling asleep) and frightening dreams while falling
asleep may occur. Individuals with narcolepsy go directly into rapid-
eye-movement (*REM*) or dream-state sleep whereas normal individuals go through non-rapid-eye-movement (*NREM*) sleep first.
Certain medications help control narcolepsy. Verses related to sleep
include Psalm 4:8; Proverbs 3:21–24, and Ecclesiastes 5:12.

Treatment for mood disorders

Most people suffering from mood disorders must get back in touch
with their basic needs for self-worth, for intimacy with others, and
for intimacy with God. Christian counselors can help them meet
those needs by urging them to take the following nineteen steps.
This plan also helps those with other disorders, and indeed all of us:

Guidelines to mental health

Accept Christ

A basic step in overcoming depression is to accept Jesus Christ
as personal Savior (see pp. 209–17). Although Christians are not
free from problems, they have a source of strength in their relationship to Christ. "Believing in Christ" includes understanding that
Christ died for one's sins and trusting him for one's own salvation.
Knowing Christ as a Brother and God as heavenly Father gains a
tremendous resource for help. One of the best ways to overcome
depression is to commit one's life daily to the purpose of glorifying
Christ.

Reprogram thinking

The new spirit within Christians (John 3:6) strengthens their ability to solve day-to-day problems. It is important to note that the
spirit is new, not necessarily the mind, emotion, or will. The mind,
emotion, and will change as one spends time in prayer and fellowship
in God's Word. Bad programming during childhood may take years
to reprogram in a more healthy direction.

It helps to monitor our thoughts. Critical, negative thinking reinforces a depressed mood. Changing thought patterns can lift this
mood. As the apostle Paul encouraged people, "whatever is true,

whatever is noble, whatever is right, whatever is pure, whatever is lovely, whatever is admirable—if anything is excellent or praiseworthy—think about such things" (Phil. 4:8). Some people are much too hard on themselves. Everyone makes mistakes and commits sins from time to time. Dwelling on accomplishments rather than failures is good mental exercise. Unhealthy introspection makes people critical, pessimistic, and negative about themselves.

Learn to deal with feelings; feelings are important but should not rule one's life. Scripture often emphasizes behavior or actions, as in Philippians 2:13 and 4:13. We have little direct control over our emotions, but maximum control over our behavior. Understanding how fickle our feelings are helps us to keep them from controlling our lives. A more stable focus for behavior bases life on sound logic and biblical convictions.

Much depression and grief would be avoidable if we refused sinful behavior. Individuals depressed because of sin may react by doing even more sinful things to relieve their emotional pain. Solomon's advice about sinful behavior was, "Avoid it, . . . turn from it and go your own way" (Prov. 4:15). Depressed individuals benefit from learning to deal with their guilt. Confessing sin to God (1 John 1:9) and making things right with another person (Acts 24:16) handles true guilt. Getting rid of false guilt depends on educating oneself about the grace and mercy of God. Those who learn to reprogram their thinking can overcome depression.

Deal with anger

Many depressed people fail to realize how angry they are. Dealing daily with anger as advised in Ephesians 4:26 prevents clinical depression from developing. Regardless of whether it should or should not be present, anger should be admitted. Sinful, inappropriate anger arises from four sources:

1. Selfish demands are violated. Selfish people are angry much of the time and often have serious problems with depression.
2. Perfectionistic demands are violated. Perfectionists expect too much of themselves, of others, and even of God. As a result they are frequently angry, mostly toward themselves.

3. Suspicion arises. People often become angry toward those most like themselves. Some people deceive themselves about their own faults, but they are suspicious of any other person who shows those same qualities. They may dislike that person without understanding why.

4. Anger becomes directed at God. Such anger is always inappropriate, but forgivable.

To deal with anger recognize the types of situations that cause intense feelings and try to understand why. That helps to control and handle anger better in the future. Insight into the development of one's personality in the past helps one deal with present anger and depression.

Verbalize anger and forgive the offender, even if the anger is appropriate. Verbalizing anger keeps one from repressing it and feeling frustrated and depressed and also helps one forgive, no matter what response one receives in return. It is wrong to suffer depression for another person's sin. God often uses tactful verbalization of anger to convict an offender of sin. The offender respects the person more for being assertive, under emotional control, and responsible in handling anger. Verbalizing anger tactfully and in obedience to God's Word prevents gossip, which God hates (Prov. 6:16–19). After verbalizing anger, one must forgive. Forgiving starts with an act of will. It takes time to reprogram hurt feelings but another person can be forgiven immediately by an act of will. Forgiving does not erase all recall but means no longer holding something against another person.

Stop trying to get even; God will have vengeance on all who deserve it—or through divine grace he will forgive those who repent. God wisely decides to show a person vengeance or grace.

Do not repay anyone evil for evil. Be careful to do what is right in the eyes of everybody. If it is possible, as far as it depends on you, live at peace with everyone. Do not take revenge, my friends, but leave room for God's wrath, for it is written: "It is mine to avenge; I will repay," says the Lord. On the contrary: "If your enemy is hungry, feed him; if he is thirsty, give him something to drink. In doing this, you will heap burning coals on his head." Do not be overcome by evil, but overcome evil with good. [Rom. 12:17–21]

Develop an intimate relationship with family members

To counteract depression, spend time with mate, children, or relatives, removing any barrier that exists in the family relationship. Much of a person's self-worth is based on the family's loving acceptance, so be willing to take the initiative in resolving family conflicts. We should not wait until relatives "repent" for hurting our feelings; we should assume total responsibility for healing old wounds.

Depressed individuals need to be intimate with others, but because they fear rejection, they seldom get close enough. Sometimes only a concentrated effort breaks the *rejection syndrome*—fearing rejection and thus rejecting others. Typically, persons in this cycle expect people to fall short, often because their parents failed to meet their needs when they were young. Out of anger and hostility they test the love of those closest to them. Inevitably they are rejected because they set themselves up to be rejected, and their dependency needs increase with their anger. Only by changing behavior patterns can one break out of such a cycle. One must learn to make more realistic demands of others and to risk getting close to others. One must refuse to use depression to manipulate others.

Build close friendships

Friendship overcomes depression. "Two are better than one, because they have a good return for their work: If one falls down, his friend can help him up. But pity the man who falls and has no one to help him up" (Eccles. 4:9–10). A friend is someone who is warm, concerned, caring, sensitive, loving, accepting, and willing to give of self to another. It is important for Christians to share their burdens with a friend (Heb. 10:24–25). Because loneliness hurts and everyone fears rejection, a person must assume full responsibility for building friendships. "A man of many companions may come to ruin, but there is a friend who sticks closer than a brother" (Prov. 18:24). That kind of friend helps overcome depression.

Christians who become depressed can benefit from associating with other members of the Body of Christ. The apostle Paul urged:

Then we will no longer be infants, tossed back and forth by the waves, and blown here and there by every wind of teaching and by the cunning and craftiness of men in their deceitful scheming. Instead, speaking the truth in love, we will in all things grow up into him who is the Head, that is, Christ. From him the whole body, joined and held together by every supporting ligament, grows and builds itself up in love, as each part does its work. So I tell you this, and insist on it in the Lord, that you must no longer live as the Gentiles do, in the futility of their thinking. [Eph. 4:14–17]

As depressed persons relate to others and become less self-centered and self-absorbed, depression lifts.

Establish a routine that brings satisfaction

A depressed person needs a specific plan to bring about change. If a particular problem causes depression, different options for a solution should be listed and a plan implemented for daily activities. Time should be allotted for intimacy with God, including prayer and Scripture meditation; time for developing good mental health; time to relax and unwind, and time to build an intimate marriage and parent-child relationships. Only *after* those priorities, time should be set aside to earn a living. Finally, any time remaining should be used to develop one's God-given talents. Often new interests and activities help ease depression.

Reach out to others

The ultimate step in overcoming depression is to reach out to others—to "love your neighbor as yourself" (Matt. 22:29). By becoming aware of the needs of others, one can often help another person physically, emotionally, or spiritually. "Each of you should look not only to your own interests, but also to the interests of others" (Phil. 2:4). Helping others often helps us see our own problems more objectively, and almost always lifts us out of depression.

Focus on a specific plan of action

Little things determine how we feel: the time we get up in the morning; our first response to our mate; and whether we eat breakfast. Have some quiet time with the Lord, think about a Bible verse for encouragement, avoid being overloaded in our work, have enough social contact, eat a good diet, and exercise. Individuals who force themselves to work out a specific plan of action consisting of perhaps ten things to do daily for the next week almost invariably see improvement in their lives.

A patient considering suicide was asked in the emergency room what was troubling him. He said that because he awoke that morning feeling depressed over not going to work, he began watching television. When he started to identify with situations in soap operas, he became depressed. Asked if he might be doing something he thought was wrong which could be intensifying his depression, he admitted that one thing in particular made him feel very guilty. His attitude was much improved by giving him help to change that behavior.

A housewife who was depressed outlined her daily schedule. She slept late in the mornings because she felt too depressed to get up, then she felt depressed about sleeping late. She felt that she ought to cook her husband's breakfast and felt depressed about not doing it. By making specific plans to change her daily activities she was able to overcome her depression. Her list included: (1) Get up early at least three mornings a week, regardless of how I feel. (2) Memorize one encouraging Bible verse every week. (3) Have more social contact. (4) Do things around the house that will make me feel better for having done them. Changing her activity and ventilating her feelings started her toward recovery.

The authors ask individuals depressed about a situation to list the options they have and the steps they can take to resolve that situation. We urge them to commit themselves to implementing their plan for at least a week at a time. If, after a few weeks, the plan is not working, we suggest making a new plan and trying some new options. Many depressed individuals see no other things to try. When they list all the options—probable, possible, and even ridiculous options—they can hardly believe the number that come to mind. Only after all options have been listed does evaluation begin; that keeps the process of creativity from being hindered. Sometimes one of the ridiculous options turns out to be most practical for setting a new course.

Develop new interests and activities

Depressed individuals often need to get out of a rut. Going to a movie with one's spouse, driving home by a different route, developing new friendships, or taking up a new athletic activity are examples of small actions that sometimes help people begin to restructure their lives. Positive results usually appear over a period of several weeks.

Use the Word of God as a resource

The promises in the Bible enable believers to "participate in the divine nature" (2 Pet. 1:4). Such a powerful resource should not be neglected in the struggle to overcome depression. Access to God's own nature establishes tremendous stability. Although lust can make people emotionally weak and prone to emotional problems (1 Pet. 2:11), the Word of God brings strength. Initially one can memorize Scripture verses that address a problem; but after hours of meditating on Scripture, the individual begins to love the Word (Jer. 15:16). It is not familiarity with the Bible that frees us from depression but the habit of applying its precepts to our lives. Psalms 43 and 69 especially may help depression.

Focus on assertiveness

Unhealthy aggressiveness runs over other people and hurts them unnecessarily. But passivity is also wrong. Instead of speaking up when we ought, we internalize our feelings and become bitter. Depressed individuals tend to be passive, letting others run over them. Anger builds until eventually it explodes in some aggressive behavior. Healthy assertiveness tactfully expresses the way we actually feel, in love. Assertive people keep others from being irresponsible.

Deal with dependency needs

Depressed individuals seldom know how to take care of their dependency needs in a healthy way. Fearing rejection, they do not get close to others. They may go to the extreme of becoming an independent "superperson" who helps others. In spite of such a defense mechanism, the basic problem of their underlying depression complicates their lives. They need to deal with their dependency needs by taking a chance on getting close to others. Changing certain patterns may help them stop rejecting others out of fear of rejection. If they have put on excess weight to keep other people from getting close, they need to lose weight. If they have been abusing alcohol to keep others at a distance, numbing their brain to keep from being hurt by others, they need to deal with their alcohol problem in a healthy way. One who needs no one but helps all finds dependency needs met less and less frequently. Those who fall into this pattern can help others without hurting themselves if they realize their problem and get their lives into balance.

Be careful with introspection

Although insight is essential in overcoming depression, insight can become dangerous if it becomes stuck in introspection. Depressed individuals tend to be overly introspective anyway, so the authors encourage limiting time spent in introspection to therapy sessions, or perhaps to periods of talking with a close friend. Someone who spends hours trying to figure everything out becomes overly self-critical. If the person cannot stop being introspective, he or she should set aside a certain portion of the day for thinking about their problem and refuse to think about it at any other time. Dwelling on problems all day long uses up emotional reserves and deepens depression. Introspection by depressed individuals is seldom objective, so the evaluation is probably unrealistic. When negative thoughts intrude the person should get busy doing something to avoid pessimistic self-examination.

Accept responsibility for depression

Many depressed individuals begin to get over depression by putting themselves in charge of their own lives. An old proverb says "Pray to God, but keep rowing to shore." Individuals who say, "I just can't get over this depression," often really mean that they *won't* get over their depression. Some subconscious reason makes them cling to the pattern. They may gain attention from it, or manipulate others with it, punishing themselves or someone else, or even use it as an excuse for not getting out and doing something more productive.

Realize there is hope

Christian counselors can help people find hope, often the first step in overcoming depression. One Christian man said he had been depressed for twenty years and had seen a half-dozen therapists. Then someone convinced him that there was hope for him, and that he *could* get well! Within a month he felt better than he had for twenty years. There *is* hope.

Manipulate the environment

Stress can be relieved either by learning to cope from within or by changing one's external environment. Depressed individuals should be encouraged to do whatever they can to alter and relieve external stresses. If their depression is partially due to working too hard, they can be encouraged to work fewer hours. Some external stresses can be relieved by stopping sinful behavior.

Respond—don't react

Many depressed individuals react strongly to stressful situations, sometimes even becoming overly aggressive and attacking others. When they learn to discipline themselves to respond rationally rather than to react aggressively, they begin to feel better about themselves and the way they handle stressful situations.

Increase self-esteem

Christ's admonition to love our neighbor as we love ourselves implies that we should have a healthy self-image. We are able to give to others only if we have a healthy opinion of ourselves. Although many Christians confuse the sin of pride with the godly attribute of loving ourselves in a healthy way, pride and feelings of self-worth are really opposites. Generally, the more inferior we feel the more we compensate with false pride. A "better-than-thou" attitude toward others usually covers up feelings of inadequacy.

Learn to laugh

Laughter relaxes us as can almost nothing else. Many depressed individuals improve as soon as they learn to laugh at their own perfectionistic demands or other shortcomings.

Therapy for mood disorders

Individuals unable to overcome depression by using the preceding guidelines may need the help of a psychiatrist or clinical psychologist. A Christian professional will consider possible spiritual and psychological causes of depression, while being alert to any physical problems that may produce symptoms.

Drug therapy

Medication prescribed by a psychiatrist or medical doctor often holds the key to successful treatment of mood disorders (see appendix B). Depression and manic-depression often relate to the depletion of certain chemicals in the brain or elsewhere in the body.

A wide variety of medications may be prescribed to help those with mood disorders. One major group of medications is the *tricyclic antidepressants*, which include Elavil, Sinequan, Tofranil, Aventyl, and Vivactil.

Dosage levels of these medications vary. A typical example would be 150 milligrams of Tofranil daily. Often the medication is given at bedtime to allow any sedative effects to wear off before morning. In fact, the sedative effects are often helpful but these medications vary in that respect. For example, Elavil acts as a sedative, Vivactil tends to act more as a stimulant, and Tofranil runs a middle course between the two.

Another major category of medications, the *MAO inhibitors*, include Marplan, Nardil, Parnate, and Eutonyl.

Such drugs have been used to treat *atypical depression*, in which features of hysteria, phobia, or anxiety may be prominent along with typical depressive symptoms. MAO inhibitors are used less often today because they have been associated with troublesome side-effects, including elevated blood pressure. Hypertension can occur when someone using MAO inhibitors eats cheese, chocolate, pickled herring, canned figs, yeast, game, red wines, chicken livers, broad-pod beans, beer, meat extracts, or yogurt. Individuals on these drugs also have to be careful about certain other medications, such as amphetamines, adrenaline, nonadrenaline, dopa, dopamine, certain cold remedies, nasal decongestants, and the novocaine used by dentists.

Amphetamines may work by affecting the level of chemicals in the brain. Many individuals taking amphetamines alone to control their depression have an additional depression after about two weeks from the onset of the medication. For that reason, and because they are so addicting, amphetamines are not a good antidepressant medication.

Lithium produces dramatic results in the treatment of manic-depression. When administered in the manic phase of manic-depressive psychosis, lithium seems to prevent the depressive phase from coming on and helps abate the manic phase. The individuals calm down, talk at a normal rate, and are no longer extremely euphoric; their mood is essentially normal and they do not become depressed.

Research tends to indicate that lithium is not as effective in a depressive phase. The exact mechanism is not known. Some feel that it works by influencing the electrolytes of the body more or less directly, but others are studying its possible effects in the brain.

The major tranquilizers sometimes treat certain cases of depression, even though in general they are not antidepressants. They decrease anxiety and are most generally used in cases of psychosis. Many of these drugs, in fact, precipitate a depression, or deepen a depression. A few, however, (for example, Mellaril) seem to have some antidepressive qualities. The authors have noted that the major tranquilizer Navane may have some antidepressive qualities.

Factors affecting dosage

Most psychiatric drugs are fat-soluble and concentrated in lipid tissues. Since women's body tissues contain a higher percentage of fat, women generally require more of a given drug than do men of the same weight range. Also, individuals who smoke seem to require higher dosages.

Food intake influences how much of a drug is needed. Fasting for religious or other reasons can endanger individuals on psychiatric drugs. In fasting individuals the blood level of a psychiatric medication can be much higher than for individuals on a normal diet who take the same dose.

Concurrent use of other drugs can alter the amount of antidepressant medication needed. For example, since barbiturates lower the blood level of the tricyclic antidepressants, higher antidepressant dosage is needed for a person also taking barbiturates. Other agents that lower the blood level of the tricyclic antidepressants include expectorants containing ammonium chloride and substances that lower the pH, such as massive doses of vitamin C. Major tranquilizers can affect the blood level of antidepressants being taken concurrently. Such amphetamines as Ritalin may enhance the effects of tricyclics by slowing down their elimination from the body. Antacids interfere with the absorption of the tricyclic antidepressants.

Elderly patients have some difficulty in absorbing antidepressant drugs but, on the other hand, seem to benefit from lesser amounts. Tricyclic antidepressants can cause cardiac problems; they must be used with extreme caution in patients with heart disease. Sometimes MAO inhibitors and tricyclic antidepressants are used concurrently, but only with extreme caution. Usually it is done only in a resistant type of depression, with the tricyclic antidepressant started first and then an MAO inhibitor, such as Parnate, added later.

Vitamin and hormone therapy

General practitioners have long used vitamin B_6 or such thyroid preparations as Cytomel to treat depression. Research indicates that certain individuals do respond to such treatments, but more do not. Some cases of depression respond to use of antidepressants with thyroid extract.

Low-dose estrogen replacement is often used for short periods along with antidepressants. The exact effect of estrogen on depression is uncertain. Although it does help relieve hot flashes, estrogen therapy is increasingly suspected of causing potentially dangerous side-effects.

Megavitamin therapy has been suggested as a panacea for emotional disorders. Scientific research generally fails to confirm that megavitamins are effective in the treatment of any emotional disorders.

Medications that cause depression

Some medications, such as reserpine, which is given for high blood pressure, will precipitate a depression. Some birth control pills, major tranquilizers, and minor tranquilizers (such as Valium) can also precipitate a depression. Ritalin, which initially elevates the mood, can have a depressant effect two weeks later.

Substances used to combat depression

Although alcohol is a depressant, millions of people use it in an attempt to drown their depressions. Alcoholism is a major social problem, most affecting those with an underlying depression. One in every three alcoholics significantly benefits from antidepressant medication. (See chapter 8 for more on substance abuse.)

The smoking of tobacco seems to provide a euphoric and tranquilizing effect which may temporarily relieve tensions but it hardly seems worth the risk of developing cancer. Some depressed individuals turn to marijuana for a euphoric feeling and temporary lifting of their depression. Yet marijuana smoking can cause permanent brain damage, lung damage, persistent personality changes, memory impairment, chromosome alterations, and motivational disturbances. Although marijuana does affect the pleasure centers in the brain, giving a temporary euphoria, in the long run it produces loss of motivation and even more depression.

Somatic therapies

Physical methods of treatment, such as electroconvulsive treatment, sleep therapy, and drugs, are known collectively as *somatic therapies*. These include:

Shock treatment

At one time electroconvulsive treatment (ECT) was used extensively for many kinds of emotional disorders, especially psychosis (see chapter 6). Today it is rarely used as a first level of treatment for depression. Memory impairment may be a negative side-effect from ECT. Scenes of shock treatments in movies may be frightening, but these are usually exaggerated. While ECT is relatively safe, there are better methods available to treat depression.

Today ECT is sometimes used with those who do not respond to tricyclic antidepressants or for those who have negative reactions to these medications. In addition, some suicidal persons cannot afford to wait the two or three weeks for antidepressants to take effect.

A standard ECT treatment involves five to eight sessions. Unfortunately 30 percent to 40 percent of those undergoing this procedure relapse within a year, probably because the underlying psychological and spiritual problems have not been dealt with.

How does ECT help depression? No one really knows, although some evidence suggests that the electrical current induces chemical changes in the brain, much as do antidepressant medications. In recent years it has become more popular to shock only one side of the brain, the nondominant hemisphere, to reduce the amount of memory loss.

Insulin coma therapy

Another form of "shock therapy," almost never used anymore, is insulin coma therapy. A coma was brought on by the injection of insulin, but each patient had to be monitored very closely.

Sleep therapy

Another type of therapy rarely used today is continuous sleep therapy. Introduced in 1922, drugs induced the therapy's long periods of deep sleep. For over a week at a time patients were awakened only for feeding and elimination of waste. The results were not particularly encouraging.

Hospitalization

If a depressed individual seems a suicide risk or near the point of a break with reality into psychotic depression, hospitalization is necessary. During hospitalization more intense psychotherapy may be given and medication adjusted rapidly. Getting away from a stressful environment and into a friendly, supportive atmosphere can be of great benefit. Trained psychiatric nurses and other staff assist in counseling, teach people helpful insights, and observe daily behavior, relaying such information back to the psychiatrists. Meeting other depressed individuals who are improving brings hope. Hospitalization costs less in the long run than prolonged outpatient psychotherapy, or at least may be covered by insurance. Hospitalized patients frequently return to full employment more rapidly.

Treatment for cyclothymia

With help, many cyclothymic individuals can identify the maladaptive behavior that accompanies their "mood swings." Recognizing the goals of their behavior, they can learn better ways to attain them. Often the individuals come to realize that their moods are ineffective ways to get along with people. Anxiety expressed in the mood swings may be more apparent than real. People sometimes appear or pretend to be hypomanic if they perceive that the only way to be accepted is to be "the life of the party." They may appear to be depressed if they see sorrow as a means of obtaining attention and affection.

Hypomanic hyperactivity often covers unconscious depressive feelings. By staying excessively busy, cyclothymic individuals do not have time to look at their true feelings. Cyclothymic individuals may need help to get in touch with their anger and other emotions. They must learn to verbalize those true feelings without being ashamed of them. They must also forgive those who wrong them.

4

Problems
with Stress
and Adjustment

Stress is an everyday fact of modern life. However, the person who experiences hurricanes, earthquakes, or seeing someone murdered must cope with more than a normal level of stress. Furthermore, some have less stress resistance than others. Depending upon one's experience and personal disposition, occupational or social stresses can result in poor adjustment in some area of life.

Traumatic stress

Post-traumatic stress disorder—The person has experienced a very traumatic event, which is reexperienced psychologically in some way.

Traumatic events create extreme, unusual stress. Natural disasters, violent criminal attacks, airplane crashes, being in the midst of battle in a war, automobile accidents, and similar sorts of experiences all may cause serious psychological repercussions.

In the *post-traumatic stress disorder* the person reacts to a traumatic event by reexperiencing the event repeatedly. He or she remembers it over and over, dreams about it, relives the event mentally or becomes very upset when something similar to the trauma occurs (such as the anniversary of the event). Very often the individual avoids anything related to the event, or becomes less responsive when around reminders. Often the person has sleep disturbances, angry outbursts, problems concentrating, startles easily, or is irritable.

While almost anyone has a period of adjustment after trauma, the problems described above last for at least a month afterward. Occasionally the problems do not develop until six months or longer after the traumatic event. Post-traumatic stress symptoms can continue for months or even years.

Whenever a person has experienced a traumatic event, it is important for them to be able to talk out the event. Victims of automobile accidents or rape need to describe the event and their feelings about what happened. Pastors, friends, and counselors need to listen, encouraging the individual to talk so that post-traumatic stress is less likely.

Very often those who have endured trauma go through three stages (Carson and Butcher 1992, 157): (1) In the *shock* stage the person becomes stunned or unresponsive. Sometimes they simply wander around or do not recall the event. (2) In the second stage of *suggestibility* the person seems to have no mind of his or her own, willingly doing whatever told. Persons recovering from a disaster may express concern for others involved, but they have not yet bounced back. (3) During the *recovery* phase, they may still be anxious, but gradually they come back to normal. During this third stage post-traumatic stress disorders are most likely to develop.

The Bible records no clinical descriptions of psychological disorders, and thus we must infer only the possibility of disturbance from the biblical record. A post-traumatic stress reaction might be suggested in Jeremiah's lamentation over Jerusalem. Under siege by

Babylon, the city of Jerusalem suffered famine until the enemy broke through the walls. Later a commander set fire to the temple and most of the buildings in the city and took many of the residents as captives (Jeremiah 52). Lamentations represents Jeremiah's reexperiencing of this horrible event. Yet the book is more than that, as Jeremiah had long predicted the destruction. The horrors of the event may have shocked Jeremiah, in spite of the fact that he had prophesied it would occur. The book ends with an affirmation of God, "You, O Lord, reign forever; your throne endures from generation to generation. . . . Restore us to yourself, O Lord . . . renew our days as of old" (Lam. 5:19–21).

The affirming of God's sovereignty and his ability to restore us may, indeed, be a key factor in overcoming post-traumatic stress. Jeremiah states, "Because of the Lord's great love we are not consumed, for his compassions never fail. They are new every morning; great is your faithfulness" (Lam. 3:22–23). In addition, the terrible event may also provide an opportunity for self-examination, "Let us examine our ways and test them, and let us return to the Lord" (Lam. 3:40). Victims of trauma often blame themselves for the death or harm to others, even when they had no realistic possibility of preventing it. Yet in some traumatic events, such as the fall of Jerusalem, different actions could have prevented the disaster or minimized its effects.

Causes of post-traumatic stress

How suddenly the disaster strikes and the seriousness of its threat are central factors contributing to the severity of the reaction. Often, the disorder results when counseling is not available or not used. Rest, perhaps with the help of sedatives, and repeatedly talking about the event generally help the person avoid a prolonged reaction. Obviously, the coping ability and outside resources available to the person also affect the trauma's influence.

During World War I the term *shell shock* described the adverse reactions soldiers experienced around exploding bombs. During the Korean and Vietnam wars the terms *combat fatigue* and *combat exhaustion* were substituted. Gary Collins (1972, 153) points out that the noise, adverse living conditions, sleeplessness, and awareness that death or injury could occur at any moment produce anxiety, fatigue, and even depression. Perceived failures add guilt to the emotional reactions. Yet, the normal means of coping used in everyday life are not available or do not work.

These reactions, if not adequately dealt with, became post-traumatic stress disorders. Many factors account for these problems, including the anxiety and fear experienced by soldiers, the unpredictability of the situation, the inability to take action in some cases, the requirement that the soldier kill, and the length of time in active combat. While most soldiers never require psychotherapy, it is not surprising when negative reactions occur.

In recent years a number of psychologists and counselors have proposed a variation of post-traumatic stress disorder, termed *post-abortion syndrome* (Rue 1986; Reardon 1987; Franz and Gans 1987, 1988). Normal grief reaction is denied because of the circumstances of abortion. The person becomes less able to make good decisions, sleep well, or be sexually responsive. The submerged grief often does not appear until as long as ten years after the abortion. While several studies of the effects of abortion do not agree that such a syndrome exists, in nearly all of these the research methods were seriously flawed. Indeed the few studies conducted in a scientific manner indicate that many women suffer from such a syndrome and may even require hospitalization for the resulting psychological problems (Rogers, Nelson, and Phifer 1987, 26–28).

Terri Reisser (1987) found that seventy women she was counseling shared feelings of depression, anxiety, and guilt. They experienced sexual or marital problems and often felt as if they had been unduly influenced to have the abortions. Reisser identified eight stages in these women: (1) initial *relief* because the unwanted pregnancy no longer existed; (2) *denial* of the hurtful emotions resulting from abortion; (3) *anger* towards those who had helped them get abortions because they felt such individuals should have stopped them (sometimes this anger was turned towards themselves); (4) *bitterness and depression*, leading to distrust of others or, less often, clinical depression; (5) taking on personal *responsibility*, admitting their guilt and no longer blaming others; (6) *forgiveness* of self and others, while accepting forgiveness from God; (7) *reconciliation* through grieving for the aborted child, and (8) *hope* by beginning to help others.

Case history

On November 6, 1977, an earthen dam burst holding a lake of water above the campus of Toccoa Falls (Ga.) College. The result was a flood that claimed the lives of thirty-nine faculty, staff, and students, injured many others, and destroyed homes and other buildings. Several years later one of the survivors reported some symptoms of post-traumatic stress. Mary lost both her father and brother in the flood. Immediately after the flood she and her mother moved off campus, so she was able to avoid the college. For several months she spoke to others only when she had to, and later described herself as acting mechanically. She experienced reduced involvement with the world in general and was less interested in everyday activities. Mary then began to have vivid dreams about the flood and her mother, dreams that often left her crying and wide-awake. She eventually married, and only through extended discussions with her husband about the experience was she able to cope more effectively.

Adjustment disorders

> *Adjustment disorder*—Intense stress, though less extreme than post-traumatic stress disorder, resulting in problems in social relationships or occupational difficulties.

An *adjustment disorder* results from more common stresses, such as divorce or separation, severe marital problems, forced relocation, major problems at work, unemployment or economic hardship, death of a loved one, physical illness, leaving home, or retirement. The reexperiencing of the trauma found in post-traumatic stress does not occur.

The individual with an adjustment disorder develops problems at work or in relationships beyond what would be normally expected from such stresses. For a full-time student, the problems could include difficulties with school work. The problems in adjusting come in eight specific varieties. The diagnosis could be adjustment disorder with:

1. anxiety (if worry or nervousness is the result)
2. depression
3. conduct disturbance (such as fighting, vandalism, or reckless driving)
4. a mixture of emotions and conduct (conduct disturbance with either anxiety or depression)
5. mixed emotions (anxiety and depression)
6. physical symptoms (unaccounted for by a physical examination)
7. withdrawal
8. inability to work or study

The adjustment problems surface within three months of the stressful event. In addition, adjustment difficulties involve a pattern of behavior, not just one isolated difficulty. Usually the problem decreases or goes away after the stressful event ends or when the person learns to adapt.

Causes of adjustment disorders

The most obvious cause of an adjustment disorder is the stressful event, yet some may react rather extremely to minor stresses while others seem to be able to cope with extreme stresses successfully. The amount of stress an event places on a person is the sum of several different factors, among them the kind of event involved, how threatening it seems, and how long it exists. Several stresses added together increase the stress effects of each. A couple who has their first disagreement will probably be less stressed by it than a couple considering divorce after a long series of arguments. Stress also increases when the problem demands immediate action.

People differ in their abilities to deal with stress because of their individual perceptions of the event. Uncertainty of our ability to deal with a situation heightens its stress. Sometimes a better understanding of what will happen or what has happened decreases stress. The resources available to help us deal with difficult events also affects the amount of stress that results. When family and friends are informed and supportive, stress tends to decrease; whereas if others are also highly stressed, our reactions to stress tend to be more negative. Our faith in God, the pastor, and fellow believers can also be a tremendous support in the face of stress.

Case history

Robert C. Carson and James N. Butcher (1992, 154–55) describe a retired school teacher who had a close relationship with her husband for forty years. When her husband died of a heart attack, even though friends and family members visited her and her daughter invited her to come for a visit, the woman withdrew from everyone for many months. She sat alone in the dark house, not answering the phone and answering the door only reluctantly. She would not even leave home to go grocery shopping. Normal grief reactions often include many of the symptoms of an adjustment disorder, but they do not last as long. Typically the most severe symptoms of grief subside within a month or two, although episodes of acute grief or sadness may occur for several more months afterward. The story of this teacher shows that this division between a disorder and normality must be judged by how intensely and for how long the person reacts.

The adjustment of one who grieves normally creates a time of disordered living. Within its grip, though, Christians do have a support base; in the words of Paul: "We do not want you to be ignorant about those who fall asleep, or to grieve like the rest of men, who have no hope" (1 Thess. 4:13). The message Paul intends is *not* that we have no grief. Even Jesus grieved at the tomb of his friend, Lazarus. Rather, we should not be overwhelmed with grief after the death of a fellow believer, because we have assurance of seeing our friend again in heaven.

Treatment for stress and adjustment disorders

As has been mentioned earlier, it is vital for the person to come to terms with the original stress or trauma that resulted in the disorder. Sometimes friends and family facilitate this by listening to the person retell the event, perhaps many times. In a sense, the individual can heal himself or herself in this manner, if loved ones care enough to hear the repeated accounts.

Adjustment disorders

Effective crisis intervention for those with adjustment disorders helps them ventilate feelings and gives them information about needed resources. Being a good listener is a key role of the counselor.

For those who often encounter stress, "stress inoculation therapy" can help. Those who hold to this approach believe that people give themselves self-defeating messages. People tell themselves, "I'm falling apart," "I can't handle this" or "This is the worst thing that has ever happened to me." Within counseling the individual learns new self-statements such as "I can make a plan" and "Yes, I can make it." When overwhelmed with fear, the person learns to think "Don't try to get rid of all fear; just keep it manageable."

Physical relaxation also helps those with adjustment disorders. In stressful situations the person learns to relax their muscles and think peaceful thoughts, which can increase the power to cope. Some recommend hypnosis to increase relaxation.

Post-traumatic stress

Post-traumatic stress disorders may be helped by physical relaxation as well. Occasionally the client will bury the painful event, so that a professional therapist is needed to bring events back to the conscious mind where they can be directly confronted. One way of accomplishing this is though a four stage cycle:

1. Think through the traumatic event, describing it and all its possible sensations.
2. Describe feelings that accompanied the event, as well as feelings experienced in the retelling.
3. Emphasize thoughts about the experience, especially mental links among the sensations, feelings, and actions.
4. Take action by changing the reactions.

Repeated cycling through these four steps enables the person to regain repressed memories and express the emotions felt at the time. With repeated telling of the event the person "works through" the hidden emotions and becomes able to cope with memories.

Occasionally medication may be needed to encourage needed rest. Finally, we must never overlook the importance of prayer and reading the Scriptures in counseling these problems.

Rape

Rape is a distinctive form of stress which requires some specific comment. After a rape has occurred, women may feel guilty that they did not respond differently. A woman who knew the rapist may feel partly responsible for what happened, as well as betrayed by someone she trusted.

Victims of rape may express themselves by crying openly to vent their fear and anxiety. Others, however, react calmly and in apparent control. With either style, the victim often blames herself. Dependency upon others often increases after rape, and physical problems such as insomnia and nausea are relatively common.

After the immediate reaction, a second phase may last several months. A woman may move to a new location and change her telephone number. Nightmares commonly recreate the rape; an aspect resembling nightmare flashbacks of post-traumatic stress disorder. Victims' fears often surface—of being alone, of sexuality, or of locations similar to that in which the rape took place. Crisis telephone services may help victims of rape, where such supportive counseling is possible. Women generally able to cope well in crises probably will not develop a disorder following the experience, but those who have had prior psychological problems may experience severe reactions to a rape.

Post-abortion syndrome

Women suffering from the delayed reaction to having an abortion need to mourn the loss of the child (Rue 1986, 20, 22–29). This involves the need to admit that a human life has been taken so guilt may be dealt with and God asked for forgiveness. Women struggling with guilt need to remember that the apostle Paul aided in the murder of Christians; if he could be forgiven so can they.

Some counselors recommend memory healing in helping overcome guilt. This involves relaxing and recalling the abortion experience. This is accompanied by picturing Christ (and perhaps the infant) forgiving the mother for the action. The woman may, in the process of imagining, role-play asking the infant to forgive her, and the counselor can role-play the infant granting forgiveness.

Vincent Rue (p. 29) offers seven guidelines for counseling women who show post-abortion syndrome:

1. Use empathy so that the depth of pain and feelings of loss can be better understood.
2. Accept the woman without rejection and encourage her to bare feelings.
3. Speak of the death of the child, recognizing it is a terrible tragedy, but legitimate the grief by talking openly about it.
4. The counselor should resolve his or her own fears regarding death.
5. Encourage the client's ability to cope and take charge of her life.
6. Encourage communication with family and friends, promoting interaction.
7. Help the client realize that others also have had abortions and that God's love is greater than any sin.

5

Anxiety Disorders

Anxiety, characterized by apprehension, dread, tension, restlessness and worry, underlies many psychological problems. An anxious individual may believe misfortune, danger or doom lurks just ahead. Often irritable, overdependent, and fearful, the anxious develop any of a number of physical complaints with little or no genuine organic cause. Anxiety also affects the individual spiritually; Luke 8:14 observes that anxiety can choke spiritual growth.

Anxiety can be either normal or abnormal. Psychologists have long noted that individuals are more efficient and productive when they have some anxiety. As anxiety becomes intense, however, efficiency decreases proportionately. Scripture also considers realistic concern as healthy (see 1 Cor. 12:25; 2 Cor. 11:28, and Phil. 2:20). Fretting and worrying, however (as in Phil. 4:6 or 1 Pet. 5:7), are not considered healthy. The Greek word often translated *anxiety* is used about twenty-five times in the New Testament, usually in the negative sense (worrying or fretting), but occasionally in the positive (realistic concern).

Generalized anxiety and panic attacks

Generalized anxiety—Excessive worry and apprehension about problems for six months or longer, not related to mood cycles or another psychological problem.

Panic disorder—One or more unexpected panic attacks not triggered by a known reason for concern.

Persistent anxiety unrelated to any object, thought or action marks *generalized anxiety disorder*. No specific stress can be determined. If specific stress produced the anxiety, an adjustment disorder is indicated (see chapter 4). Tension, shown as trembling or an inability to relax, and such physical symptoms as a pounding heart, dizziness, sweating, or stomach complaints result. Edgy, impatient, or irritable, the person worries a good bit and may ruminate over past mistakes or misfortunes.

The continual worry and anxiety manifested runs contrary to the Scriptures. Matthew 6 has a number of verses which speak to this issue: "Therefore I tell you, do not worry about your life" (v. 25), "Who of you by your worrying can add a single hour to his life?" (v. 27), "Therefore do not worry about tomorrow, for tomorrow will worry about itself. Each day has enough trouble of its own" (v. 34). The command for chronic worriers is 1 Peter 5:7: "Cast all your anxiety on him because he cares for you."

The generalized anxiety disorder differs from the panic disorder in that episodes are more intense but generally last only a few minutes. The person diagnosed as having panic disorder must have several such attacks each month, and often there are several each week. Nearly 2 percent of the adult population have panic attacks. During a panic attack the person feels fearful and physical symptoms occur, such as a rapid heartbeat, shortness of breath, discomfort in the chest, dizziness, numbness, the feeling of being smothered, hot flashes, sweating or having cold hands, faintness, and trembling. Often the person feels as if he or she is dying or "going crazy." Sometimes the individual has feelings of unreality or fears he or she might do something uncontrolled. The experience is terrifying for the few minutes of the attack.

As in generalized anxiety disorder, nothing in particular seems to bring on the panic attack. If something can be identified, another diagnosis must be made. For example, if an object or situation brings on the attack the person has a *phobia*. If a thought or action precipitates the anxiety it is an *obsessive-compulsive disorder*, if stress precedes the attack a *stress disorder* will probably be diagnosed.

Sometimes a panic disorder occurs in combination with *agoraphobia*, the fear of being in public places where escape or help would be unlikely. As a result the individual tends to avoid travel and often wants to be with a companion. Agoraphobia may be due to a fear of something embarrassing happening, such as loss of bladder control or falling down, so the person simply avoids public situations.

Causes of generalized anxiety and panic disorders

Like most of the anxiety disorders, generalized anxiety and panic disorders often stem from early childhood experiences, often related to inner conflicts. A young boy is constantly told to grow up, but when he shows any independence his parents spank him. Those with many such experiences as children are more prone to anxiety as adults. When the individual encounters a situation that creates anxiety as an adult, the early childhood anxiety also surfaces. Usually only the emotions surface, not the actual memories of early events. This may explain overreaction to events in adulthood. When many such events occur, the anxiety no longer has a specific target and thus the person either has generalized anxiety or panic attacks.

While this has been a popular thesis, others believe there may be a biological or genetic component in such disorders. While genetic influence may exist with the panic disorder, the precise role of such an influence is far from certain.

Learning may also account for some of these reactions. Children may imitate parents or others who manifest generalized anxiety. If this is rewarded by attention and "getting their way," the pattern may become a way of life. In addition we must not overlook the powerful influence of rewards that may exist for adults who have these disorders.

Phobias, obsessions, and compulsions

Phobia—Unreasonable fear of an object, person or situation. If the individual must be near it, anxiety results; thus avoidance is likely.

Obsessive-compulsive disorder—Obsessions (recurrent, uncontrollable thoughts) or compulsions (recurrent, uncontrollable actions).

We all have fears, some of them reasonable and normal (fear of poisonous snakes); others are not all that reasonable (fear of non-poisonous snakes). A fear is not a *phobia*, however, unless it interferes with a person's relationships or daily routine or causes great distress. The person must realize the fear is unreasonable, yet suffer anxiety when around the thing feared. People can become phobic of almost anything. Common phobias include *acrophobia* (fear of high places), *hydrophobia* (fear of water), *astraphobia* (fear of thunder and lightning), *claustrophobia* (fear of enclosed places), *xenophobia* (fear of strangers), *zoophobia* (fear of animals), and *necrophobia* (fear of dead bodies). *Agoraphobia*, which often occurs with panic disorders, has already been mentioned.

Social phobia is a relatively common problem in which the individual fears public situations in which he or she may choke, be unable to talk, say something foolish, or do something else embarrassing. Perhaps the most common variety of social phobia is when the individual fears to speak in public. When asked to do so, such individuals often break into a cold sweat, have problems breathing, feel their heart pounding, and feel panicky. Others fear to eat in public, write in public, or use public lavatories. These do not technically classify as phobias unless they significantly interfere with work, school, or relationships.

Obsessive-compulsive disorders are characterized by recurrent obsessive thoughts that interfere with everyday life, or compulsive, irrational actions. The most frequent obsessions are thoughts of violence, doubt or contamination, and common compulsions include repeated hand washing (sometimes dozens of times a day), checking things over and over, and repeatedly touching something. In any six-month period, 2.5 percent of American adults have such a disorder (Karno, et al. 1988).

When Pontius Pilate condemned Christ to be crucified, the Bible records that he washed his hands (Matt. 27:24), indicating that he was not responsible for the injustice. Extrabiblical church tradition states that Pilate thereafter developed a compulsion of washing his hands many times a day in his attempt to symbolically remove his guilt for permitting the death of Christ. The tradition may not be true, but the account makes sense because guilt and anxiety feelings often cause such compulsions.

There also can be an obsessive or compulsive component in some religious activities. When the Old Testament tells us that "all our righteous acts are like filthy rags" (Isa. 64:6), the prophet does not put down righteousness, but rather criticizes ritual (righteous acts) apart from a clean heart and good motives. The Bible regularly stresses that religious actions by themselves accomplish little or nothing.

Gary Collins (1972, 134) finds a great deal of compulsive and obsessive activity in the church. Rituals may be used to avoid or at least alleviate anxiety about sins. In more informal churches personal devotions, daily Bible reading, and even church attendance may become a means of avoiding anxiety rather than an expression of love for God. For some Christians rituals add meaning to worship, but compulsive religious activities only provide a temporary relief from anxiety. The joy of Christian living, says Collins, becomes lost to the drudgery of legalism and slavery to religious compulsion. Christians must deal directly with the underlying anxiety and guilt rather than cover up problems in compulsive activity.

Causes of phobias and obsessive-compulsive disorders

Phobias are understood by some to be *anxiety that becomes attached to something*. This assumes that a general anxiety, probably from early childhood experiences, becomes targeted to some specific object or situation. The anxiety aroused by that object or situation is perceived as fear, and avoidance results (see fig. 2).

While this process may indeed explain some phobic disorders, many phobias result from a specific learning process. Learning theory explains that fears tend to develop when something previously feared is paired with a new object or situation. For example, many decades ago psychologist John Watson (Watson and Rayner 1920)

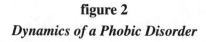

figure 2
Dynamics of a Phobic Disorder

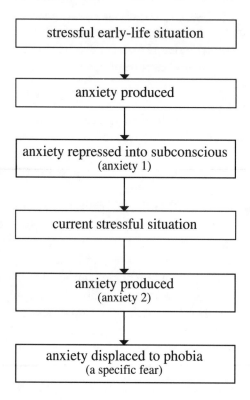

presented a rat to a baby named Albert. The little boy was interested in the rat and showed no fear. Later, Watson again presented the rat to Albert, and then made a loud noise. The loud noise frightened the baby, and the rat was removed. Still later, the rat was presented to Albert, who showed signs of fear and avoidance.

Many people's fears develop in a similar manner. For example, falling from a tree as a child may produce a fear of heights because the falling produced fear which was associated with high places. A person might develop a fear of snakes because they imitate the reactions of others (such as parents) when they first see a snake.

While learning theory gives us a straightforward explanation about

figure 3
Dynamics of an Obsessive-Compulsive Disorder

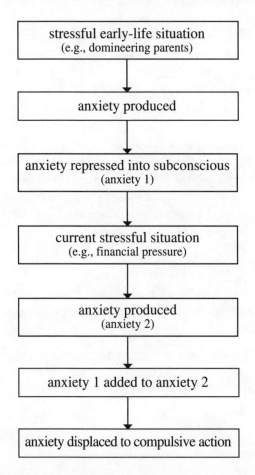

how fears develop, the question remains as to why some fears become so extreme while others are minor. The difference may relate to the anxiety theory mentioned earlier—fears become phobias because of the presence of anxiety.

Similar explanations for the obsessive-compulsive disorder have been offered. The underlying anxiety from early childhood can become attached to an action (compulsion) or thought (obsession). The reoccurrence of the action or thought triggers a message from the unconscious mind that an anxiety needs to be dealt with directly (see fig. 5.2).

Learning theory offers another explanation for obsession and compulsion, however. One person may become obsessed with checking to be sure the doors are locked several times each night; another becomes obsessed with attempting suicide. The obsessive person probably found some payoff for such thinking, a reward that made the behavior more likely to occur again. Yet, as in phobias, the emphasis upon learning does not explain why these repeated behaviors sometimes go to an irrational extreme and occur in situations where they are never rewarded. Both learning theory and the concept of anxiety have something to offer in the explanation.

To illustrate, a young girl experiences extreme anxiety while a black dog jumps on and bites her. She later represses the entire event. As an adult she does not understand why she develops anxiety symptoms whenever a black cat crosses her path.

Somatoform disorders

Somatization disorder—A number of physical symptoms reported over a span of several years for which there is no adequate physical explanation.

Hypochondriasis—Preoccupation with disease and interpreting physical sensations unrealistically. Reported problems are inconsistent with medical findings. Unrealistic fear of disease.

Somatoform pain disorder—Preoccupation with pain in the absence of medical findings.

Conversion disorder—Loss of some physical function of the body or altering of that function. Psychological, not medical factors, account for the change, and symptoms are not voluntary.

Body dysmorphic disorder—Preoccupation with some body defect.

When physical symptoms or problems result from anxiety, a *somatoform disorder* results. *Soma* comes from a Greek word meaning *the body*, and in someone with a somatoform disorder bodily symptoms or problems develop which are unexplained by medical findings. Either no medical problems exist, or diagnosed medical problems do not begin to explain the symptoms reported. These people are not faking the problems (That is called a *factitious disorder*), but rather the symptoms result from psychological problems, usually anxiety-related.

The *somatization disorder*, which is sometimes called *briquets syndrome*, takes in a number of physical complaints that cannot be explained by any findings. These complaints are usually vague yet dramatic, involving many organs of the body. This disorder, more commonly found in females, generally begins during the teen years. About 1 percent of American women have this disorder, which often begins with complaints of menstrual problems. The *DSM* lists seven broad categories of the symptoms these individuals commonly report:

1. being "sickly;"
2. neurological symptoms or conversion symptoms;
3. gastrointestinal symptoms;
4. female reproductive symptoms;
5. sexual symptoms;
6. pain symptoms, and
7. cardiopulmonary symptoms

For a diagnosis of somatization disorder at least thirteen different symptoms must be reported from several of these categories, each significant enough to seek medical help or to make some change in the person's life. Not one of the thirteen may be fully explained by an actual physical problem, and the problems occur within a span of several years.

Clearly such individuals have problems more severe than do hypochondriacs. Those with *hypochondriasis* show extreme interest in disease and in keeping healthy and often believe they have disease (or have a morbid fear of disease) in spite of reassurances from medical sources to the contrary. Physical symptoms again have little or no basis in medical findings. Hypochondria is less severe and more general than the somatization disorder.

Collins (1972, 126) notes that hypochondriacs and others with somatoform disorders often make their way to churches in hopes of finding relief from their problems. They seek a pastor or other church member on whom to unload all of their physical and other problems. Often they become very unpopular because they are often demanding and have little awareness that the listener may have other things to do.

The *somatoform pain disorder* involves the experience of pain apart from physical findings. Such pain may allow the person to avoid some activity they find unpleasant and sometimes results in attention and support.

In a *conversion disorder* psychological conflicts become converted into physical symptoms. Usually these symptoms in some way symbolize a conflict or some unacceptable impulse. Examples of conversion reactions include paralysis of some part of the body, blindness, deafness, or lack of skin sensation. The vocal chords may become paralyzed so that the person can only whisper. Paralysis may affect as much as one-half of the body. Voluntary muscles of the body may become impaired, resulting in tics (muscular twitches), convulsions and recurring movements of the body. Smith (1977) describes her own difficulties with a conversion disorder that involved paralysis, and her subsequent healing through Christian counseling.

Other than physical symptoms those with a conversion disorder show no major mental abnormalities. They are generally indifferent to the symptoms and the problems they produce. About 50 percent of those with a conversion disorder lose their symptoms within a year.

While we must be wary of distorting Scripture, Paul's blindness on the road to Damascus (Acts 9) might be considered a conversion reaction, reflecting his lack of spiritual vision in persecuting Christians. It may be significant that the Bible does not say Paul was healed of the blindness, but rather that he was filled with the Holy Spirit (Acts 9:17). Yet we must also note that something like scales fell from his eyes, which may imply something more physical was involved.

Faith healers and supposed miracle cures are often sought by those with somatoform disorders (Collins 1972, 129–30). Because they tend to be highly suggestible, those with such disorders may be influenced easily by healers or by visiting a shrine. They may unconsciously desire the attention given them when they are prayed for, and the supposed healing before a crowd increases the attention even further. Very often the healing lasts only a short time. The problem then recurs or the unconscious conflicts surface in the form of another physical problem. Nolan (1974) explores these possibilities in his research of many people supposedly restored to health by one well-known faith healer.

Certain instances of people collapsing on the stage of an evangelist ("going under the spirit" it is sometimes called) may be experiencing a temporary conversion reaction.

Collins notes that such people are not necessarily insincere nor do they consciously seek the attention. Many psychologists believe all "cures" seen in healing meetings may actually be relief from somatoform symptoms. Yet Scripture clearly teaches that divine healing occurs (James 5:13–15). Certainly among some the forgiveness of sins helps to relieve anxiety, which may be at the root of a somatoform disorder, a psychological correlate for healing. This would not make the cure any less wonderful, although perhaps it becomes less mystical. Some biblical healings were clearly supernatural and not merely a psychological phenomenon. As Collins concludes, "Psychologists can explain some of what is called divine healing, but they cannot account for all of it. God still answers the petitions of His people as they pray for the sick" (Collins 1972, 130–31; see Grazier 1989 for documentation of supernatural healing).

The *body dysmorphic disorder* involves being preoccupied with a defect the person has imagined. Sometimes the reaction is greatly disproportionate to some slight physical problem. Usually the imagined problem involves the face.

Causes of somatoform disorders

As with other anxiety disorders, there may be underlying childhood difficulties and traumatic events behind the somatoform disorders. The stress becomes displaced into physical symptoms which continue in one form or another until the underlying difficulty is relieved.

Somatoform disorders sometimes result from identifying with someone who has one or more genuine physical problems. When someone dies, a close loved one may develop symptoms of the terminal problem or problems because of unconscious psychological imitation. Sometimes the physical problems are related to the "secondary gain" or rewards the person receives for having the disability. Attention, manipulating others, freedom from unwanted tasks, and financial rewards all tend to perpetuate the difficulties. While these rewards are not usually believed to be the cause of the problem, which more likely rests in unconscious imitation and anxiety, they make such problems more difficult to treat.

Examples

The first three examples illustrate a conversion disorder:

A right-handed mother feels a sudden urge to kill her misbehaving child. She rapidly represses that unacceptable urge. Instantly her right arm becomes paralyzed. During the Vietnam War many American soldiers became paralyzed in one arm, nearly always the individual's primary shooting arm. Under hypnosis a soldier could use the arm, but it again became paralyzed when the person was not under hypnosis. A similar situation is found in a woman with multiple, lifelong sexual conflicts, who loses all sensation in her genital area and no longer enjoys sex with her husband.

The fourth example illustrates hypochondriasis:

A man in his forties develops a legitimate lower-back problem. Laid up for six weeks, he is pampered, does not have to do anything responsible, and enjoys watching television all day. Because of all that "secondary gain," he unconsciously convinces himself that his back is still in terrible condition even after it has healed completely. His wife goes to work to support the family, and he is able to avoid responsibility without feeling consciously guilty and without the criticism of his wife, who believes her husband to be physically ill. Eventually his unconscious guilt (or boredom) gets to him, he attends a "faith healing" service, and is miraculously healed. He has not consciously deceived anyone during the entire course of events.

The fifth illustrates a somatization disorder:

A college professor tactlessly corrects one of his students in class. The student becomes angry but is afraid to be aware of his anger because he might get in trouble with the professor if he speaks out.

The student's body responds with almost immediate tightness of lower-back muscles. Lactic acid accumulates and puts pressure on nerve endings in his back muscles within a few hours. Several days later he becomes immobilized by severe back pain and sees a physician. The physician will either give him pain medication or refer him to a psychiatrist. A dishonest physician might diagnose the problem as a "pinched nerve" and operate unnecessarily.

Dissociative disorders

Psychogenic amnesia—Memory impairment as a result of psychological difficulties.

Psychogenic fugue—Amnesia accompanied by suddenly leaving the home or workplace and assuming a new identity.

Multiple personality—Two or more distinct personalities exist within the individual.

Depersonalization disorder—Repeated episodes in which the person has a sense of unreality, feels in a dream, or acts mechanically, yet retains contact with reality.

Among the cluster of disorders usually termed the *dissociative disorders* the individual's identity or consciousness changes. The alterations usually begin and end abruptly, beyond the individual's conscious control.

Amnesia

With *localized amnesia* the individual has a total loss of memory about occurrences during a limited time, perhaps a few hours or a few days; with *general amnesia* an entire lifetime of experience might be forgotten. By definition the amnesia is the result of psychological problems, most likely unconscious conflicts and anxiety, rather than physical problems. Amnesia due to a brain dysfunction (a tumor or blow to the head, for example) is called *amnestic syndrome* (see chapter 7).

The individual may appear quite normal prior to and just after the amnesia. A person with *continuous amnesia* forgets each event as it happens. At other times systematized amnesia occurs in which specific, related past events are forgotten but other things are recalled.

Psychogenic fugue

Psychogenic fugue combines amnesia with wandering, which can take the person far from home and results in the development of a new identity. This can occur for a period of several days or longer, during which time they forget their past but do not seem aware that they have forgotten anything. If and when they regain their memory of the past they usually do not recall the time period involved in the fugue state. There is no evidence that they are acting out some memory of a past event, nor does their behavior appear very strange in the new identity.

Multiple personality

Multiple personality involves two or more separate personalities, one of which dominates. The transition between personalities may occur suddenly and dramatically. Each personality has a separate set of associated memories and behavior patterns, including different relationships and attitudes. Amnesia for one or more of the other personalities often exists, so that one personality may have little or no recall of what another experiences. In other cases personalities will be aware of the existence and activities of another personality. Often the personality that characterizes the person during most of his or her life is emotionally restricted, moralistic and proper. The secondary personality often exhibits the opposite behavior and attitudes.

Multiple personality has often gained media attention through popular books and dramatizations, such as *The Three Faces of Eve* in the 1950s and *Sybil* in the 1970s. A vivid first-hand account by a Christian, *On Stage as One*, was written anonymously with the help of Jan Meier. At this writing the account has not been published, but excerpts appeared in *Christian Psychology* (1985–1986).

Sometimes people have confused multiple personality with demon possession. Some biblical descriptions of demonic activity, particularly those in which the demon speaks through the person (such as Acts 19:15), sound very much like multiple personality. Yet the disorder differs in other respects.

James Friesen (1991, 222) has attempted to distinguish multiple personality from demon possession using seven criteria. Friesen believes multiple personality is a common disorder, whereas many other psychologists believe it rare. The seven traits of demons Friesen believes are not found in multiples are:

1. The spirits are arrogant and devious, not relational.
2. After the client knows of the different voices, he or she does not experience them as part of the self.
3. Spirits stir up confusion, lust, and fear in spite of therapy.
4. Spirits impose undesired behavior and then blame the person.
5. Spirits are voices but not personalities.
6. Demons produce feelings of bitterness and hatred.
7. The person pictures the entity within as varying in form, from human to nonhuman.

Depersonalization

The *depersonalization disorder* instills a feeling of unreality. The *DSM* notes that the person may feel like an outside observer of his or her body or feel outside one's mental processes. Sometimes the person feels as if in a dream or like a machine. By definition the feeling must occur persistently, not as a single episode, it must cause significant distress, and yet the person must remain in contact with reality. A mild depersonalization experience occurs in 30 percent to 70 percent of young adults, but it is not a disorder unless it meets the other criteria listed.

Causes of dissociative disorders

Trauma is often linked to dissociative disorders, trauma too painful to allow in the consciousness, so it is blocked from memory. That suppression of the memory may be accompanied by a more general loss of memory (amnesia) or memory loss accompanied by escape from the context associated with trauma or stress (fugue). Occasionally the individual attempts to deal with general stress by deliberately suppressing memories, which eventually become inaccessible due to amnesia. Those with amnestic disorders are often self-centered and very suggestible.

Multiple personality generally is linked to severe personal trauma, often early in life. Psychologists point out that, in a sense, everyone is a mild multiple, acting in somewhat different ways depending upon context and those we are with. True multiple personalities take this to an extreme where the changes in behavior are more generalized (including changes of name). The person is not fully conscious of those differences. Personalities may separate because the core person is threatened by the presence of inappropriate desires, so those desires become part of a separate person (an alternate personality). Some believe multiple personality can be subtly shaped by encouragement from others—even the inadvertent suggestions of a counselor!

Case history

Jules H. Masserman (1961) describes a woman who was raised in a very conservative religious environment. Her parents frequently accused one another of being unfaithful, but vented their hostility on the daughter through extreme demands and prohibitions throughout childhood. In college she studied to become a missionary. She married a man chosen by her parents, entering into a marriage devoid of love. Six unhappy years on the mission field ended when her husband settled into a pastorate in a small town. Here the husband become increasingly involved in the demands of the church and a lifestyle marked by prohibitions. The woman responded by daydreaming a lot about her earlier and happier college life. When she was age thirty-seven her youngest and favorite child became sick and died. The next day she disappeared. Four years later she was discovered in the distant town where she had gone to college, working as a piano teacher and performer. She had lost all memory of the past, including her identity. When a childhood friend identified her, she at first completely denied her former identity. With extensive therapy she regained her memory of the past. Her husband was very understanding and helped her to readjust to a life marked by much happier circumstances.

Treatments for the anxiety, somatoform and dissociative disorders

Disorders covered in this chapter vary considerably, as do their treatments. As with most disorders, individuals may respond differently to counseling methods depending upon the causative factors involved and the individual's personality.

Generalized anxiety and panic disorders

Many counselors spend considerable time in counseling to help the anxious client uncover underlying fear. Once located the fear can be treated as a phobia. Sometimes general relaxation methods decrease anxiety, yet if the source of the anxiety is not addressed, the results may be temporary.

Some therapists use medications to treat anxiety, particularly Librium and Valium. These can be addicting and may have such side-effects as headaches, poor coordination, and impaired judgment. Recent research has linked certain tranquilizers to increased aggression. In general, supportive counseling seems to be as effective as medication.

A more dynamic approach to counseling these disorders is to locate buried childhood experiences and repressed wishes, using a technique called *free association*. Here the client speaks freely about whatever comes to mind. As he or she begins to relax, unconscious conflicts and problems from early childhood surface and can be discussed. Sometimes the client relives troublesome early experiences, with the counselor verbally role-playing the other person in the memories. This may be repeated in the four-step process explained in chapter 4.

Phobias

When the person has a single phobia the favored treatment is *desensitization*. This involves several steps. The individual learns to relax by tightening and relaxing the muscle groups of the body, one at a time. Eventually, with practice, the person can completely relax the body. Then the counselor and client construct a list of fears, starting with the most fearful situation and progressing downward to less and less feared contexts. Someone who fears snakes might imagine holding a snake as the most feared situation, looking at a snake in a cage as less fearful, and reading a book about snakes as the least feared.

After the list is made the counselor describes the least feared of the situations on the list. Sometimes slides or pictures help visualize the fear context. If the client begins to experience fear and anxiety, he or she immediately initiates the relaxation exercises. After the client becomes able to imagine the lowest feared situation without fear, the therapist moves to the next level on the list. After a few sessions the client should be able to imagine the most feared situation without anxiety.

The client and counselor may then move from the imagined situation to an actual situation. If in the process the client begins to experience fear, they stop and being relaxing again. The basic assumption is that relaxation and anxiety are incompatible.

When the phobia is more complex or there are several phobias, desensitization may be combined with such techniques as assertiveness training, modeling (imitation), and group therapy. Helping people change their self-talk, as described in chapter 4, may also help.

Sometimes *implosion* (also called *flooding*) is used with phobic individuals. The counselor guides the client to imagine terrible variations of the feared object or situation. This process, which is very unpleasant for both counselor and client, appears to work well because the exaggerated extremes cause the original feared object to seem less terrifying.

In the book of Exodus we see an example of using *modeling* and *rewards* to overcome social phobia. Moses, in Exodus 3 and 4, complained to God that he could not lead the Israelites and confront Pharaoh. He pled, "O Lord, please send someone else to do it" (4:13) because he was ashamed of his speech. This might be considered a mild form of social phobia. God responded by gradually helping Moses overcome his phobia. Aaron became Moses' model, even though the words came from Moses (4:15). Aaron does indeed speak for Moses to Pharaoh in chapters 7 and 8. Next Moses performs the actions God demands, but still does not speak (9:8, 23). Finally Moses himself speaks to Pharaoh in 9:29. Moses gradually overcame his phobia, given time, patience, and careful instruction from the Lord.

Obsessive-compulsive disorders

No single technique works all of the time for obsessive-compulsives. Sometimes medication helps. Anatomic differences affect the brains of many of these individuals. There may be an imbalance of the chemical seratonin in the brain. In any event, psychiatric medication at times really helps.

Thought-stopping has been used to help control obsessions. This involves linking an irritating event with the recurrent, undesired thought. Initially the client is instructed to allow the obsession to come to mind, and then the counselor yells "Stop!" The loud, unexpected sound often ends the obsession. The client is then instructed to do much the same at home when the obsessions begin. Once control over the obsession has been achieved, the client can begin lowering his or her voice when saying "Stop." Eventually just thinking the word will end the obsession. In a variation on this approach the client wears a rubber band around the wrist, snapping it whenever the obsession occurs. Pain is associated with the undesired thought. The same idea can be used with compulsions.

The somatoform disorders

Somatoform disorders also are difficult to treat, in part because clients avoid or undermine therapy, insisting the problem is actually physical, not psychological. Changing the environment has reportedly been successful for some. The family must become involved because they must no longer allow the client to avoid tasks or obtain sympathy and attention for symptoms, but rather reward the client when he or she does not act sick.

Problems due to early childhood experiences may be treated through relaxation, reliving the experiences, ventilating feelings, and working through any trauma or childhood problems. Faulty perceptions may need to be corrected, and poor models understood for what they were.

One rather effective technique is simple suggestion. The client is told the symptoms will go away, and if they believe this statement the problems often do. Conversion clients are particularly suggestible. But if the underlying causes are not dealt with the problems may return, sometimes in a different form. In one study 75 percent were cured or much improved using suggestion (Carter 1949).

Dissociative disorders

If people develop dissociative disorders to avoid underlying anxiety, help comes as the client deals with that underlying anxiety so that retreat is not necessary.

Free association and directed regression can uncover the original stressful or traumatic event in childhood. The client may find relief by uncovering the awful memory. Discussing the long-forgotten experiences repeatedly incorporates the unpleasant events into the total person. Desensitization and thought stopping have also been successful with some dissociative disorders.

With all of the disorders in this chapter, underlying anxiety likely contributes to the problem. Thus some general biblical principles can be harnessed to help the person decrease anxiety, and thus help overcome the problem. These include:

1. prayer (Phil. 4:6);
2. meditation (Phil. 4:8);
3. joining a fellowship group;
4. exercise;
5. sleep (Ps. 127:2);
6. talking with a close friend;
7. living one day at a time (Matt. 6:34);
8. paying more attention to the concerns of others (Phil. 2:3–4);
9. not procrastinating (procrastinating increases anxiety), and
10. limiting the amount of time spent worrying, perhaps to fifteen minutes in the evening (When tempted to worry, defer thoughts about the problem until then.)

Other helpful verses for combating fears and phobias include Isaiah 41:10 and 1 John 4:18. Also see Minirth, Meier, and Hawkins (1989) for more detail on anxiety in general, and Hemfelt, Minirth, and Meier (1990) regarding obsessive-compulsive behavior.

6

Psychosis

The term *psychosis* means losing touch with reality. The *DSM* states that the person with psychosis creates a new reality by incorrectly perceiving the world and one's own thoughts, in spite of evidence to the contrary. Psychosis does not include minor distortions of reality that are the result of misjudgment; this is a part of most mental disorders. Psychosis often involves *delusions* (false beliefs about reality in spite of obvious contrary evidence), *hallucinations* (perceptions not based upon reality, such as hearing voices), or persistently incoherent thoughts that cause nonsensical speech.

Schizophrenia

Schizophrenia—Psychotic for at least one week, but with indications of a mental disturbance lasting at least six months. Social functioning, work, or self-care deteriorates as a result.

The most severely disabling of all the psychological problems, *schizophrenia* traps troubled persons in their own inner world of fantasies and daydreams until they withdraw from the external world. They are detached or preoccupied, and immobilized when required to make choices. They lack motivation and goal-directed behavior. They often have peculiar behavior, poor personal hygiene, and dress eccentrically.

While this disorder severely disorganizes daily behavior, the person often returns to near normal functioning given the proper treatment, although some symptoms usually remain. Those who abruptly become schizophrenic following a definite crisis have the greatest hope of recovery if the problem began well into adulthood, and they functioned well prior to the beginning of the disorder.

Usually schizophrenia begins in adolescence or early adulthood, more often among the lower socioeconomic groups. Approximately 1 percent of the population experiences some degree of the disorder.

Prior to becoming schizophrenic the person may show suspicion, shyness, withdrawal or eccentricity. Poor grooming or hygiene, peculiar behavior, inappropriate emotions, unusual speech or beliefs, lethargy, surreal perceptions, and superstition often characterize the individual prior to the actual beginning of the disorder.

Schizophrenics usually have delusions or hallucinations or both, but sometimes they simply speak incoherently or display unusual emotions. Occasionally they move excitedly, purposelessly or hold some rigid position for long periods of time.

Delusions

A delusion is an irrational belief held in spite of solid evidence to the contrary. Commonly schizophrenics have delusions of persecution, thinking people spy on them or spread rumors about them. More rarely they have delusions of grandeur, such as believing they are Christ, Hitler, or Napoleon. The person with delusions of reference believes things in the environment have a special personal significance. They may believe, for example, that a certain television program is intended specifically for them. Others may be convinced that their thoughts are being controlled, broadcast to others, or taken out or inserted into the head. Delusions often include irrational levels of jealousy.

Hallucinations

The individual with hallucinations hears, sees, or feels things that are not present. Most commonly schizophrenics may think they hear someone calling their name or insulting them, and sometimes they hear music no one else can hear.

Incoherence

Schizophrenic individuals may ramble from one topic to another, making it impossible for others to follow their train of thought. The loose associations between different ideas indicates an underlying disorder of thinking, probably due to a chemical imbalance in the brain which can be corrected with medication. Speech tends to be vague, overly abstract, repetitive, and illogical. Facts become distorted and conclusions reached with little or no evidence.

Emotions

The face and voice generally convey the emotions a person feels. Schizophrenics often show either no emotion or inappropriate emotion through their speech and facial expressions. Sometimes the individual stares and speaks in a monotone, even when speaking of exciting or horrible events. Sometimes the individual might smile or laugh while telling of a sad personal experience.

The *DSM* lists five varieties of schizophrenia:

1. *catatonic.* Individuals live in a stupor, not reacting to the environment or being relatively inactive. They resist attempts to move them, hold a rigid posture (such as holding the arms outward as if they were Christ on the cross), or make purposeless, repeated, excited movements.

2. *disorganized.* The incoherent speech and loosened associations between ideas predominate, with grossly disorganized behavior and inappropriate emotions.

3. *paranoid.* Delusions or auditory hallucinations related to one single theme occupy the individual. However, they do not manifest the incoherence, unusual emotions, and loose associations characteristic of the catatonic and disorganized schizophrenics. The guidelines for the paranoid schizophrenic became much more restrictive with the 1987 edition of the

DSM, and many previously diagnosed in this category have had to be reclassified.

4. *undifferentiated.* Incoherent speech, delusions, hallucinations, or extremely disorganized behavior marks undifferentiated schizophrenics. However, they do not meet other guidelines for the first three types.

5. *residual.* The person has been schizophrenic in the past and continues to have several related symptoms.

For a vivid first-hand description of schizophrenia read *A Promise of Sanity* (Owens 1982). This Christian writer's observations of her own schizophrenic thinking, as well as the way certain medications affected her, may be unparalleled. Not all react to psychiatric medications as did this woman, however.

Daniel 4:33–34 records an apparent schizophrenic episode in the life of King Nebuchadnezzar of Babylon: "But when his heart became arrogant and hardened with pride, he was deposed from his royal throne and stripped of his glory. He was driven away from people and given the mind of an animal; he lived with the wild donkeys and ate grass like cattle; and his body was drenched with the dew of heaven, until he acknowledged that the Most High God is sovereign over the kingdoms of men and sets over them anyone he wishes." While Nebuchadnezzar may, or may not, have been schizophrenic, he certainly was psychotic.

Causes of schizophrenia

Most of the evidence suggests a biological basis for the disorder. Relatives definitely stand at greater risk to develop the problem. The identical twin of a person with the disorder has far more risk than a fraternal twin. Biochemical imbalances in the brain are strongly associated with the symptoms of schizophrenia, as well as certain abnormalities of brain tissue.

However, a number of psychologists have long argued that environment also influences the disorder. Likely both the environment and heredity contribute to the development of schizophrenia.

Disturbing, traumatic early-childhood experiences seem to increase susceptibility to schizophrenia. The general communication patterns of families may play a part. Specifically, the mothers of schizophrenics tend to be domineering, rejecting, overprotective parents who ignored the needs of their children. In such a family the mother's emotional fulfillment derives not from the father but from the children, so she fosters their dependence upon her. The father of the schizophrenic, in contrast, tends to be more distant and passive, uninvolved with his children. He often rejects his son, acts seductively towards his daughter, and frequently criticizes his wife. Both the mother and father of a schizophrenic are more likely to be emotionally disturbed than the general population.

The idea that faulty communication patterns of the family contribute led to a classic description called the *double bind* hypothesis. In this theory the parent communicates contradictory messages to the child. For example, a parent may communicate love and acceptance through the words they use, but at the same time communicate hatred and rejection through the tone of voice and body language. Regardless of which message the child responds to, the parent indicates the child misunderstood. One can easily see that a child in such a situation never gets any reinforcing feedback that they understood what the parent communicated, so the child gives up and withdraws.

Case history

The following interview took place in a hospital ward with a woman who had been actively schizophrenic for about thirty years. Prior to her schizophrenic break at age twenty-five she had been a wife and mother to several children. While she always sat passively in her chair all day long, her moods varied from agitated, to happy, to uninterested. Regardless of her mood, the content of her speech remained the same—the themes of doom and destruction, and her own role as a prophet. Note the strong religious content of her speech, which is not unusual for schizophrenics. Perhaps schizophrenics are attracted to religion as their only hope, or perhaps they gravitate to unhealthy forms of religion. Regardless, the religious content—like everything else they perceive—is severely distorted.

Donald Ratcliff: Good morning.
Client: I'm saved. He's the more madder.

D.R.: How have you been doing this morning?

Client: I wanna be careful now—I don't want to talk too much no way.

D.R.: Uh huh.

Client: I'm not angry. I'm not angry. I overlook it all, but I was pulled down here like an [animal]. They'll wake up all of a sudden and they'll see what two guides means. We'll be overlooked then. We'll be changed completely—the whole creation.

D.R.: Uh huh. When will that happen?

Client: (stutters) When no one is expecting. Power come down from above have all the redeemed and the doomed and death and sin will be gone forever.

D.R.: Huh.

Client: And they'll say his holy's name. All the suffering and nothing on this earth changed, uh, all creation a eternally paradise.

D.R.: Hmm—uh huh.

Client: We'll all understand each other as we should.

D.R.: You seem happy about that.

Client: Yes.

D.R.: Uh huh.

Client: But I wasn't born for this earth, that's why I was marked like I am. Holy Spirit providing for my grave, like God wanted. God wanted me, my heart, and soul, and spirit. I wanna watch out so God would come up to my soul creation. They don't know what two guides mean. They'll be overlooked the end of the age.

D.R.: Uh huh. Who are the two people that guide you:

Client: (stutters) More getting at the end of the age. These people coming over here with the north born chapter they're raging for nothing, not knowing what two guides mean, too. That way. That's why this world's getting bounced. All it is is animals, more than human creatures. No wonder God's having this world come to an end faster every day. But it was the same way when Christ was on this earth. And I'm gonna the same thing for God his holy Son did. I don't have to be afraid, take my last breath, my home's above. I know not care to bless, but where I'm going to is certain. That's what this earth is certain I'm taking my holy Creator's sake. But I who did am accountable for more, because I have a different spirit, and the spirit paths. And I overlook them, I'm talking, I'm doing.

D.R.: Who is the . . .

Client: (stutters) I won't be accountable, but that way be harm, the end of the age. The right then to go to them.

D.R.: Who is the holy Creator?

Client: The one who created this earth.

D.R.: Oh, he created, I see.

Client: Yes. The holy Creator, he created this earth, and he was before he created this earth. He's forever, because he's holy. I'm holy and saved, and free, and I overlooked (stutters) they don't know what two guides mean. They'll be overlooked and we'll be changed.

D.R.: Now you say . . .

Client: And I wouldn't need to understand so like they should, and not get so mad, because (stutters) talk loud and upset. I overlook more. You know why I can't be understood.

D.R.: Ah, uh huh. You can't be understood.

Client: They've got the evil spirit after me.

D.R.: I see. Uh huh.

Client: This world's one side. I overlook it as I go through it. I doubt I couldn't do it. (stutters) the right and wrong and my guides are, so I should overlook.

D.R.: Uh. Now you say you are marked. How are you marked?

Client: Because I'm marked with this disease so I'd be an outcast in this earth. So I overlook it. But people wouldn't think about it. If they did, they'd know what two guides was. But they overlooked the end of the age.

D.R.: Uh huh.

Client: Sure.

D.R.: Uh huh. Who are the two guides again?

Client: The evil spirit and God almighty.

D.R.: I see.

Client: (stutters) God marked me what God almighty means. They'll be overlooked and we'll be changed. Sure.

D.R.: Well, it's been pleasant talking with you. Thank you.

Nonschizophrenic psychotic disorders

Delusional (paranoid) disorder—Delusions, though not of a bizarre nature. No prominent hallucinations or other unusual behavior.

Brief reactive psychosis—Incoherent speech or loose associations between ideas, delusions, hallucinations, and disorganized or catatonic behavior, accompanied by emotional turmoil in response to a stressful event.

Schizoaffective disorder—Major depression or manic episode accompanied by psychosis. Delusions or hallucinations are present apart from the extreme mood.

Induced psychotic disorder—Delusions occur because of a relationship with someone who has delusions.

Among other psychotic disorders, the most common is the *delusional (paranoid) disorder*, which previously was simply called the *paranoid disorder*. While the paranoid delusions of this disorder mimic those of schizophrenia, the person seems normal otherwise. Thinking is clear and orderly, apart from the delusion; thus only one aspect of the individual's thinking is out of touch with reality. They often believe they are spied on, conspired against, followed, drugged, or poisoned. Delusions may include elements of jealousy. Delusions tend to be sustained, rather than episodic as in mood disorders.

King Saul, unaware of the extent of his own extreme feelings of jealousy and hostility toward David when David became popular with the Israelites, developed the delusion that David was plotting to kill him. He projected his own wishes to murder David onto David (1 Sam. 18–31).

A *brief reactive psychosis* lasts between a few hours and a month. Usually some overwhelming, stressful event initiates this disorder.

Prior to the event the behavior is not as unusual as in schizophrenics prior to the beginning of their psychosis.

A *schizoaffective disorder* is characterized by a mixture of symptoms from a mood disorder and schizophrenia. The schizophrenia-like symptoms, such as delusions, hallucinations, or loose associations between ideas, occur as the individual goes into either the manic high mood swing or the depressive low mood swing.

The *induced psychotic disorder* or *folie a deux* occurs when a paranoid delusion is shared with another person. The individual who already has a psychotic delusion is usually the dominant individual in the friendship and generally imposes that delusion on the healthier individual. Usually the delusion is somewhat realistic and believable, often linked to the common experiences of both people.

Causes of nonschizophrenic psychotic disorders

Many of the same factors found for schizophrenia may be at the heart of other psychotic disorders. Family background, in particular, seems quite similar.

The delusional (paranoid) disorder may relate to early learning in which the child is taught to harshly categorize people as *all good* or *all bad*, denying the possibility that there might be some mixture of traits. They often come from domineering, critical families that suppress the child. These individuals often have strong feelings of failure and inferiority that contribute to their abnormality.

Example

An extremely insecure individual who is flunking out of medical school uses distortion to protect himself from the pain of reality. He convinces himself that he will soon be asked to become president of the medical school because of his tremendous insights, and he hears God's voice several times per hour reassuring him of his delusions.

Treatment for psychotic disorders
Schizophrenia

With the development of antipsychotic medication in the 1950s, many who were once hospitalized for life can now return to relative normalcy. Thus the central treatment for most schizophrenics, and many other psychotics, is prescribed drugs.

Unfortunately, Thorazine, the first of the antipsychotic medications, is still the most prescribed medication for schizophrenia. Other medications commonly used are Mellaril, Stelazine, Prolixin, Navane, and Haldol. Some of the newer drugs have fewer side effects. A fairly new drug, Clozaril, often helps when these other medications are ineffective, although it is quite expensive and can be dangerous at times. These medications have brought dramatic improvements for many—indeed the average hospital stay today is thirteen days, rather than the months and even years prior to the development of these medications.

The news is not all positive. Some of these medications have side-effects or must be monitored closely to avoid toxicity, the point at which a medication becomes a poison to the body. In addition, a large minority of people do not seem to be helped by antipsychotic drugs. Dosages are often determined by trial and error. Yet, in spite of such problems, the use of these medications has signaled a major breakthrough in helping individuals with this disorder.

Side-effects of these medications include drowsiness and allergic skin reactions for Thorazine, parkinsons syndrome for Mellaril, allergic skin reactions and other problems for Stelazine and Prolixin, restlessness for Navane, and jaundice for Haldol. Other possible side-effects include muscular disturbances, such as involuntary head and neck movements, difficulty in learning due to deterioration of brain areas, and, less commonly, sexual dysfunction, heart problems, neck and head rigidity, and loss of creativity and initiative (see appendix B). Fortunately, many side-effects can be controlled by the use of additional medications.

Other biologically-based therapies include electroconvulsive treatment (ECT, see pp. 60–61), which only seems to help severe catatonics. Megavitamin treatments and renal dialysis (purifying the blood) have rarely helped.

Counseling may supplement medication. In supportive therapy the client talks through desires and difficulties, and the therapist evaluates the home environment for sources of stress and tension. Biofeedback increases the client's attention span. The discussion of early childhood experiences generally does not help.

Other methods found to be beneficial include cognitive retraining to change negative self-statements. Halfway houses, in which residents gradually learn to take greater responsibility for shopping, employment, and running the household, have met with success. The token economy system, in which the individual receives rewards for performing tasks responsibly, succeeds for some schizophrenics. Some therapists attempt to reward rational speech and behavior, while ignoring psychotic episodes and statements about delusions and hallucinations. While such procedures appear to help some, others do not seem to be significantly affected by these measures.

Other psychotic disorders

With many of the other psychotic disorders medication and some of the above counseling methods are necessary. Several distinctive approaches have been attempted with the delusional (paranoid) disorder. It is important to realize that within psychotic disorders a physiologic disorder exists involving a neurotransmitter called *dopamine*. This physiological disorder often must be treated with antipsychotic medication for the person to be able to perceive reality.

Those with the delusional (paranoid) disorder usually resist treatment because they perceive questioning of the delusion as a threat. When the counselor expresses any doubt of a paranoid delusion, the client begins to suspect the counselor of being a part of the conspiracy. For example, if the delusion is that communists are everywhere, the counselor must be a communist if he or she questions that assumption. Rarely do delusional people seek therapy; they are generally forced into counseling by others. Methods that show some success often do not last long.

One approach, called *end around*, seeks meaning in the delusions. In the process, the counselor generates trust by the client and can eventually bring up sensitive issues related to the delusions. With this approach the counselor accepts the client, but does not affirm the delusion. If the client asks if the delusion seems reasonable, the counselor might say that it is impossible to prove otherwise (it usually is) and then emphasizes the person's feelings about the matter. Usually fear is the key emotion behind the delusion. After a good relationship has developed, the counselor gradually begins to point out the huge resources needed for the delusion to be true. It is also

helpful to point out the similarities between the client's and counselor's lives, so that the counselor becomes a new role model. Discussion of the counselor's worries and ways of coping can also help
the modeling (imitation), as does the use of humor in counseling.

While biological approaches, such as ECT and psychosurgery,
have been attempted, they often backfire by reinforcing the paranoid beliefs. Relaxation approaches to reduce anxiety sometimes
help. If the delusions are job-related, a change of occupation may be
a good step. Minimizing sources of general stress at work and home
is desirable. Yet with all of these approaches, delusions are often not
helped a great deal, particularly if they have existed for very long.

The delusional individual needs something in which he or she
can trust and have perfect confidence. A relationship with Christ is
clearly the best answer. Unfortunately many delusional individuals
have difficulty believing in God, either because their paranoia extends
to religious leaders and Christians in general or because they may
have combined religion and paranoia. With difficult disorders only a
genuine encounter with Christ and a secure relationship with the
Lord can produce any peace and hope for permanent recovery.

7

Physical Problems

Psychological problems can result in physical disorders, and certain physical problems
affect psychological health. The person acts as a unity; the psychological and the physical influence one another.

Psychophysiological disorders

Psychological factors affecting physical condition—Some event or
series of events cause or aggravate a genuine physical problem.

Anorexia nervosa—Weight is not sufficient for one's height and
age, due to a fear of becoming fat and an unrealistic perception of one's shape, size, or weight.

Bulimia nervosa—Recurring binge eating during which one feels
a loss of control, accompanied by excessive concern about the
shape and weight of the body.

Within illnesses historically known as *psychosomatic*, psychological stress directly cause physical problems, such as asthma, rapid

105

heartbeat, obesity, headaches, acne, painful menstruation, arthritis, nausea, vomiting, ulcers, high blood pressure, colitis, and hyperthyroidism. Unlike the somatoform disorders, these are genuine physical problems for which there is clear medical evidence. They usually arise from causes unrelated to psychological stress, and even when a person with a psychological disorder becomes asthmatic or arthritic, other physical factors may be responsible. Yet many suffer from such problems because of excessive stress.

In addition to "psychological factors affecting physical condition," there are two eating disorders producing physical problems from psychological factors. *Anorexia* means a drastic weight loss or not increasing weight as would be expected during the body's development. The person diagnosed as anorexic, according to *DSM* guidelines, must weigh 15 percent below what would be expected for body size and age. The disorder relates to a fear of becoming fat. The individual perceives his or her body as being fat, even when it is underweight.

Thoughts of food and calories preoccupy the person, who may exercise a great deal in spite of weakness from the low amount of food intake. Sometimes they have delayed sexual development and may lose interest in sex. The *DSM* (p. 66) states that 95 percent of those with this disorder are women. The problem has been recognized only in this century and only in Western countries. Five percent to 18 percent of those with anorexia die from it (Szmukler and Russell 1986).

Bulimia includes binge eating, in which the person consumes a massive amount of food, often high-calorie foods at one time. The individual seems to lose control. Afterward, because of concern for weight, they purge themselves by self-induced vomiting or using laxatives. They may fast, diet, or vigorously exercise to avoid weight gain from bingeing. As in anorexia, bulimics fret about the shape and weight of their bodies. Bulimia affects perhaps 15 percent of women college students (Foreyt, 1986).

Bulimia and anorexia result in severe physical problems related to starvation and/or purging. Women's menstrual cycles usually stop or never begin, anemia and dehydration are common, urinary and bowel problems often develop, and there can be damage to the digestive system.

Causes of psychosomatic illness

Psychosomatic illness may relate to high levels of stress. An arousal system normally sends hormones to various parts of the body when the person perceives some psychological threat. When fear or anger bombards various organs of the body with hormones, blood pressure and heart rate increase, digestion slows, and the body stands at "red alert," ready to fight or flee.

The high stresses many people experience in modern society produces this same bombardment, but the individual may not work off the effect of those hormones; fighting or running does not occur when the person becomes stressed. Over time, the bombardment of hormones takes its toll on the body's organs, damaging the weakest in that particular person. Ulcers result if the stomach is weak, high blood pressure or headaches occur if the circulatory system is weak, heart problems develop if the heart is weak.

The perception of stress also plays a part. Some people have more intense stress reactions to a given stressful situation. Some individuals seem to be able to cope effectively with high levels of stress without getting upset and anxious, while others have a much lower tolerance for stress. Learning and biological factors may influence an individual's response to stressful situations.

What causes anorexia and bulimia? Psychological factors appear to play the dominant role, considering the fact that the problem almost exclusively develops during adolescence or the early twenties. Undoubtedly our culture's extreme emphasis upon thin being beautiful has a great deal to do with the disorders. In many cultures, being overweight is either desirable or not a significant factor in determining beauty. In contrast, most of today's models and performers are thin. The few exceptions to this tend to be comedians— people to be laughed at. Perfectionism and an extreme desire for self-control are also common with bulimics and anorexics.

Organic disorders

Delirium—Inattention to what is occurring, disorganized thinking, and other problems due to some organic cause.

Dementia—Memory impairment and other thought problems due to some organic cause.

Amnestic disorder—Intellectual impairment without other thought problems, due to some organic cause.

Organic delusional disorder—Delusions occur due to some organic cause.

Organic hallucinosis—Hallucination occur due to some organic cause.

Organic mood disorder—Mood is persistently elevated or depressed due to some organic cause.

Organic anxiety disorder—Panic attacks occur repeatedly or there is generalized anxiety due to some organic cause.

Organic personality disorder—Personality disturbance occurs due to some organic cause.

Organic factors are behind some psychological problems. Organic factors involve deterioration of brain functioning due to tumors, head injury, infections, natural aging processes or chemical intake. Intoxication and withdrawal symptoms included by the *DSM* will be considered separately in chapter 8.

Delirium

Delirious individuals become disoriented by first losing track of time and then of place. Disorientation toward persons is rare in delirium; delusions and hallucinations are very common. Visual hallucinations, particularly of animals, occur frequently in *delirium tremens* (*alcohol withdrawal syndrome*). Symptoms of delirium frequently increase in the evening, when visual and auditory stimuli are more easily misinterpreted. Memory loss is greater for recent events than for remote events. Restlessness, with picking movements of the hands, is also common. Slurred speech, lack of muscular coordination, and loss of balance in walking may develop.

The cause of a delirium should be determined as quickly as possible by a physician. Often blood and urine tests are the only way the cause can be identified. Physical problems (for example, diabetes), insufficient oxygen in the brain, or even thyroid or other glandular diseases can be responsible for a delirium. Prompt treatment of a diabetic delirium or a delirium tremens can be life saving.

Dementia

Patients with a *dementia* account for 20 percent of all first admissions to mental hospitals. More than 50 percent of geriatric patients in mental hospitals and as many as 10 percent of the general elderly population may be affected by dementia.

Dementia is a progressively severe symptom complex caused by dysfunction of the brain, accompanied by abnormal irreversible changes in cerebral tissue. Symptoms include impaired orientation, memory, judgment and intellectual function, and inability to show deep—or any—emotions. Within the early phase of this progressive disease the person experiences forgetfulness or loss of recent memory, numerous physical complaints without identifiable cause, loss of interests and abilities, low frustration tolerance, and depression. Depression accompanies nearly early dementia because the individual senses some loss of personal thought processes.

Disorientation marks the middle phase of dementia, first to time, then to place, and finally to person. Remote memory becomes impaired along with recent memory. Concentration, calculation, and judgment deteriorate. The mood becomes shallow and changeable, often with tears coming easily. Speech slows, and the person become less emotionally expressive. Psychotic symptoms, such as delusions or hallucinations, often begin in the middle phase. In the last phase an individual may be unable to walk or talk. Generally confined to bed, the person usually is incontinent.

Diagnosis arises primarily from the progressive development of symptoms. Psychological testing reveals distortion and persistent repetition of a verbal or motor response. An intelligence test usually shows a lower performance than verbal score. An electroencephalogram identifies diffuse, slow waves. To rule out other reversible causes of poor thinking, a physician may have blood samples analyzed for toxins, infections, or deficiency diseases.

Although most dementias have an undetermined etiology, some are caused by thyroid disease, chronic liver and kidney disease, chronic high blood pressure, lack of oxygen, alcohol or drug abuse, trauma, or cancer. Dementias may, therefore, develop at almost any age, although presenile dementias, developing before age sixty-five, are less common than senile dementias occurring after age sixty-five. *Alzheimers disease* is a well-known variety of dementia.

Organic anxiety disorder is characterized by panic attacks or generalized anxiety, much like that described in chapter 5. Like the other organic disorders, symptoms closely resemble those of the purely psychological equivalent, except that some specifically organic factor may be found.

Amnestic syndrome involves impairment in short-term memory due to head trauma, chronic alcohol use, thiamine deficiency, or some other organic factor. In contrast, *organic hallucinosis* features recurrent hallucinations caused by alcoholism, LSD intoxication, sensory deprivation, seizures, or another physical problem.

With *organic mood syndrome*, disturbance in mood secondary to a specific organic factor, such as drugs, hormones, steroid medication, cushings disease, hyperthyroidism, hypothyroidism, or viral illnesses.

Organic personality syndrome involves marked change in personality due to trauma, vascular accidents, steroid medication, thyroid disease, or another physical cause. The personality change may include sudden emotional changes, temper outbursts, sexual indiscretions, marked apathy, or suspicion.

Symptoms originating from physical problems

Just as a disturbed mind affects the body in psychophysiologic disorders, a disturbed or sick body can affect the mind. Although any physical illness may manifest nervousness or depression, psychiatric symptoms particularly signal certain disorders.

Thyroid gland abnormalities

The thyroid gland, located in the neck just below the larynx, is an endocrine gland that secretes thyroxin into the blood, enabling normal growth and maturation. Thyroid disorders and some other glandular problems commonly show psychiatric symptoms.

Hyperthyroidism usually manifests a history of weight loss in spite of an increase in appetite, sweating with heat intolerance, weakness, and fatigue. Anxiety and nervousness commonly accompanies hyperthyroidism. Occasionally the individual becomes hyperactive and may manifest manic symptoms. Hyperthyroidism may also exhibit depression, especially if the onset of the disorder is slow. Hyperthyroidism is most common in individuals between the ages of thirty and fifty, but it may occur at any age. It is three times more common in women than in men.

Hypothyroidism usually produces weight gain without increase in appetite and food consumption, facial puffiness, dry skin, loss of hair, and intolerance of cold. Most commonly depression accompanies hypothyroidism, but paranoia may also appear. The hypothyroid individual may even become delirious and experience hallucinations. Once called *myxedema madness*, hypothyroidism tends to appear in the thirty-to-fifty-year age group but may occur at any age. It occurs in females five times more often than in males.

Parathyroid gland abnormalities

The parathyroid glands are four small glands embedded in the thyroid gland, two near the top and two near the bottom. The parathyroid secretes a hormone regulating the use of calcium in the body. *Hyperparathyroidism* usually causes weakness, loss of appetite, stomach ulcers, sometimes kidney stones, and often a series of bone fractures. *Hypoparathyroidism* sometimes produces muscle spasms or increased reflexes. Both disorders are often marked by anxiety and hyperactivity, although some cases exhibit depression, withdrawal, and apathy. If left untreated, these disorders can lead to a toxic psychosis, characterized by confusion and disorientation. Both disorders appear more often in women and in the forty-to-sixty-year age group.

Adrenal gland abnormalities

Tumors of the adrenal medulla nearly always produce anxiety symptoms, including fear, trembling, and sweating, with a markedly elevated blood pressure.

A *hyperactive adrenal cortex* (*cushings syndrome*) generally shows itself in a history of weight gain and fatigue. Body fat is redistributed—the arms and legs become thin, but the body takes on a bloated appearance. The individual often has a "moon" face and a "buffalo-bump" back. Bruises are frequent and the thin skin may have reddish purple marks. Psychiatric symptoms vary from anxiety or depression to serious psychosis, resembling schizophrenia.

Adrenal cortex insufficiency (addisons disease) produces weight loss, low blood pressure, increased pigmentation of the skin and gums, nausea and vomiting, and weakness. Depression and apathy are its earlier psychiatric symptoms. The individuals often develop a mild organic brain syndrome with a noticeable memory defect. Hallucinations, delusions, and psychosis occur rarely. Addisons disease is less common than cushings syndrome. Both diseases may be caused by abnormalities originating within the adrenal gland itself or by an overactive or underactive pituitary gland, which regulates adrenal function.

Pituitary gland abnormalities

The pituitary gland, just beneath the brain, secretes a number of hormones that regulate other endocrine glands. Thus tumors developing in the pituitary gland may affect the body and mind via the thyroid, adrenal, or other glands.

Deficiency diseases

Certain deficiency diseases, especially a vitamin B_{12} deficiency, can produce a blood disorder called *pernicius anemia*. That disorder commonly results in weight loss, weakness, a sore tongue, and tingling or numbness in the hands and feet. Depression is the most common psychiatric symptom, but an organic brain syndrome may develop if the disorder goes untreated. Pernicious anemia is more common in females and in the forty-to-sixty-year age range.

Hypoglycemia (low blood sugar) has been overdiagnosed in recent years as a possible cause of anxiety or depression. Its symptoms of trembling, sweating episodes, intense hunger, fatigue, and dizziness can be mimicked by clinical anxiety and depression.

Other organic disorders

Brain tumors produce depression, anxiety, and sometimes mild or even marked personality changes. Such tumors are associated with a history of headaches, nausea, and vomiting. Electroencephalography (EEG), X-ray photography, and computerized scanning (CAT scans, PET scans, and MRI scans) enable a physician to look closely enough at brain structure to make the diagnosis.

Many other physical disorders cause psychological symptoms. Cancer, for example, may bring on depression even without physical accompaniments. Most psychological disorders of this type, however, have other detectable physical complaints, which can be readily recognized by a physician.

Causes of organic disorders

Some problem in the brain, such as a brain tumor, head injury, or hardening of the arteries, causes organic disorders. Surprising though it be, the severity of the problem does not always indicate the extensiveness of the damage. The location of the brain damage or dysfunction definitely correlates to the particular kind of problem experienced. Sometimes brain damage may accentuate faulty personality traits that existed previously.

Treatment for physical problems

Psychosomatic illness can be treated with a wide variety of medications. The best treatment for these physical problems, however, is prevention. The high levels of hormones resulting from stress need to be dissipated through regular exercise and relaxation training (relaxation helps the body neutralize the effects of hormones). The person may also need to become more assertive, since feelings of helplessness can be extremely stressful. The counselor can encourage individuals to master stressful situations through role-playing and imitation. Learning to predict upcoming stressful situations also improves the individuals ability to control stress.

Peptic ulcers

A drug introduced in the 1970s, Tagamet, offers the best treatment for ulcers. This medication reduces stomach acid and aids healing in about 70 percent to 95 percent of the cases within a few months. Those with ulcers often need rest and relaxation. Counselors might teach those with ulcers to better manage their anxiety. Some psychologists report that dealing with early childhood stresses and anxiety helps some individuals. Biofeedback, involving self-control of acid secretions in the stomach, has been attempted but remains largely experimental.

High blood pressure

Hypertension may require medication. Anti-hypertensive drugs are most likely to help in severe case, but do less for mild cases. They may also have negative side-effects, such as depression and sexual dysfunction. Counseling methods include relaxation training, meditation, and biofeedback of blood pressure. Of these, relaxation training seems most effective. It may also benefit the client to emphasize that the environment is not necessarily hostile, and to encourage changes in the environment to decrease stress. Some counselors encourage their clients to release hostility through sports or other forms of exercise.

Migraine headaches

Migraine headaches, which are due to contraction and then dilatation of arteries in the head, often respond well to analgesics (pain killers), tranquilizers, and medications intended to constrict the arteries. Relaxation often aids treatment. Individuals with migraines are often perfectionistic in their personality structure, thus psychotherapy may help when the cause is not purely organic.

Asthma

When this problem results from psychological stress, it may be perpetuated to gain the attention of others. Some therapists report that if the family decreases the attention for asthma symptoms, and rewards fewer coughing spells marked improvement may follow for asthmatic children. Again, relaxation techniques often help. Biofeedback, with the person monitoring and attempting to raise body temperature, has proven useful.

Eating disorders

Eating disorders respond well to group therapy that rewards eating properly and confronts unrealistic social norms regarding weight. Faulty self-perception requires new self-talk and a redefinition of femininity, for most woman anorexics are unrealistic about what men find attractive. Counselors should emphasize that there are few payoffs in anorexia and bulimia, and severe costs in health.

Organic mental disorders

Brain surgery or medication to remove or shrink tumors obviously removes the cause of some mental disorders. If there was damage, rather than destruction, of brain tissue, hope for recovery increases. Recover most frequently occurs if the organic problem results from mild oxygen deprivation, pressure from brain trauma or tumor, infections, or pressure from excessive fluid (hydrocephalis). Since neurons generally repair themselves, treatment focuses on keeping the person alive and as healthy as possible. If neurons have been destroyed, they rarely—if ever—regain function.

Medications sometimes reduce or delay negative symptoms, although they do not cure. Antidepressants, such as Tofranil or Elavil, in low doses may help individuals overcome the depression often associated with dementia. When organic disorders produce psychotic symptoms, a major tranquilizer or antipsychotic agent, such as Haldol or Mellaril, may remediate some of the symptoms

Organic disorders may require restructuring the lifestyle. These individuals need to learn ways to cope with their problems, such as using memo pads by those with the amnestic disorder. People with dementia need a simplified environment and their days need to be structured to decrease confusion. Seldom able to care for themselves completely, they need help with hygiene, diet and rest.

Generally recovery from head trauma involves a six-stage process: (1) simple reflexes; (2) restless and purposeless movement; (3) some purposeful movements, without speech or understanding; (4) return of a few words or phrases, often delivered in an explosive manner; (5) uninhibited speech and action, although still a bit disoriented and usually unable to recall the event, and (6) return of orientation and social decorum.

The return of abilities after a stroke often comes only after systematic retraining. Such training should begin as soon as possible, preferably within the first six to twelve months after the stroke.

Counselors need to help their clients express anger and depression resulting from organic disorders. While this will not help heal the brain, it can help the person cope. Sometimes aggression develops because the individual is incapacitated, not directly from the disorder itself. Rewards for gradual improvement of physical abilities may increase motivation, while biofeedback of muscle control especially helps children. Making therapy a game is a good idea.

Organic mental disorders remind us all of the magnificent character of the brain, and the tremendous wisdom of its Creator. Each of us carries one of these, the most sophisticated organ in the universe. It offers a dim reflection of the ultimate intelligence of the universe, God himself!

8

Addictions and Impulse Control

Consideration of the use of drugs for non-medicinal purposes, sometimes referred to as substance abuse, includes the physical and psychological effects of such drugs and problem behavior resulting from their use. Since addiction involves the inability to control impulses, we will also discuss the other impulse control disorders.

Intoxication and withdrawal

Intoxication—A chemical imbalance affecting the central nervous system due to the use of drugs for nonmedicinal purposes. Problem behaviors of various types accompany intoxication.

Withdrawal—Syndrome of physical and/or psychological stresses resulting from a decrease or termination of a drug used for nonmedicinal purposes.

117

Intoxication and withdrawal problems follow the use of any of a number of drugs. The *DSM* specifically lists alcohol, amphetamines, caffeine, cannabis, cocaine, hallucinogens (such as LSD), inhalants, nicotine, opioids (such as heroin), PCP, or sedatives. Drug use can produce such organic mental disorders as delirium, hallucinosis, amnesia, dementia, delusions, or an organic mood disorder (see chapter 7).

Intoxication

Intoxication refers to drug-impaired mental and organic function leading to problem behavior, such as belligerence or poor judgment, resulting from one of the above substances. With alcohol intoxication one often observes slurred speech, lack of coordination, memory impairment, unsteady walking, rapidly changing mood, decreased sexual or aggressive inhibitions, irritability, talkativeness, or fighting. Genesis 9:20–21 records perhaps the first account of alcohol intoxication.

Alcoholics can often consume more alcohol than the average person before symptoms occur. Because of chronic intoxication, alcoholics often suffer from medical complications, such as injury from falls or a suppressed immune system. Prolonged intoxication can lead to one of the organic brain disorders, such as *alcohol amnestic syndrome (korsakoff syndrome)* in which memory loss is permanent.

Barbiturate intoxication symptoms essentially match those of alcohol intoxication, although the user dies much more frequently from barbiturates than from alcohol.

Opioid intoxication produces euphoria, depression, apathy, or psychomotor retardation. Alcohol and barbiturate intoxication does not constrict the pupils of the eyes; cocaine, amphetamine, and hallucinogen intoxication cause the pupils to dilate. Administration of an opioid by injection into a vein produces a characteristic "rush," a reaction similar to an orgasm and localized in the abdomen.

Cocaine intoxication causes excitement, elation, grandiosity, talkativeness, resistance to fatigue, and a sense of confidence. Physical symptoms include a rapid heartbeat, pupil dilation, elevated blood pressure, and nausea. Paranoid thinking and impaired judgment may exist. In susceptible individuals the intoxication may result in an underlying psychosis. *Amphetamine intoxication* in most aspects matches cocaine intoxication.

Hallucinogen intoxication produces a subjective intensification of perception, feelings of depersonalization, illusions, or hallucinations. "Flashback" hallucinations may occur later. Physical symptoms include pupil dilation, rapid heartbeat, sweating, blurring of vision, tremors, or incoordination. Maladaptive behavior patterns include marked anxiety and depression, fear of losing one's mind, paranoid thoughts, impaired judgment, and failure to meet responsibilities.

Cannabis (marijuana) intoxication stimulates euphoria, a sensation of slowed time, apathy, a subjective intensification of perception, or a preoccupation with auditory or visual stimuli. Physical symptoms include eye-watering, rapid heartbeat, increased appetite, and a dry mouth. Maladaptive behavior patterns include paranoid thoughts, panic attacks, fear of going insane, impaired judgment, and failure to meet responsibilities. Repeated intoxication will permanently change the brain waves, since toxic substances in marijuana can alter the fatty tissue of the brain. With permanent brain wave changes come corresponding behavioral changes, such as chronic lethargy and loss of motivation.

Caffeine intoxication often produces restlessness, nervousness, excitement, loss of sleep, intestinal problems, muscle twitching, or rambling conversation. Intoxication can occur from consuming as little as 250 mg. of caffeine. One cup of coffee contains 100 mg. to 150 mg.; tea is one-half as strong and caffeinated soft drinks one-third as strong as coffee.

Withdrawal

In contrast to intoxication, *withdrawal* symptoms result from reducing or ceasing to use a specific substance that was regularly used to the point of intoxication. Common symptoms include restlessness, anxiety, irritability, insomnia, and impaired attention. The person is overwhelmed with the desire to resume taking the drug.

Alcohol withdrawal produces a coarse tremor of the hands. Nausea and vomiting may also be present. Grand mal seizures are not uncommon. The symptoms of barbiturate withdrawal are almost identical to those of alcohol withdrawal. *Opioid withdrawal* may produce depression, tremor, weakness, nausea, vomiting, and joint pain. One may also see pupil dilation, sweating, diarrhea, rapid heart-beat, or fever. *Amphetamine withdrawal* may produce fatigue, disturbed sleep, or increased dreaming. Touch or smell hallucinations may occur. Violent and aggressive behavior is common. Facial expression may change a great deal. *Tobacco withdrawal* is probably caused by withdrawal of the nicotine in tobacco. A craving for tobacco usually reaches its peak in twenty-four hours. A change in mood and performance may occur, as well as dullness, sleep disturbance, intestinal disturbances, and headaches.

Not everyone reacts in the same way to a given amount of a drug. Weight, metabolism genetic factors, prior experiences, expectations, and other factors significantly influence the degree of effect from a given drug.

Substance use disorders

Psychoactive substance dependence—Some indication of not being able to control use of nonmedicinal drugs.

Psychoactive substance abuse—Continued use of a nonmedicinal drug in spite of the problems caused or dangers involved.

Intoxication and withdrawal directly result from the brain's interaction with certain substances. The *DSM* distinguishes these kinds of problems from *substance use disorders*, which refer to abnormal behavior resulting from the regular use of these substances. These are, again, classified by the specific drug used.

A combination of several factors indicates *substance dependence.* Individuals may begin to take greater dosages than originally intended, or take the drug longer than intended. They may report that they cannot control the use of the drug, or they spend a great deal of time obtaining the substance. Frequent intoxication or withdrawal symptoms also indicate dependence. Use continues in spite of problems produced. Tolerance for the drug grows, so that increasing amounts are needed to produce the intended effect and stave off withdrawal symptoms. Serious interference with everyday life also indicates dependence.

The substance abuser ignores potential and actual problems resulting from use of the drug over a period of at least one month. The behavior may become impulsive or irresponsible, until the person fails to meet important obligations. Sometimes these people develop personality disorders as a result of drug abuse (see chapter 11). If the substance abuse begins early in life the youngster may fail to complete school and have a low occupational achievement as an adult. Traffic accidents, physical injury, and illness (such as malnutrition and hepatitis) commonly complicate life.

Alcohol dependence results in several such complications. The number of those with *cirrhosis*, a fatal disease, has increased significantly in the United States, in part because of a high incidence of alcoholism. Depression commonly appears in alcohol dependency, which may partly account for the high rate of suicide among alcohol-dependent persons.

Barbiturate dependency often occurs among middle-class persons who take barbiturates for insomnia. Some individuals keep increasing the dose as their tolerance to the drug builds up, then begin to use (abuse) the barbiturate to help them feel calmer during the day. Barbiturate dependency also occurs among adolescents who use barbiturates in peer situations to reach a euphoric "high."

Opioids have long been abused. About half of the individuals who engage in opioid abuse develop opioid dependency. A majority of individuals with opioid dependency die before the age of forty because of their lifestyle.

In cocaine dependency one sees the usual symptoms of withdrawal on cessation or reduction of the cocaine. Anxiety, trembling, fatigue, irritability, and depression are common about one hour after the cocaine effect wears off. Amphetamine dependence includes either psychological dependency or a pattern of being intoxicated during the day. Social complications include fighting, loss of friends, missed work, and legal difficulties.

With marijuana dependency the person loses interest in activities that previously produced interest. Motivation decreases, which brings other social complications.

Hallucinogen (LSD) abuse has received much attention from the news media. It can be especially detrimental to certain borderline individuals who may overtly break with reality after its use.

Nicotine dependence involves a mental problem most people probably are not aware of. Research indicates that chronic use of

tobacco makes certain physical disease more likely, including bronchitis, emphysema, coronary artery disease, and vascular disease.
Perhaps 15 percent of the deaths in the United States result from
diseases either caused or aggravated by the consumption of tobacco.
The use of tobacco becomes a disorder with a repeated need to use
the substance and distress occurs when the use of the drug discon-
tinues. Smokers often feel unable to stop.

A large proportion of the adult population uses tobacco. Men
use it more than women, although use by women has increased.
Relapse rate is high among those who attempt to stop, over half
relapsing in the first six months and about 70 percent relapsing
within a year (see Minirth, et al. 1988).

The Bible has a great deal to say about alcohol. We see the first
mention of alcohol in Genesis 9, when Noah's inhibitions become so
significantly lowered due to intoxication that he lies naked in his
tent. In Genesis 19 an inebriated Lot becomes so disinhibited that
incest results. Alcoholism, accompanied by rebellion and stubbornness, called for public stoning under the Mosaic law (Deut.
21:18–21).

The Bible emphasizes that the use of alcohol is not wise (Prov.
20:1) and that it can produce poverty (Prov. 21:17, and 23:20–21).
Proverbs 23:29–35 is a classic description of intoxication:

> Who has woe? Who has sorrow? Who has strife? Who has
> complaints? Who has needless bruises? Who has bloodshot eyes?
> Those who linger over wine, who go to sample bowls of mixed
> wine. Do not gaze at wine when it is red, when it sparkles in the
> cup, when it goes down smoothly! In the end it bites like a snake
> and poisons like a viper. Your eyes will see strange sights and your
> mind imagine confusing things. You will be like one sleeping on
> the high seas, lying on top of the rigging. "They hit me," you will
> say, "but I'm not hurt! They beat me, but I don't feel it! When will
> I wake up so I can find another drink?"

A similar description is found in Isaiah 28:7 and 8: "And these also
stagger from wine and reel from beer: Priests and prophets stagger
from beer and are befuddled with wine; they reel from beer, they
stagger when seeing visions, they stumble when rendering decisions.

All the tables are covered with vomit and there is not a spot without filth."

Numerous times the Bible denounces intoxication (Rom. 13:13; 1 Cor. 5:11 and 6:9–10; Gal. 5:19–21; Eph. 5:18, and 1 Pet. 4:3). Addiction is rarely mentioned but always as something to be avoided (Titus 2:3). Clearly the Bible speaks against excessive use of alcohol, and the danger of becoming dependent suggests that the use of alcohol and other drugs for nonmedicinal purposes should be avoided altogether.

Causes of substance abuse

What causes some people to use these drugs, including alcohol and tobacco? Obviously there can be many reasons. Gary Collins (1972, 164) suggests four reasons some become alcoholics. First, children imitate parents who use alcohol to decrease tension. Second, when alcohol becomes readily available, alcoholism becomes more likely. Third, cultural values may encourage or discourage excessive use of alcohol. Fourth, alcoholism becomes more likely in the absence of other means of decreasing anxiety. Fifth, a factor not emphasized by Collins is possible genetic influence. While the majority of children of alcoholics do not become alcoholics, they are more likely to do so than the general population, even when adopted as infants by nonalcoholic parents. Research continues into the possible genetic or other biological mechanisms involved in this process.

Collins also suggests six reasons for drug addiction, which particularly apply to young people: (1) curiosity and response to group pressure; (2) an expression of rebellion; (3) relief from boredom and desire for novelty; (4) being emotionally immature; (5) anxiety relief, and (6) delinquency. He emphasizes that one reason people begin taking drugs is choice. Regardless of other factors, people still choose. They also can choose to make healthy choices later.

Impulse control disorders

Pathological gambling—Inability to resist the impulse to gamble in spite of disruption to personal, family, and vocational life.

Kleptomania—Inability to resist stealing objects.

Pyromania—Repeated, deliberate setting of fires for psychological gratification.

Intermittent explosive disorder—Destruction of property or assault due to loss of self-control.

Trichotillomania—Pulling out one's own hair.

Impulse control disorders involve a failure to resist an impulse or temptation to perform some action, even if it harms the individual and others. The individual feels a release after the act has been committed.

Gambling

Pathological gamblers become preoccupied either with the gambling itself or with trying to win money. Often the person gambles more or for a longer time than he or she originally intended. He or she may increase the frequency of gambling behavior or the size of bets to create excitement. When unable to bet the gambler commonly becomes irritable or restless. The person tries repeatedly to win back lost money, may attempt to stop gambling without success, and may gamble instead of meeting job or social obligations. Defaulting on debts or arrest for forgery or fraud may occur. Important activities are often sacrificed to gamble, and the urges continue in spite of problems made worse by the behavior.

Legalization of state lotteries has made gambling more popular in the United States. Unfortunately, the poor are more likely to gamble and more likely to suffer when they lose. Gambling often increases the role of organized crime and the incidence of pathological gambling. Other forms of gambling, legal and illegal, often follow public lotteries. The head of the national Center for Pathological Gambling believes that "compulsive gambling [will be] the mental health problem of the 1990s," while the director of the National Council on Compulsive Gambling in the late 1980s stated that the United States is "headed into a decade in which gambling will be the addiction of choice" (Brushaber 1989). Perhaps 3 percent to 4 percent of the population compulsively gamble, and at least 20 percent of those in therapy for the problem have attempted suicide (Atkins 1991).

C. Donald Cole (1983, 3) makes a convincing case that gambling is a sin. Love of money provides some motivation to gamble (1 Tim. 6:10). Cole underscores that the idea of getting rich without work, basic to gambling, undermines biblical ideals of disciplined work habits and the relationship between rewards and work. Throughout the Bible, beginning in Genesis 3:19, the principle of earning a living through work is the clear teaching. He considers gambling a form of covetousness. Gamblers want what others have, so the many verses against coveting apply equally to gambling. False values and wrong priorities contrast with the principle of making wise investments emphasized in the parable of the talents (Matt. 25:14–30). See also the observations by David McKenna after he served on a governor's committee that considered the issue of legalizing gambling (McKenna 1977).

Kleptomania

Kleptomania is stealing out of an overwhelming compulsion. The objects are not taken because of their value or usefulness to the person, but because the theft decreases tension and creates pleasure in itself. Such thefts are not planned or done with the cooperation of others.

Pyromania

Pyromania, the setting of fires, also results from increased tension prior to the act and relief or gratification from seeing the fire or the destruction from the fire. Those who set fires because of pyromania are often easy to catch because—unlike those who set fires for money—they generally stay and watch the fire after they set it.

Intermittent explosive disorder

An explosive disorder causes occasional uncontrolled bursts of rage. The extremely hostile manner in which explosive individuals strike out at their environment contrasts markedly with their normal behavior since they quietly hold their anger in until they explode. The outbursts may be verbal or physically aggressive, breaking furniture, throwing objects, or striking an adversary. Between outbursts the explosive person often feels sorry or repentant.

Under a calm, friendly, loving facade, an explosive person can be a latent volcano of anger, taking offense at the slightest provocation.

Expressions of violent anger camouflage feelings of helplessness and weakness. Boasts of physical strength may be used to ward off possible attackers. Appearing to be out of control, explosive episodes are intense, even sadistic. Often such episodes follow a period of continued irritability and hostility or a fantasy in which the patient is troubled by a feeling of inadequacy. At times explosive persons appear withdrawn, pouty, and obstinate. Their despondency seems to invite "mothering." Allowing someone to help them soothe their ruffled feelings, they may begin to resent feeling overly dependent and again react violently and destructively. The fluctuation between bravado and pouty withdrawal constantly confuses friends and associates.

An explosive male generally relates poorly to women, seeking instant gratification of his needs, He often has a "madonna-prostitute complex" in which he views women as either degraded or sanctified. If they satisfy him he views them as "just whores"; if they reject him the idealized woman is a snob. The explosive male often harbors deep fears of impotence and latent homosexual urges. He attempts to counteract these with such pseudomasculine defenses as weight-lifting, fighting, reckless driving, or excessive drinking. Diagnosis of an explosive personality disorder often follows the consequences of explosive action, such as physical abuse or even murder.

Causes of impulse control disorders

Some individuals have an abnormal EEG pattern. Explosive behavior often has a neurological basis. The explosive personality, in fact, was once referred to as an "epileptoid personality." Even in the presence of neurological abnormality, however, disordered behavior usually does not occur without a psychologically traumatic past. As children, individuals with an explosive personality may have been tattered, abused, or rejected. Hostility toward such treatment manifests in their own aggression. Such behavior could also be a learned response to the example set by abusive parents. Parents who tolerate temper tantrums and reward hostile attitudes reinforce explosive tendencies. Individuals with an explosive personality usually have a poorly developed superego and thus cannot readily suppress or repress their hostility to a level accepted by society.

Other impulse control problems arise from a variety of factors. Compulsive gamblers often have an early history of separation from their parents by divorce, death, or desertion. An early childhood gambling model may be imitated. Competitive personalities more likely develop pathological gambling compulsions. Cultural acceptance of gambling, such as through state lotteries, has been associated with greater incidence of pathological gambling. Pyromaniacs are usually males and tend to be lonely and frustrated.

Case history

Sam was a long-term institutionalized man who could become violently angry for little or no reason. One day, upon minor provocation, he began a fight with a fellow resident. The incident ended when he beat the resident to death with a shovel. Not only did he have an intermittent explosive disorder, he set fire to several group homes to which he had been transferred; apparently he was also a pyromaniac. When interviewed, he held two highly polished chicken bones, with which he played rhythms. He spoke of loving God and was generally friendly, but began to sweat and become agitated when his past problems were mentioned. He had problems getting along with people, and seemed happiest when he was tending his garden in a corner of the institution grounds.

Treatment for substance abuse and impulse control disorders

Smoking

Rewards for positive changes and punishments for nonimprovement have reportedly helped people stop smoking. This involves a gradual decrease in the number of cigarettes smoked (or decrease in the amount of tobacco in other forms) according to goals set up in advance. While programs often withdraw tobacco gradually, some authorities believe that stopping all at once is more effective. Other methods used include aversion or punishment, in which pills are inserted in cigarettes to make them taste bad. The biggest problem with this approach is the ease with which an individual can circumvent the program. Flooding has also been attempted, in which the person must smoke several cigarettes within a short time, far in excess of the normal amount. With any approach, support from other family members is especially crucial.

Alcoholism

A number of methods have been used to help alcoholics. Aversive programs include Antabuse, a drug that will make the person sick if they use alcohol. Again, this is easy to short-circuit, simply by not taking the pill. A variation of aversion is electrostimulation, which pairs the smell and taste of alcohol with a brief, harmless, but painful electrical shock. In effect a phobia develops toward alcohol.

Alcoholics Anonymous (AA) emphasizes self-labeling, in which the person admits he or she is an alcoholic, and pseudo-group therapy at regular meetings. The alcoholic develops rituals in response to a crisis, such as calling a fellow A. A. member when there is an overpowering compulsion to drink. A. A. stresses social contact with other nondrinkers because bars offer the only social contact many alcoholics have. The organization points to God as a source of help, although God is defined vaguely as a "higher power."

Other methods attempted include biofeedback of blood alcohol level, to sensitize the person to his or her level of intoxication. Counseling involves discussion of conflicts, anxiety, and self-esteem problems and works to change self-talk. Family therapy intervenes when relationships have become severely disrupted or the family unintentionally encourages the alcoholism through codependence (see Hemfelt, Minirth and Meier 1989, 11–13).

Drug abuse

Therapies for those with other kinds of drug disorders include live-in communities with other former drug abusers. A number of these exist, some more effective than others. Confrontation when a member slips up and takes drugs is often paired with acceptance and affirmation for those who stay off drugs. Unfortunately, many such communities exclude professionally trained people. Minirth-Meier Clinics offer programs for substance abusers.

Methadone maintenance programs satisfy the craving for heroin but do not remove the addiction. Methadone also can be injected to get a high. This medication also has side-effects.

The Seed program shows promise. Similar to AA, it emphasizes love of God, family, and country. A high rate of success (90 percent) is claimed, but accusations have surfaced that some are held against their will in near prison conditions. A similar, but more non-religious program is known as Straight.

Recent studies stress the importance of follow-up care to help addicts leave their drug habit. Weekly group meetings must follow residential care, for example, for alcoholics or other addicts.

Christians have often emphasized the importance of accepting Christ as Savior as a part of any drug treatment program. The temperance and prohibition movements, generally led by Christians, spared many from the problems of alcoholism. Some of those most concerned with the effects of alcoholism and other addictive disorders are taking a second look at such movements. Prohibition, long considered a dismal failure in motion pictures, actually resulted in much lower hospital admissions and a general decrease in consumption. Some suggest massive tax increases on alcohol to cut consumption, in effect a modern form of prohibition.

Christians should also participate in teaching young people and others about alcoholism and drug abuse. Effective teachers, however, must have accurate information. Rescue missions and such other ministries as Teen Challenge have become keys to reaching substance abusers with the message of Christ. Pastors can also reach out to those needing help. Genuine, widespread revivals historically result in decreased alcohol use and would probably have the same effect with drug usage. The Great Awakening of the late 1700s and early 1800s came during the "gin age" when many families were destroyed by an alcoholic parent. As Gary Collins (1972, 177) states, we must attempt to eliminate the widespread spiritual vacuum that drug and alcohol users try to fill, by offering real meaning and purpose in life through surrender and submission to Christ.

Impulse control disorders

Six counseling therapies have been suggested for pathological gamblers. First, Gamblers Anonymous has helped many by using most of the principles found in AA. Second, group therapy focusing on marriage relationships has sometimes been successful. Third, aversion therapy, in which impulses to gamble are counteracted by punishment (snapping a rubber band on the wrist, for example) have been attempted. Fourth, irrational beliefs or self-statements may be treated by changing self-talk and beliefs. Fifth, many gamblers simply need to learn more appropriate forms of recreation. Sixth, since faulty values (materialism, lack of financial planning or savings . . .) lie at the heart of much gambling, values change may be needed. Salvation helps in this area.

Pyromania demands quick intervention. If family problems are involved, group therapy with the entire family may be required. Changing self-talk is sometimes a useful counseling approach, as are public confession and restitution, such as working to pay for the damage caused. Some counselors encourage their clients to perform the action until it becomes aversive, such as striking one thousand matches or more, one at a time. This approach is called *satiation*.

Aversive treatments help stop kleptomania. For example, the client might be videotaped while role-playing shoplifting. When played back, the client imagines actually stealing. When the object is taken, the client receives electrostimulation. Highly motivated clients may take self-shockers while shopping, giving themselves unpleasant shocks when they have the impulse to steal.

Treatment of an explosive disorder carries poor prognosis for the long range. A careful EEG study and neurological examination should be conducted to determine if a neurological abnormality is present. Hospitalization, often necessary, can benefit because hospital regimentation can provide behavioral modification through social-ization. The arousal of anxiety often associated with deepening dependency and closeness must not be allowed to undermine treat-ment efforts. If anxiety does occur, appropriate use of anxiety-reduc-ing drugs and anticonvulsants may help the individual pass through the moments of crisis. Since explosive persons often cannot readily control themselves, they are not good candidates for group ther-apy. Acting out their aggressive impulses, they represent a physical risk to other members. Psychotherapy helps these individuals develop healthier modes of expression of anger and adequate gratification of their needs.

Individuals with explosive disorders usually can be taught to rec-ognize signs of an impending crisis. Such symptoms may include headache or lightness in the chest or other subjective or "aura-like" phenomena. Toxic factors such as alcohol may also precipitate violent outbursts. It is extremely important to help explosive persons work through their depressive feelings, especially loneliness, isolation, and nonachievement. They need to develop self-respect and gain a new self-image. Self-respect enforces self-control and self-reliance.

9

Sexual Problems

Sexual disorders result from psychological and physical factors, although only the psychological fall within the concerns of this book. Psychological sexual problems include *dysfunctions* of the sexual-response cycle and *paraphilias*, in which the person becomes sexually aroused in response to unusual objects or situations.

Sexual dysfunctions

Hypoactive sexual desire—Consistent lack of desire for a sexual relationship and absence of sexual fantasies.

Sexual aversion—Persistent avoidance and aversion to sex.

Female sexual arousal disorder/male erection disorder—Regular lack of pleasure or inability to become physically excited during sexual intercourse.

Inhibited female orgasm/inhibited male orgasm—Consistent delay or absence of orgasm during sexual intercourse.

Premature ejaculation—The male penis ejaculates after minimal
stimulation, allowing little or no control over orgasm.

Dyspareunia—Recurrent pain in the genitals related to sexual
intercourse.

Vaginismus—Muscle spasms in the vagina during sexual intercourse that impede sexual relations.

Most sexually active people have occasional problems. Many newly
married men have some difficulties with premature ejaculation and the
new wife may have problems achieving orgasm immediately. Such
problems usually disappear in time with patience, sensitivity, and practice. There may be occasional times when one spouse may have less
sexual desire than the other, or no desire at all. Even chronic sexual
difficulties arise in most marriages; time and discussion of any personal problems usually facilitate resumption of normal sexual activity.

For some, though, the problems listed above become a regular
part of life, so that only occasionally (or never) does the normal sexual cycle occur. The *DSM* (p. 291) lists four stages that comprise
the sexual cycle: (1) *appetitive*, increased sexual fantasies and desire
for sexual activity; (2) *excitement*, a sense of sexual pleasure and
physiological changes (The male develops an erection; muscle tenses
in the woman's pelvis and the vagina secretes a lubricating fluid.); (3)
orgasm, a peaking of sexual pleasure with release of sexual tension and
rhythmic contractions of the muscles, the penis emitting semen, and
(4) *resolution*, general muscular relaxation; males (but not females)
resist further sexual activity during this stage.

Hypoactive sexual desire, or inhibited desire, involves the persistent, pervasive lack of sexual interest. Among possible organic reasons, a number of medications lower sexual desire. Among psychological causes, depressed individuals often lack all sexual desire. When
some organic factor or another psychological disorder appears, a doctor does not diagnose a sexual disorder. Such disorders are considered
secondary by-products of some more basic problem. Sometimes sexual desire is inhibited with the spouse but not other individuals.

Someone with a *sexual aversion* actively dislikes or is disgusted
by sexual behavior. The person does not just lack desire; he or she is
repulsed by, and therefore avoids, all things sexual. Inhibited sex-

ual excitement, seen in lack of erection for the male or lack of lubrication and excitement for the female, is sometimes referred to as *frigidity* in women or *impotence* in men. An *inhibited orgasm* means orgasm seldom or only happens following the normal excitement phase of arousal. Sometimes women may be able to achieve orgasm when the clitoris is directly stimulated, but not during intercourse.

Premature ejaculation involves the involuntary, undesired release of semen. This may occur before intercourse, while attempting intercourse, or shortly after intercourse begins. Age, how often the individual has sex, and the presence of a new situation may relate to this problem. Pain during intercourse by either a man or a woman, called *dyspareunia*, refers to discomfort not caused by a lack of lubrication by the female, which would be *female sexual arousal disorder*, or to *vaginismus*. The latter problem is an involuntary spasm of the muscles in the outer third of the vagina which interferes with sexual activity.

Few biblical passages seem to mention the disorders in this section. The Bible teaches that married couples should not avoid sexual relations except for times of special prayer (1 Cor. 7:5). The Song of Solomon graphically portrays the sexual desire of Solomon for his Shulamite bride, including foreplay (7:7–8 and possibly 2:6) and erotic enticement of the husband by the wife (1:2, 12–16; 3:1; 4:16). That compliments and loving words prior to physical sexual activity are important can be seen throughout the Song of Solomon. Sexual problems often occur when a spouse fails to use romantic enticement and adequate foreplay.

Causes of sexual dysfunctions

Some develop sexual dysfunctions because of well-meaning parents who so strongly teach their children not to engage in premarital sex that the child only learns that any sexual relationships must be avoided. When this general notion is maintained into adult life, a pattern of dysfunction may result. The parent should teach a healthy view of sexuality, that physical relationships are good and desirable when reserved for marriage.

Anxiety also may cause problems. Fears related to difficulties of life or anxiety about sex itself disturbs the normal sexual-response cycle. Sometimes sexual dysfunctions result from feelings of being rejected by the spouse or because one or both sexual partners have extremely high standards for their performance.

Sin, such as lust, adultery, or premarital sex, result in many sexual problems. Sin produces certain psychological and physical consequences. Many of these dysfunctions may also be related to unhealthy learning, at any point in one's lifetime. Sexual desire may decrease simply because of an unresponsive spouse. Rape may create sexual aversion because sex is associated with pain and trauma.

Paraphilias

Exhibitionism—Repeated urges and fantasies about exposing the genitals to strangers, resulting in distress or the act of self-exposure.

Fetishism—Repeated sexual urges and fantasies involving non-living objects, resulting in distress or sexual actions with those objects.

Frotteurism—Repeated sexual urges and fantasies involving touching and rubbing a person without consent, resulting in distress or the actual activity.

Pedophilia—Repeated sexual urges and fantasies involving children, resulting in distress or molestation.

Sexual masochism—Repeated sexual urges and fantasies of being humiliated or hurt, resulting in distress or masochistic activity.

Sexual sadism—Repeated urges and fantasies about hurting someone, resulting in distress or actually performing sadistic activity.

Transvestic fetishism—Recurrent sexual urges and fantasies about cross-dressing, resulting in distress or this activity.

Transsexualism—Recurrent discomfort about being one's gender, accompanied by a long-standing preoccupation with sex change.

Voyeurism—Regular urges and fantasies about seeing an unsuspecting person naked or engaged in sex, resulting in distress or actual voyeuristic activity.

Other paraphilias or disorders—Zoophilia (sex with animals), telephone lewdness, or distress related to homosexual thoughts or activities.

Paraphilia is characterized by arousal in response to sexual objects or situations that are not part of the normative arousal patterns and by gross impairment in affectionate sexual activity between human partners. *Fetishism* involves the use of nonliving objects (such as undergarments, shoes, boots, hair, nails) as the preferred method of producing sexual excitement. The object selected is often associated with someone the individual knew intimately during childhood. *Transvestism* means cross-dressing (males as females, females as males) by heterosexual individuals for sexual arousal. *Zoophilia* is characterized by the use of animals for producing sexual excitement (see Lev. 20:15–16). *Pedophilia* refers to a preference for sexual activity with prepubertal children. *Exhibitionism*, in which individuals repetitively expose their genitals to an unsuspecting stranger for the purpose of sexual excitement, occurs almost exclusively in males, generally in their middle twenties. Exhibitionists often are in conflict-laden marriages. In *voyeurism* individuals (generally men) repetitively seek situations in which they can "peep" at unsuspecting persons who are naked or disrobing. *Sexual masochism* means an individual feels sexual excitement through his or her own suffering (being beaten, bound, or humiliated). Masochistic sexual fantasies often relate to childhood. *Sexual sadism* excites by inflicting physical or psychological suffering on another. In *gender-identity disorder* the individual feels a dislike for his or her anatomic sex. In *transsexualism*, best known of the gender-identity disorders, the individual wishes to live as a member of the opposite sex.

Causes of paraphilias

Exhibitionism, the most commonly reported sexual crime in the United States, sometimes results from emotional immaturity. The individual may feel shy or inferior and cannot achieve sexual fulfillment with his wife. Sometimes exhibitionists expose themselves because of personal stress, the act expressing inner conflicts. It may also result from brain deterioration among elderly men, or appear as part of a psychotic episode.

Fetishism most likely develops because the person masturbates while holding, touching, or viewing the object, or there is an accidental pairing of orgasm with the fetish object. Continued masturbation with the fetish, a common ongoing pattern among people with this problem, perpetuates the disorder.

Pedophilia may result from several possible causes. Sometimes the person has never been able to have a mature, satisfactory relationship with same-age peers, and thus is only comfortable with children or young adolescents. This is by far the most common pattern, with sex play gradually developing into more overt sexual behavior. Sometimes the offender discovers that the wife (or girlfriend) is adulterous and then initiates the molesting. At other times the problem is more of a learned activity. Older boys exploit younger boys in institutions where there are no normal sexual outlets. Finally, some develop this problem because they are aggressive, antisocial personalities.

Masochism and sadism most likely result from early experiences in which either the giving or receiving of pain became associated with sexual arousal. Many people with these problems were taught very negative views of sexuality. Their actions may express contempt for sexual expression. They may feel inadequate and anxious about achieving sexual satisfaction through more normal sexual activity. Occasionally sadists and masochists have a personality disorder or other psychological problem that feeds the sexual disorder.

Transvestic fetishism, dressing in clothing of the opposite sex, is probably best understood as learned behavior. Often men who dress like women were rewarded for wearing feminine clothes as small children, and the behavior became sexualized in adulthood. The Mosaic law strongly condemns this particular behavior (Deut. 22:5).

Voyeurism may begin as curiosity; the youth who wants to know about a naked body of the opposite gender or sexual activity. This curiosity, combined with feelings of inadequacy, shyness, and other inward issues, results in experimenting with watching others undress or have sex. The lack of negative consequences, combined with arousal, often increased by masturbation, may account for the development of this disorder. Other disorders in this section are also probably best accounted for by combinations of reward, punishment, and association.

Although the *DSM* no longer lists homosexuality, the authors regard it as a mental problem. In the Bible it is considered a serious sin (Lev. 18:22; 20:13; Rom. 1:24–27; 1 Cor. 6:9; 1 Tim. 1:10; and

Jude 1:7). As with heterosexual sin, the individual chooses to participate in homosexual behavior. An early history characterized by an overprotective mother who forms an alliance with her son against a hostile detached father does make male individuals more prone to homosexual temptation. Females with a hostile, competitive mother and a passive father are more prone to be tempted to become lesbians. Such individuals often seem to fear heterosexual relationships.

Homosexuality may often originate in childhood or early adolescent sexual experiences, so that the first arousing activities are homosexual. In such cases the behavior is learned, with sexual arousal being the reward. Eventually the person begins to label himself or herself as homosexual and may not explore heterosexual sources of arousal. Unfortunately, many homosexual pedophiles seek out children and young adolescents, and those sexual experiences incline the victim toward homosexuality. Painful experiences with the opposite sex, including the mother, sisters, or other females for men or with the father, brothers, or other males for women offer another possible explanation. Perhaps the most common factor found among male homosexuals is their perception that their father rejected them. Lesbians commonly felt rejected by their mother. They both seem to search for what they did not have. Of course, the physical closeness of being with one of the same gender never gives the emotional closeness they so desire from the parent. The possible role of genetic factors remains uncertain.

Treatment for sexual disorders

Dysfunctions and paraphilias

In treating sexual dysfunctions a medical exam must initially rule out any physical causes. This step includes a full analysis of medications being taken and other potential medical problems.

Assuming the dysfunction appears primarily psychological in origin, a method called *sensate focus* may be employed. The counselor either instructs the couple, or provides materials to teach them how to regain a normal sexual-arousal cycle. The training helps the couple practice sexual behavior between counseling sessions, focusing on pleasure, not orgasm. Indeed, the couple usually *avoids* orgasm and intercourse. Instead, they begin by exploring the spouse's body (except for the sexually sensitive areas). Over the course of therapy, the couple moves to caressing breasts and genitals without having intercourse and finally intercourse after adequate foreplay, but without focusing on orgasm. Often the sequence must be repeated one or more times.

The exercise of the kegel muscle may help women achieve greater arousal. The woman regularly tenses the muscle used to stop urination. Some women exercise this muscle in preparation for marriage. Assertiveness training may help men or women who avoid sexual behavior due to shyness and self-consciousness. Problems with premature ejaculation may be solved if the woman employs the "squeeze technique," squeezing the man's penis to help him avoid orgasm.

Often sexual dysfunctions signal other interpersonal problems, such as ineffective communication, and couples always need to resolve these problems prior to having sexual relations. Communication about sex is important, such as telling one another which actions feel good and which do not. In rational emotive therapy unhealthy self-statements are examined for underlying irrational beliefs and expectations about sex. A helpful Christian book on sexuality is Ed and Gayle Wheat's *Intended for Pleasure* (1977). Another is *Sex in the Christian Marriage* (1988) by Meier, et al.

The best approach to dealing with a sexual disorder usually combines such techniques as insight therapy, behavioral techniques, medical help when indicated, and spiritual guidance.

Homosexuality

While homosexuality has been taken out of the *DSM*, partly because of political pressure on the American Psychiatric Association, it is still treated by many psychologists. Indeed, the diagnostic category *Sexual Disorder Not Otherwise Specified* includes what is termed *ego dystonic homosexuality*—homosexuality that causes personal distress. From a Christian perspective, all homosexuality should cause personal distress because it breaks God's law and God's plan for the family.

Several Christian organizations have developed communities in which homosexuals can develop nonsexual friendships with those of the same gender and learn how to relate to those of the opposite sex. Often run by former homosexuals, the leaders serve as models for those in the program. Unfortunately, if the leader falls back into homosexual behavior, which sometimes occurs, the ministry may be disgraced and discredited.

Dealing with irrational beliefs and self-talk may help. For example, individuals who feel that they *must* have sexual activity only with their own gender learn that this is untrue and is, in fact, irrational. Modeling, through a close relationship with a heterosexual of the same gender, might be attempted. Churches can be particularly good settings for modeling. Such efforts can supplement explorations of the hurtful memories of childhood, offering forgiveness for those who have wronged the homosexual, if this is considered part of the cause for the homosexuality.

The homosexual needs to fully realize that this behavior is an abomination to God and seek the Lord's forgiveness with genuine repentance. But the person also needs to receive the forgiveness of the church and find acceptance within a Christian community once the past way of life has been forsaken. Counseling for homosexual temptations and thought sins should continue, even after the sinful behavior ceases. Churches should restrict certain kinds of involvement for homosexuals and others with a history of a paraphilia to minimize temptation. It would not be wise for a former homosexual to teach an all-male class of teenagers. God can help the person overcome any sinful behavior, and the church must forgive, but one must avoid naïveté when incorporating such individuals, for the grip of sexual temptation is strong.

Sexual disorders, as drug addictions and many other problems, often have an easily recognized sin component. However, a distinction needs to be drawn between someone who falls into sin and one with a pattern of practicing sin. If someone is in the practice of sin, then he or she is not a Christian (1 John 3:6) and needs to know Christ.

10

Child and Adolescent Disorders

A large section of the *DSM* deals with disorders that first appear in childhood or adolescence. Many of these commonly last into adulthood; they are not confined to children and adolescents. Thus adults will be given such diagnoses if they apparently had some of the symptoms as children and the problems still exist. The reader should also be aware that children sometimes have some of the disorders that have been discussed in other sections as well.

Mental retardation and learning disorders

Mental retardation—An intelligence quotient (I.Q.) of 70 or below when measured before age eighteen. Self-care abilities unusually deficient.

143

Developmental arithmetic disorder—Math skills are significantly below what is expected for the child's I.Q. and educational level.

Developmental expressive writing disorder—Writing skills are significantly below what is expected for the child's I.Q. and educational level.

Developmental reading disorder—Reading skills are significantly below what is expected for the child's I.Q. and educational level.

Attention-deficit disorder (with or without hyperactivity)—Persistence of developmentally inappropriate and marked inattention.

Developmental articulation disorder—Consistently not using speech sounds appropriate to the child's age.

Developmental language disorder—Expressive or receptive language use significantly below what is expected for the child's I.Q.

Mental retardation and learning disabilities accompany a low level of academic performance in school or low performance in one or more specific areas (arithmetic, writing, or reading). There is also a "not otherwise specified" category, which could include any other academic area, such as spelling problems.

Mental retardation

Mental retardation occurs in at least 1 percent of the population. Diagnosis must take into account the child's or adult's score on a test of intelligence, in which one qualified examiner gives one child the test, usually a Stanford-Binet or a Wechsler adult or child test), the level of adaptive behavior (self-care skills), and the age at which the problem began (before age eighteen).

An individual, rather than a group, test ensures precision and guards against the situation overly influencing the results. Adaptive behavior is important because some may be able to live independently in spite of a low I.Q.; thus a test score should not be enough to label a person *retarded*. Finally, the problem must begin before age eighteen because it is assumed the brain develops until that point, and once the brain has developed completely, its development could not be retarded (slowed). Adults with brain damage from an automobile accident, for example, may have a low I.Q. and poor adaptive behavior. However, they would be considered to have dementia, not retardation, because the brain was fully developed at the time of the accident. The same accident occurring to a child might produce retardation, because the brain is not fully developed.

The level of retardation is determined by examining both the I.Q. and the adaptive behavior. The four I.Q. levels are: mild (50–55 to about 70), moderate (35–40 to 50–55), severe (20–25 to 35–40), and profound (below 20–25). The range of scores varies a bit at each end of the levels because of differences in tests and the possibility of test error.

The American Association for Mental Deficiency (AAMD) specifies a number of adaptive behaviors typical of different levels of retardation. For example, adults of normal intelligence generally do not need help purchasing clothes, do not require reminders for personal care and health care, can go to other towns alone without help, can write about and discuss current events, can handle money without guidance, and have hobbies that require rapid or complex thinking, such as tennis or playing the piano.

A *mildly* retarded person can write simple letters, use the telephone, hold a semiskilled job, make change at stores, walk about freely, and use a bicycle or trampoline. *Moderately* retarded individuals would probably lack these skills, yet they would be likely to comb and shampoo their hair, not need supervision with bathing, cut their meat and mix foods while cooking, wash, store, and select daily clothing, possibly read sentences with comprehension, make minor purchases without a note, add coins, and initiate most of their own activities. *Severely* retarded people would lack these abilities, but could still eat without spilling food, bathe with some supervision, be toilet-trained, not need help buttoning and zipping clothes, wash their hands, use complex sentences, make their bed, sweep the floor, set and clean the table, make purchases with a note, use coin machines, and prepare such simple foods as sandwiches. Someone at the *profound* level probably lacks most, if not all, of these abilities.

Three-fourths of the retarded fall in the mild range (55–69 on the Wechsler scale) and are said to be educable. An individual with an I.Q. of 40–54 on the Wechsler scale is said to be trainable.

Learning disabilities and developmental disorders

Specific developmental disorders, another category of disorders includes *developmental reading disorder*, an impairment in reading skills not due to inadequate schooling. A person with a developmental reading disorder may have poor language skills, poor left-right discrimination, awkwardness, hyperactivity, impulsiveness, poor concentration, distractibility, and short attention-span. Letter reversals or inversions are common. Some symptoms disappear as the children mature. Others tend to develop antisocial behavior. Often there is a family history of similar problems.

Developmental arithmetic disorder, another specific development disorder, causes significant impairment in the development of arithmetic skills not related to age, overall I.Q., or poor schooling.

Short attention-span, poor concentration, and distractibility characterizes *attention deficit disorder*. This disorder has been called by a variety of names, including *minimal brain dysfunction (MBD)*, *hyperkinetic reaction of childhood*, and *minimal cerebral dysfunction*. Attention deficit disorder involves a short attention span and may be accompanied by excessive motor activity. Children are impulsive, distractible, disorganized, and inattentive and may be restless, overactive, and overdemanding. They frequently fail to carry through a parental request. Frequently these children show signs of a neurological disorder, secondary to immaturity of the nervous system. Some hyperactivity in children relates to anxiety. Some children outgrow the symptoms at puberty; others retain attention difficulties into adult life.

With *articulation disorders* a child does not use speech sounds appropriate for his or her age range. A six-year-old usually uses the sounds for *f, l, r, z, sh*, and *th*. If the child has difficulties with one or more of these special training by a school speech therapist would be appropriate. On the other hand, a normally developing four-year-old might not be able to use these sounds.

Developmental language disorders include failure or delay in developing any language. Delayed acquisition is more common; lack of *any* language can signal mental retardation or *autism*. The disorder may involve a lack of expressive language (talking) or deficient receptive language problems (understanding what someone else says). In either case, the difficulty significantly interferes with the child's daily life or school achievement. The prognosis is good for this disorder, with only a few such children needing speech therapy.

Causes of mental retardation and learning disabilities

While most cases of mental retardation have an unknown origin, some can be traced to genetic problems, such as the presence of an extra chromosome that produces *downs syndrome* (what used to be called *mongolism*). The intake of alcohol by the expectant mother can produce *fetal alcohol syndrome* causing retardation. Poor nutrition by the mother prior to the birth of the baby may result in retardation or learning disabilities. Oxygen deprivation or injury during the birth process is also linked to this problem. Injuries, ingesting poisons, and other accidents after birth also may produce learning disabilities or retardation, although most such accidents do not. In some cases, a poor home environment in which the child is emotionally and mentally deprived of stimulation can contribute to retardation or learning disabilities.

Speech disorders

Cluttering—Speech that is unintelligible due to uneven pauses and spurts of language while speaking and faulty phrasing.

Stuttering—Repeated or prolonged sounds that impede fluency of other speech.

Elective mutism—Regularly refusing to speak in at least one social situation.

Communication difficulties are fairly common among children. Some problems are mentioned above as developmental disorders. Others involve fluency in speaking. A qualified speech therapist usually is better equipped than a psychologist to help a child develop better speech skills.

Cluttering and *stuttering* both interfere with the fluency of speech. Stuttering (stammering) repeats or prolongs sounds, syllables or words. While 4 to 5 percent of children have a transient problem with stuttering, the chronic variety occurs in only 1 percent of the population and is three times more common in males. Sixty to 80 percent of children spontaneously recover from stuttering.

In a sense, lack of fluency in speech is universal for young children when they are first learning to speak. Moses had a speech problem. He said to God, "I am slow of speech and tongue" (Exod. 4:10). Paul also described himself as being deficient in speaking ability (2 Cor. 10:10, 11:6). Yet the Lord mightily used these men, in spite of their personal weaknesses. In fact, the Bible indicates that God may be better able to use imperfect people because "my power is made perfect in weakness" (2 Cor. 12:8).

Causes of speech disorders

Problems in using or understanding language often stem from trauma or disease that slowed these abilities. Some children appear to be predisposed to such problems from infancy. Stuttering often stems from a more basic emotional problem. The child may be shy and self-conscious. Some experiments (reported by Rosenhan and Seligman 1984, 525) indicate a perceptual processing problem. If given headphones in which the person's speech is delayed by a half second, some individuals stop stuttering (interestingly, those without stuttering problems often begin to stutter when given this treatment). Focusing a lot of attention on early speech problems may cause the child to become more self-conscious and thus perpetuate or worsen the problem. In some cases, ignoring stuttering in early childhood is the best measure.

Elective mutism, a continuous refusal to speak in spite of language skills usually results from early emotional or physical trauma, marital strife in the family, or a protective, controlling mother. The parents may have used silence to express their own anger and to control others.

Autistic disorders

Autistic disorder—Social interaction impaired by problems with communication and imagination, a lack of interests and limited actions, beginning in infancy or childhood.

Pervasive developmental disorder—Problems in interaction and communication not severe enough to be considered autistic or schizophrenic.

Children with autism show little or no responsiveness to other human beings. Autistic children fail to develop normal attachments. As infants they may not cuddle. They have an indifference or aversion to affection and physical contact. In early childhood they fail to develop friendships. Language is either absent or slowly develops. The children may repeat over and over some word said to them (*echolalia*). The facial expression is inappropriate or flat. Autistic children may become fascinated with moving objects and show ritualistic or generally bizarre behavior. About 40 percent of autistic children have an I.Q. below 50 and only 30 percent have an I.Q. of 70 or more. Only one in six eventually makes a good social adjustment and two-thirds remain severely handicapped.

In *pervasive developmental disorder* the child shows a disturbance in relations with people and an inability to form peer relations. One sees bizarre behavior, extreme irritability over minor events, inappropriate facial affect, peculiar posturing, and speech abnormalities. Self-mutilation (head-banging) may be present. Pervasive disorders are distinguished from childhood schizophrenia by an absence of delusions, hallucinations, or incoherence.

Causes of autism

Autism and the pervasive developmental disorders are probably the result of some kind of brain dysfunction. Lack of oxygen during birth, encephalitis, meningitis, the mother contracting German measles during pregnancy, and untreated phenylketonuria (a hereditary chemical imbalance among some newborns) are among the physical factors found to be related to these disorders. While certain child-rearing methods were once thought to be related, recent research indicates that this is not the case.

Behavior disorders

Conduct disorder—Antisocial behavior that lasts for at least six months.

Oppositional defiant disorder—Regular defiance and disagreement with others, especially adults, without adequate cause.

Children with a *conduct disorder* persist in antisocial behavior that violates the rights of others, chronically lying, bullying, using abusive language, and stealing. Other behaviors include vandalism, reckless driving, superficial friendliness for self-seeking purposes, chronic disobedience, extortion, and breaking and entering. Nine percent of boys and 2 percent of girls have this disorder prior to age eighteen. If the problems persist into adulthood, an antisocial personality disorder may result (see chapter 11).

Children with an *oppositional disorder* demonstrate pervasive opposition to adults. They show frequent argumentativeness, stubbornness, passive resistance, belligerence, lack of response to reasonable persuasion, and provocative behavior.

Causes of behavior disorders

Conduct disorders have been linked to early rejection by the parents and inconsistent child-rearing, often through harsh punishment or indulgence without discipline. Very often the child was moved from foster parent to foster parent (or from relative to relative), and quite often no father or father substitute was available. Many were hyperactive as small children, and a surprising number come from large families or have fathers who are alcoholics. Probably some of these same factors are implicated in the oppositional defiant disorder.

Tic, habit, and elimination disorders

Tic disorders—Involuntary, repetitive, purposeless movements of muscles or vocalizations.

Stereotypy/habit disorder—Repeated nonfunctional but intentional actions.

Functional enuresis—Urinating in bed or clothes repeatedly.

Functional encopresis—Passing of feces repeatedly in inappropriate locations.

Tic disorders are characterized by motor movements, usually of the eye or face (such as squinting), but the whole head or an entire limb may twitch. Sometimes vocal tics occur, in which the person may make a noise with their voice (such as clearing the throat) or shout some word uncontrollably.

A *chronic tic* occurs several times a day, almost every day, either regularly or intermittently, over a period of at least one year. If episodes have occurred for at least two weeks but less than a year, the diagnosis is *transient tic disorder*. *Tourettes disorder* involves multiple vocal and motor tics, often obscene words repeated endlessly. A fairly rare disorder, this occurs three times more often in boys.

Stereotypy/habit disorder involves the intentional performance of actions repeatedly for no apparent purpose, including rocking, head banging, hand shaking, picking at the body, and biting nails. Moderate nail-biting is not considered serious among preschool children. About 20 percent of college students still bite their nails. While thumb-sucking appears to belong to this category, it probably would not because it does not cause physical damage to the child (except for possible displacement of teeth in older children) and it does not interfere with regular activities. Twenty percent of children continue to suck their thumbs after age six.

Enuresis, urinating in the clothing or in bed repeatedly, is another common problem with children. To be diagnosed as enuresis it must occur at least twice a month for five- and six-year-olds, or at least once a month for older children. The child must also be at least five years old physically and at least four years old mentally. Enuresis occurs in 8 to 10 percent of the population beyond age five, and in only 5 percent at age ten. About one to two percent persist even through high school.

Encopresis (soiling), like bed-wetting, can be expected in the preschool years, with the normal range for neurological readiness for toilet-training extending to four years of age. If a child is over four and still soiling from time to time, the parents should consult a professional counselor for help after ruling out possible physical causes.

Causes of tic disorders

With the exception of tourettes syndrome, nervous tics signal emotional conflicts requiring counseling and usually go away as the conflicts are resolved. Brain impairment causes some cases, since nonspecific brain wave changes sometimes present themselves in tic disorders, particularly tourettes. Stereotypy/habit disorder may reflect anxiety, although rocking and head banging sometimes involve neurological impairment.

Enuresis and encopresis may be the result of developmental delay, in which the body simply matures more slowly than normal. In some cases, stress influences these problems, so that the bowel or bladder difficulty is secondary to the underlying conflicts. Some children experience control problems because they sleep soundly or because they have not learned to pay attention to their body's inner cues that elimination is needed. Poor potty training techniques, involving excessive punishment, can be responsible because of the child's frustration.

Anxiety, identity, and attachment disorders

Separation anxiety disorder—Anxiety results from being separated from the attachment figure.

Avoidant disorder of childhood or adolescence—Contact avoidance with unknown people that interferes with social relationships.

Overanxious disorder—Persistent excessive worry or anxiety.

Gender identity disorder of childhood—Extreme distress over being one's own gender, or desire to be the opposite sex.

Identity disorder—Distress related to identity in any of several areas.

Reactive attachment disorder of infancy or early childhood—Difficulties related to social interaction. The child does not respond or initiate interactions or is socially indiscriminate.

In *separation anxiety disorder* a child intensely fears separation or threat of separation from parents, home, or familial surroundings. Such children may react strongly to going to school, visiting friends, or doing errands, possibly fearing that something may happen to their parents during that time. The anxiety may be expressed in phobias, nightmares, physical complaints, fears about dying, trouble going to sleep, or fear of the dark. Constant attention may be demanded.

In *avoidant* (shyness) *disorder of childhood or adolescence* the anxiety involves contact with strangers. Although close to family members, the child avoids strangers to a degree that interferes with peer functioning. The avoidant behavior persists with strangers even after prolonged exposure, the children often standing behind their parents or furniture when strangers arrive. Extreme avoidant behavior must persist for at least three months before this diagnosis is made.

Overanxious disorder refers to a more generalized anxiety. The children have excessive worry about the future and many fears, even without a recent precipitating stress. They may have difficulty falling asleep. Such children may transfer the anxiety to their bodies and have many physical complaints. Their anxiety may center around approval and acceptance, especially by authority figures. Perfectionistic in tendency, they worry about their own competence in a variety of areas. Generalized anxiety must exist for at least six months for this diagnosis to apply. Fears and stress are common sources of anxiety.

Fears

Fear of animals, common between the ages of three and five, should cause no concern. The parents' patient explanations and reassurances should help the child cope. Nightmares and night terrors are also common in preschoolers, who spend a large portion of their sleep time in dreaming. Nightmares awaken children, but with night terrors children thrash around in bed and cry out without waking. In fact, parents may have a hard time waking a child during a night terror. For most children, night terrors go away as conflicts are resolved. Medications can be given to eliminate night terrors but usually are not necessary. A night light in the preschooler's room, allows a child to see that there are no animals or bogeymen. A child who comes to the parents' bed at night after a nightmare should be taken back to the child's own bed and calmly spoken to for a few moments. Young children also occasionally sleepwalk, but parents should not worry—if the sleepwalker stays in the house! Medications can stop sleepwalking in severely persistent cases.

Depression and stress

Childhood *depression* following the loss of a loved object, a divorce, the death of a parent, or the transfer of a father overseas can be a serious problem. Weekly counseling sessions usually succeed. Psychiatrists sometimes supplement counseling in serious cases

with low doses of antidepressant medication. Social withdrawal, prolonged sadness, and either a marked increase or decrease in activity
accompany serious depression.

Preschoolers, developing rapidly from the dependent toddler stage
to the independent school-age stage, have many adjustments to
make. Going to Sunday school or to the pediatrician or dentist,
moving into a new home, or having a new baby brother or sister,
can be very stressful for a preschool child. The best way for parents
to reduce such stresses is to prepare their children ahead of time by
talking about them in words children can understand. Parents should
always be truthful. It can be distressing for children to go to sleep at
night, then wake up to find a strange babysitter there and their parents gone. Parents should tell their children that they are going out,
even if the children will be asleep before the babysitter comes, so
they will not be surprised.

Gender identity disorder of childhood is somewhat similar to adult
transsexualism (see chapter 9). With this disorder the child is
extremely distressed over being his or her own gender and actively
states that they want to be the opposite sex, or sometimes insists
that they already are the opposite sex. These children are often preoccupied with wearing clothing of the opposite sex and repudiate
their own anatomy. Boys may reject masculine toys and prefer the
pastimes of girls. By definition this disorder begins prior to puberty.

Identity disorder, most likely in adolescents, involves considerable
concern about long-range goals, choosing a career, friendships, sexuality, religion, morality, or loyalties to their group. For this diagnosis, worries must become so intense that they interfere significantly with the teenagers social, academic, or occupational life and
persist for at least three months.

Reactive attachment disorder occurs prior to age five. These
youngsters either do not respond to others or they respond to anyone without discriminating between loved ones and strangers.

Causes of anxiety disorders

Children with the separation anxiety disorder often come from
close-knit families and are characterized as being conscientious, con-

forming, and eager to please. The disorder may develop after a stress, such as the death of a relative or pet, an illness of the child or a close relative, or a change of residence and school. This disorder should not be confused with normal separation anxiety seen in infancy and the early preschool years.

The avoidant disorder is often the result of modeling a parent who tends to avoid others. Or the child may not learn social skills, and thus feels uncomfortable being around anyone outside the immediate family or friends. Again, normal early childhood "stranger anxiety" should not be confused with this problem, which by definition develops after age two and one-half years.

The gender identity disorder often results from prior learning. The child may have been exposed to sexually inappropriate behavior. A mother who hates men may reward her son for dressing and acting like a girl and punish him when he shows typical male interests. Among boys the father may be absent or unavailable, while physical and emotional closeness with the mother may be rewarded. Girls with this disorder have usually lacked rewards for gender-appropriate behavior. One-third to two-thirds of boys with this disorder become homosexuals in adolescence. Most adult transsexuals have this disorder in childhood, but the majority of children with gender identity disorder do not become transsexuals.

The identity disorder can be understood as an extreme form of the normal identity struggles most adolescents face. It may be that the many options in lifestyle, values, and occupations that exist today may have contributed to the problem, as may conflicts between peer and parental value systems. While most adolescents have some struggle with identity, it is unclear why some develop the mental disorder.

The reactive attachment disorder occurs when a care-giver persistently disregards the child's basic emotional or physical needs, or there is a repeated change of care-giver. The stress of continually facing new people causes the child to refuse to interact with others or to interact with everyone indiscriminately. In many cases research has discovered that the care-giver is severely depressed, lacks a social support system, or thinks a great deal about infanticide. The problem also shows up in children when a care-giver has difficulty controlling his or her impulses and was abused or deprived as a child.

Treatment for child and adolescent disorders

Some psychologists believe that nearly all disorders among children reflect a problem family rather than a problem child, although this would probably not apply to cases of mental retardation and autism. It is important to change negative situations in the home and arrange therapy for the parents if necessary, so parents can actively influence their children toward healthier behavior.

Perhaps the two most commonly used approaches to helping children are medications and behavior modification. For example, Ritalin effectively helps most hyperactive children. Even though it is a stimulant, for physiological reasons it tends to settle children down and to focus their concentration. Certain medications can help eliminate tics within twenty-four hours, although the tics will return soon after the medication is discontinued if the underlying conflicts are not resolved. Communication disorders often improve with speech therapy.

Behavioral interventions involve rewards, punishment, and helping children make associations. For example, bed-wetting is probably best treated with the bell-and-pad approach. This device, widely available from catalog stores, detects the release of urine in the bed and then rings the bell. The bell awakens the child, making him or her more aware of the sensation of a full bladder. The bladder sensations become associated with the bell and waking up, and eventually the child learns to wake up and go to the bathroom when the bladder is full. Rewards reinforce proper elimination in the bathroom. Punishment is less effective, although older children may be required to clean up the bed after a night accident as long as excessive shame is not used.

Warm acceptance and reinforcement teach autistic children to interact. The process often takes several years of intensive treatment. The prognosis for children with autistic symptoms prior to age two is quite poor.

Working with childhood anxiety often requires group experiences as well as behavioral reinforcement. Teaching relaxation skills, perhaps in the context of desensitization techniques, and assertiveness training may help those with anxiety or avoidant disorders.

Tic disorders often require in-depth therapy to locate underlying conflicts. Those around the client also need instruction to stop unknowingly rewarding the behavior by giving the person attention for the actions or vocalizations. Behavioral approaches are usually adopted for mental retardation, learning disabilities, and many speech disorders.

Play therapy helps children explore underlying conflicts behind their behavior. Youngsters often lack the ability to reflect and verbalize their problems, but generally they are familiar with the idea of playing. In play therapy the child plays out their problems, often using dolls or other materials. Once the problem is understood, the counselor may enter into the play of the child, promoting better understanding and resolution of conflicts.

Conduct disorders and oppositional disorders do not usually respond to individual counseling unless the person's environment changes significantly. Emphasis upon punishment less effectively encourages change in these children than rewarding more desirable behavior. Membership in gangs often perpetuates the problem, and thus a change in friendships can change behavior. Some treatment facilities for problem teens use regimented environments based upon rewards and privileges for positive, desirable behavior. Such methods have reportedly helped some youths achieve permanent change.

Christians have often reached out to troubled children and young people. Christian developmental centers help meet an important need in our society, particularly with retarded children and adults who function at the severe and profound levels. Some churches have developed special programs and religious education classes for the moderately and mildly retarded, often based upon the principles of behavioral psychology (Ratcliff 1985). Teen Challenge and other similar groups reach young people who may have conduct and oppositional disorders, bringing youths to Christ and helping them acquire a new way of life. An excellent source on helping children is Paul Meier's *Christian Child-Rearing and Personality Development* (1977).

11

Personality Disorders

Deeply ingrained maladaptive patterns of behavior, often present throughout life, constitute *personality disorders*. Therefore, personality disorders are diagnosed by behavior patterns (perfectionism, suspicion, emotionality), rather than by such symptoms as anxiety or depression. The severity of the behavior patterns ranges from a few examples of a particular *trait* to a full-blown *disorder*. Having a few traits is normal. Everyone has some of the traits characteristic of a personality disorder. Few individuals have enough of the traits to be regarded as having a personality disorder. When the traits significantly impair function, year after year, they have a personality disorder.

Passive-aggressive behavior

Passive aggressive personality—Passive resistance to social and occupational demands.

159

Individuals with the *passive-aggressive disorder* are inwardly aggressive but express their aggressive tendencies passively. They express anger, for example, primarily in subtle, nonverbal ways—rarely openly and verbally. The behavior of passive-aggressive individuals expresses resentment at not having their emotional needs met. They learn to accomplish their goals by passive manipulation.

Passive-aggressive individuals use obstructionism, pouting, procrastinating, and intentional inefficiency as manipulative tools. A passive-aggressive wife, for example, might unconsciously keep her husband from making an appointment on time when she is angry over something that happened the night before. Especially if her husband is compulsive about being on time, the wife passively expresses her aggression toward him. Another unconscious way of passively expressing aggression is pouting. Instead of resolving a disagreement maturely, the passive-aggressive person pouts and walks away. Procrastination sometimes reflects suppressed anger. Asked to mow the yard, for example, a passive-aggressive son expresses hostility by putting it off. When he can no longer get by with that, the boy may passively express aggression through intentional inefficiency. He may mow the yard but intentionally leave streaks and do a poor job. If, as a result of his inefficiency, he is relieved of the task, he has learned how to avoid responsibility. Passive-aggressive personalities reach their goals indirectly, learning to manipulate people by their passive behavior.

Individuals with passive-aggressive personalities generally have poor interpersonal relations. At times they appear submissive, but toward people who have no authority over them or cannot fight back they can be rude, overbearing, and inconsiderate. Complaining of unfair treatment, acting slighted when someone disagrees with them, nagging, delaying repayment of borrowed money, and doing careless work can be very aggravating to others. Within the church, passive-aggressives tend to be half-hearted Christians, irresponsibly "waiting on the Lord" for everything while criticizing others as being "less spiritual." They may brag about being prayer warriors or even be attracted to full-time Christian employment in which they depend on others for support.

Causes of passive-aggressive behavior

Passive-aggressive personality develops when a person's dependency needs exceed normal limits. Parents who overprotect their children and show mixed reactions toward them encourage a helpless, clinging attitude and inhibited development of independence. Expecting other people to gratify all their needs, the children grow up dependent on others to protect them or to aid them in the performance of daily chores. They tend to have a low tolerance for frustration. Basically insecure, they seek constant reminders that they are being loved. Unfulfilled needs produce anger and depression; they feel very alone. Craving satisfaction may lead to excessive eating, drinking, smoking, or using addictive substances. Because they need so much nurturing, passive-aggressives seek to please those they depend on and cannot tolerate criticism. The threat of any loss brings on anxiety. Unable to handle interpersonal tension, such individuals seek an infantile and blissful state.

Domineering and controlling mothers often produce the passive-aggressive personality. Children who never learn to make independent decisions suffer anxiety when separated from their mothers, sometimes developing a phobia to school and putting up a fuss to stay home. In school a boy like that may be the "teacher's pet" but his peers label him a "sissy" or a "momma's boy." Adult praise reinforces his passivity. When he grows up he may perform well when told what to do, but has difficulty making his own decisions. A passive-aggressive male may choose a forceful mate or mother substitute. Such a wife will probably soon tire of his dependency and seek divorce. Feeling unloved and overburdened, the husband often seeks solace in alcohol, an outward gratification of his oral dependent needs. A passive-aggressive woman generally does not face the same kinds of conflicts, because male-dominated society reinforces dependent behavior in women and encourages them to be submissive.

The passive-aggressive personality sometimes develops to express resentment against excessive parental demands. Such parents never meet the basic trust and dependency needs of their children. If open expression of hostility is not accepted by the parents, the children find more subtle means of rebellious behavior. At the same time the children are forced to repress resentment, their parents reject their affections and show hostility toward them. A cycle of inhibition and rejection develops. Such children soon learn that negative behavior (nail biting, bedwetting, eating problems) will at least get them attention, so they willingly take punishment at the price of greater gain. Parental inconsistency is also linked to this disorder.

Passive-aggressive children usually cause problems in school, violating class rules and frequently fighting with other students. By their teenage years they may lean toward antisocial personality, engaging in delinquency, drug usage, and theft or other misdemeanors. If they control and channel passive aggression constructively, such students may achieve academically but will never be popular socially because of their poor manner of relating to others. Passive-aggressives often use physical complaints to escape duties imposed on them. Backaches, cramps, or migraine headaches can serve as a means of escaping from work.

In marital relationships, the passive-aggressive man seeks his own gratification and may be unwilling to give much to his mate. Husbands who push their wives beyond their level of endurance cause many divorces. Their lack of adaptive skills and irritating personal habits make it difficult to establish satisfying personal relationships. Realizing that their dreams cannot be achieved because of their own inadequacies may produce such bitterness and loss of self-esteem in passive-aggressive men that they contemplate suicide.

Examples

An alcoholic represses his hostility toward a domineering, mothering, compulsive wife. He dares not express anger toward her or even be aware of it, so he gets even with her by coming home late from work, putting off daily chores, and eventually dying of liver disease. A more subtle example would be a passive-aggressive pastor who represses his anger toward the church leadership for two or three years but accumulates unconscious grudges toward them. He gets even by unexpectedly splitting the church over a noncrucial issue. Many Scripture passages, such as Romans 2:5–6, deal with stubbornness and other passive-aggressive behaviors and attitudes.

Obsessive-compulsive behavior

Obsessive-compulsive personality—Behavior pattern characterized by inflexibility and perfectionism.

Of the various personality types in Western culture, the *obsessive-compulsive* shows the highest incidence of depression. Individuals with this personality disorder tend to be self-sacrificing, overly conscientious, perfectionistic "workaholics," frequently drawn to fervent religious expression. Over 90 percent of the physicians and 75 percent of the ministers tested by the authors lean primarily toward obsessive-compulsive personality traits. Lawyers, musicians, engineers, architects, dentists, computer programmers, and other professionals usually have many obsessive-compulsive traits. That is probably why physicians, dentists, and musicians have the highest suicide rates. Missionaries frequently fall into the compulsive category. Men outnumber women with this problem.

At first glance it hardly seems fair that society's "dedicated servants" should be the most likely candidates for depression and suicide. But those who study the depth of unconscious human dynamics realize that, to a large extent, depression, suicide, and even happiness are all choices. The selfishness of perfectionists is very subtle. A man out "saving humanity" at a work pace of eighty to 100 hours a week may selfishly ignore his wife and children. Burying his emotions, he works like a computerized robot. However loving and compassionate he may be, his activity unconsciously compensates for his own insecurity and fulfills a strong need for society's approval and a driving urge to be perfect. Such individuals are self-critical and deep within themselves feel inferior. They may spend the bulk of their lives working at a frantic pace to amass wealth, power, and prestige to prove to themselves that they are not a "nobody." In their own eyes, and in the eyes of society, obsessive-compulsive individuals epitomize human dedication.

For example, an obsessive-compulsive medical researcher spends seven days (and nights) a week in the lab to save humanity from various diseases while his or her family suffers from loneliness and children become delinquents. Such individuals often get angry at family demands on their time, reasoning, "How could anyone have

the nerve to regard my working for others as selfish?" The strong
need of obsessive-compulsive individuals to compensate for inferiority
feelings often blinds them to the truth that their families are correct. That is one reason why so many children of pastors, missionaries, and doctors become rebellious.

Of course many pastors, missionaries, and physicians do spend
time with their families and have intimate fellowship with their
spouses. It all depends on one's willingness to establish biblical priorities. The Bible says Christians should not be pastors unless their
families are well-governed and their children are well-behaved (1
Tim. 3:4, 12). Those who cannot say no to parishioners' demands
should not be pastors. Pastors who devote excessive hours to "the
Lord's work" and neglect their families can seldom see that they are
building bigger and better churches for their own pride and selfish
motives.

In their middle years, with a mixture of godly and selfish motives,
dedicated people may find themselves overwhelmed with anger
toward God for supposedly expecting so much of them, toward family and associates for similar reasons, toward their children for
rebelling, and toward themselves for not being perfect. They may
become clinically depressed. In a weak moment of immense pain
and hopelessness because they lack insight into the truth, they may
even commit suicide. The authors pray that this book will help prevent such wastes of human potential. Legalistic perfectionism is
unnecessary, depression is a waste of valuable time, and suicide dev-
astates those left behind.

Actually, a degree of compulsiveness can help people be hard-
working, conscientious, and genuinely moral. If medical students
were not organized and industrious, for example, they would never
make it through the grinding demands of medical school and private
practice. Compulsive traits help seminary students and ministers
accomplish great tasks for God, provided they also know how to
relax and enjoy life. The apostle Paul, who obviously had some
healthy compulsive tendencies, may have had to overcome some
unhealthy ones. Legalistic Christians with obsessive-compulsive tendencies are unlikely to relax and have fun because they are absorbed
in overly rigid concepts of right and wrong. Their consciences are
ruled by guidelines stricter than any found in the Bible. They often

feel false, not real, guilt because they violate their own laws rather than God's. This false guilt commonly causes depression because it produces pent-up anger towards the self. Perfectionists feel true guilt when they sin, but they also carry a burden of false guilt over thoughts or actions that do not actually violate God's laws. Legalistic Christians need to receive the grace and mercy of God. Rather than being absorbed by the letter of the law, they need to relax and enjoy the abundant life God desires for us (John 10:10).

Causes of obsessive-compulsive personality

Some causes behind obsessive-compulsive personality traits have been noted. Compulsive perfectionists typically come from families in which children must meet extreme standards for toilet training, cleanliness, etiquette, and performance in general, and where the children perceive their parents' love as being conditional on the child's performance. Often the interpersonal dynamics of such families center around talk rather than healthy, loving contact with each other. Much of the talk may be about morality and responsibility, seasoned with criticism of neighbors, church leaders, and others. Some parents criticize each other in the children's presence or ridicule the religious convictions of the children's grandparents. Instead of learning the good news of salvation by grace and of forgiveness of sin through Jesus Christ, a child may hear much about morality as a way of being superior to others and of getting to heaven.

In such a cold, rigid, unforgiving, critical environment, children learn to suppress emotion and deny healthy sexual feelings. They become overly self-critical, unable to tolerate their own mistakes. They pick up their parents' tendency to save money and develop legalistic and ritualistic tendencies. Having learned to protect themselves against their insecurities and fears of failure by various defense mechanisms, they become compulsive "drivers." Their success in school, business, or other tasks they can approach unemotionally tends to reinforce their behavior patterns—until something breaks down.

Example

To explore the unconscious dynamics of the compulsive personality, let us take a close look at a typical man. Once an excessively insecure, perfectionistic child, John P. Workaholic ("P" for Perfectionism) is now a *magna cum laude* college graduate.

John P. Workaholic is perfectionistic, an over-conscientious worker, unable to relax. He demands much from himself and those close to him. His strong conscience makes him prone to depression. In spite of his hard work, John knows he has never done enough.

John exhausts his physical and mental reserves. Even though financially successful, he is never satisfied because deep within he keeps demanding more of himself. John seems coldly intellectual because he majors in facts rather than in feelings. He detests feelings because they are harder to control than facts, and John has an intense *need* to control himself, his thoughts, and those around him. His aversion to feelings pertains not only to uncomfortable feelings but also to warm feelings, which are equally hard to control. By maintaining rigid control, John keeps in check many of the deep insecurities he feels. Whenever those insecurities surface, he feels depressed.

John has an obedience-defiance conflict. Obedient and submissive but pulled by anger, he occasionally lets that anger escape. Then he develops an intense fear. That fear is, in fact, a fear of authority that drives him immediately back into obedience. His fear reminds him of his mother's or father's rejection whenever as a child he became angry toward them. That fear produces his traits of being dutiful, conscientious, and concerned. Thus many of his "good" traits are really motivated from an unhealthy source, John's fear of parental rejection. As a child John was expected to live up to a performance standard, so he got the idea that love results from high performance.

As an adult John feels insecure in his relationship to others, including God. Since he perceived that his parents' love was conditional, he secretly asks the Lord into his life hundreds of times because deep within he does not feel God could possibly accept him on an unconditional basis.

His constantly critical nature affects the entire family. John is torn by both his critical nature and his intense anger. One has to observe John's mannerisms for only a short time to realize that anger reflects in his facial expressions, in many of his movements, and in his rigid posture.

The time frame to which a compulsive individual relates is usually the future. John ever strives and plans for future goals. Never satisfied with the present, he always commits more of himself. When John gets depressed, though, his thinking shifts from the future to the past, and he begins to worry over former mistakes and failures.

John uses several major defenses to deceive himself. He *isolates* most emotions so that he seldom thinks about his feelings. He can go through a funeral with apparent calmness, while being torn apart within. Another of his unconscious mechanisms is called *undoing*, that is, trying to undo things he has done wrong. Another unconscious defense mechanism is called *reaction formation*. John guards against impulses and feelings by doing exactly the opposite of what he would really like to do. For example, John may carry on a private crusade against sexual promiscuity to counteract the strong sexual desires he represses. These and other defenses temporarily keep John from becoming depressed. To become suddenly aware of all his anger, fears, guilt, and sinful desires would be overwhelming, so he deceives himself. He really needs Christian psychotherapy or guidance toward positive discipleship so he can begin to understand himself and change with the help of Christ. That is what sanctification is all about—dealing responsibly with the truth about ourselves through the power of God and the insights of close friends.

John has many unconscious rituals that help him control his anxieties and avoid intimacy. Intimacy would arouse emotions, and emotions are hard to control. John's church is probably ritualistic, too, which helps him avoid coming close to others. He is chiefly concerned about time, money, and dirt. As a young child his mother pushed him and hurried him to bed or to the bathroom, so he worries about time. Money is important because money brings him status and power. Dirt has become symbolic of the sinful desires and motives John unconsciously represses. Usually very neat and clean himself, he demands that his wife keep their house spotless.

Since John cannot control his insecurities in an uncertain world, he develops a false sense of omnipotence and behaves with a confident demeanor. He usually succeeds in fooling his associates and even himself. He has a strong urge to know everything and to be in utter control. In spite of his outward confidence, John often has a hard time making decisions; he might make a wrong choice—and he cannot stand being wrong.

John wants ultimate truth in all matters, including theological questions. When things are not clear-cut, he turns to rigid rules to control the uncertainty. Engaging in philosophical discussions of certain topics avoids responsibility as well as emotion. For example, if he can talk enough about what it means to be a good father and husband, he can avoid being one.

Although usually punctual, orderly, tidy, and conscientious, at times he may revert to opposite traits. His perfectionistic traits, derived from a fear of authority, exist alongside a nonperfectionistic trait, such as untidiness, derived from defiant anger at having to be obedient. John can be very stubborn, a trait learned when as a young child he obstinately resisted the wishes of his parents.

Histrionic behavior

> *Histrionic personality*—A personality pattern characterized by seeking attention and emotional display.

The personality type nearly opposite from the obsessive-compulsive is known as the *histrionic personality*. Emotional, extroverted, dramatic, impulsive, naive, and frequently seductive, histrionic individuals tend to be attractive to the opposite sex and popular socially, possessing a great deal of charisma. Just as obsessive personality traits are somewhat more common in males, histrionic traits are somewhat more common in females. The stereotypical sex roles imposed on men and women in our culture play a role in producing the male-female distribution of these personality traits.

Perfectionists *become* depressed more often, but histrionics *act* depressed more often. Although histrionic women in particular may complain of depression, they seldom show the physiological symptoms of true clinical depression—unless they have recently read a good book on the subject. Such cases are called theatrical depressions. Histrionic individuals (both male and female), like individuals of any other personality type, do become clinically depressed at times. But from early childhood, histrionic individuals learn either to fake depression or to put themselves into a temporary depression to manipulate people. They "get depressed" when they want attention or to punish an authority figure, usually a parent, romantic attachment, or mate, for not letting them have their own way.

When perfectionists tell a counselor that they feel seriously suicidal, they usually should be admitted to a hospital immediately for their own protection. But when histrionic individuals tell a counselor that they feel like committing suicide, it may be better to reply, "Well, that's one option. What are some other ways you could show your spouse that you are feeling angry toward him (or her)?" After discussing a few other options, such as telling one's mate how one feels instead of showing it so dramatically, some so-called suicidal depressions are resolved within a few minutes. Suicide attempts, however, must be taken seriously. Although such an attempt may be faked, the possibility of accidental death exists.

Histrionics also have a higher than normal incidence of the passive-aggressive personality traits of obstructionism, pouting, procrastination, intentional inefficiency, and stubbornness. Such ways of getting even with a person on whom one is dependent without being openly hostile are used by almost everyone at least some of the time, but individuals with true histrionic personalities behave in almost all of those ways almost all of the time. Personality disorder is a matter of degree.

Within the Christian community, histrionic individuals tend to emphasize emotional experiences rather than to rely on God's Word. They have many spiritual ups and downs, sometimes blaming the devil for everything to exempt themselves from personal responsibility and guilt. Some become religiously grandiose and claim special powers and gifts. Even in church-related activities histrionic persons unconsciously seek attention. They frequently get angry at God for not doing things their way, dropping personal devotions whenever God does not do what they tell him to. Even among Christians, predominantly sexual temptations confront histrionic personalities.

The Book of Proverbs warns young men against the adulteress and her histrionic traits:

> For the lips of an adulteress drip honey,
> and her speech is smoother than oil;
> but in the end she is bitter as gall,
> sharp as a double-edged sword.
> Her feet go down to death;
> her steps lead straight to the grave.
> She gives no thought to the way of life;
> her paths are crooked, but she knows it not

Now then, my sons, listen to me;
do not turn aside from what I say.
Keep to a path far from her,
do not go near the door of her house,
lest you give your best strength to others
and your years to one who is cruel,
lest strangers feast on your wealth
and your toil enrich another man's house.
At the end of your life you will groan,
when your flesh and body are spent.
You will say, "How I hated discipline!
How my heart spurned correction!
I would not obey my teachers
or listen to my instructors.
I have come to the brink of utter ruin
in the midst of the whole assembly."

Drink water from your own cistern,
running water from your own well.
Should your springs overflow in the streets,
your streams of water in the public squares?
Let them be yours alone,
never to be shared with strangers.
May your fountain be blessed,
and may you rejoice in the wife of your youth.
A loving doe, a graceful deer—
may her breasts satisfy you always,
may you ever be captivated by her love.
Why be captivated, my son, by an adulteress?
Why embrace the bosom of another man's wife?

For a man's ways are in full view of the Lord,
and he examines all his paths. [Prov. 5:3–21]

Causes of histrionic personality

As with the obsessive-compulsive personality, the roots of the histrionic personality reach back into childhood. The old-fashioned word
spoiled comes to mind in the typical childhood backgrounds of adult
histrionics. As children they often had decisions made for them, so

that they failed to learn how to think for themselves. They learned to get their way by pouting or crying. Often they were praised for their looks rather than for character, "rewarded" in various ways for being sick, and given the wrong kind of attention if they ran away from home or feigned a suicide attempt. They were thus taught to be vain, overly dramatic, and manipulative. As teenagers they began to act and dress seductively to manipulate. Attitudes toward the opposite sex were picked up from unhappy and sexually frustrated parents.

Histrionic traits sometimes relate to sexual abuse before age five or six. It may be that their later sexual behavior unconsciously "plays out" those early sexual experiences in an attempt to understand them, since they were too young to understand what was happening at the time.

Case histories

As a five-year-old girl very attached to her father, Jane was sleeping in his bed one night when he had a heart attack. An ambulance came to take him to the hospital and as he was being carried from his bed, he promised Jane he would return. He died at the hospital, however. Told of her father's death, Jane made use of massive denial techniques and continued for several years to look for him in closets and under the bed. Even into her teenage years she occasionally hallucinated that her farther had walked into her room to say a kind word to her. Stuck in the denial stage of grief, it took Jane two years of weekly psychotherapy, beginning at age fourteen, to overcome it completely.

At fourteen, Jane was admitted to the psychiatric ward of a general hospital after repeatedly running away, using some drugs, and behaving in some bizarre ways. For example, in the school bathroom she cut up her back with a razor blade, then ran into the classroom to tell a female teacher on whom she had a crush that her sister had cut her. She did almost anything to get attention. In the hospital ward, when she was seen talking to inanimate objects, she was first thought to be psychotic; later it became obvious that even that behavior was a dramatic attention-getting device. After intensive psychotherapy for six weeks in the hospital, Jane had weekly outpatient psychotherapy sessions for two years. During that period, Jane ran away once again (for half a day), overdosed half a dozen times in attempts to manipulate her mother, smoked marijuana intermittently, and threw probably a hundred temper tantrums—all of which represented a dramatic improvement over her previous behavior. By the time she went to live in a youth home for girls at age sixteen she had matured quite a bit. When first seen at age fourteen, Jane was operating at about a three-year-old level of psychological maturity, even with an I.Q. of 135. By the time she was sixteen, she was behaving much like a girl of ten to twelve most of the time.

In her childish understanding, Jane blamed her father for leaving her when she needed him so much. In reality she might have been worse off had he lived, because he was treating her as a substitute wife. After his death Jane both loved and hated her farther. She became bitter toward men in general and became more seductive as she grew older, developing all classic histrionic personality characteristics. Seeing a Christian therapist regularly, she learned to trust and identify with an older male who would not yield to her seduction and manipulation but who showed her genuine Christian love in a matter-of-fact way. During the course of therapy she put her faith in Jesus Christ. Although she a Christian, she found herself trying to manipulate God the same way she had manipulated her father. As many people, Jane thought God must be a lot like her father, so she had difficulty accepting God's omniscience and omnipotence and the divine mixture of genuine love and perfect justice.

An attempt was made to teach Jane's mother how to handle her at home. But her mother, who had arthritis and a heart condition, could not force herself to discipline Jane as she needed. At last report, however, Jane was doing well at the youth home where she was placed.

A priest in the Roman Catholic church, Paul complained that his superiors constantly misinterpreted his actions. Whenever his superiors walked into the church and found him caressing a female parishioner, they accused him of behaving seductively. In his view he was only showing such women sympathy for their marital and other problems. He felt that his bishop was harassing him because of his liberal ideas about women's rights and the women's liberation movement. His personality stemmed from his relationship with his mother, who had pampered him all his life and continually praised him for his appearance rather than his character.

Dynamics of a histrionic personality

Conscious or subconscious seduction of persons of the opposite sex, which we have seen in both Jane and Paul, characterizes histrionic individuals. They seem to do it to prove that the other person is good-for-nothing, like everyone else of the opposite sex. Most prostitutes are histrionics. Female histrionics who entice a man sexually may tell everyone that he seduced her and thus ruin his reputation. Some make up stories about ministers or physicians who supposedly have seduced them.

Perhaps we can best illustrate the unconscious dynamics in the mind of a histrionic individual by closely examining the behavior of an imaginary one, as we did for the obsessive-compulsive personality.

Marilyn S. S. (for "Subtly Sexy") Charisma is a sociable, well-liked adult woman in her second marriage. Her first husband, who she married at age seventeen, was handsome but dependent. They married when she became pregnant. Unconsciously Marilyn had wanted to get pregnant to punish her father. She and her husband conflicted from the start. Since both were too irresponsible to work out their personality conflicts through counseling, they divorced, blaming their break-up on "incompatible personalities." (*Incompatible* personalities are actually *unwilling* personalities. Any two personality types can, with God's help, quality counseling, and some swallowing of pride, develop a happy marriage—but both partners must be willing to make some changes. See appendix A.)

Marilyn could not stand being independent after the divorce, so she soon married an older man who seemed stable, confident, and successful in his profession. She did not understand that he was, for her, a father substitute, a compulsive individual whose stability and confidence were only a facade.

Marilyn at times becomes emotional and excitable or depressed; at other times she is likable and pleasant. She can be extroverted and out-going, the life of a party. She has charisma; people tend to gather around her because of the excitement radiating from her life. People find her enjoyable, vivacious, often theatrical, and physically attractive. She expresses herself dramatically. A charming individual, she puts others at ease while she feels only stress within. Although emotional on the surface, she has trouble relating to others on a deep level. She emphasizes feeling rather than logic. Marilyn concentrates on the present rather than the future or past; her obsessive husband focuses on the future, planning and setting goals.

Marilyn's friends hardly notice her self-centered vanity. She has occasional romantic affairs, especially when her husband is out of town. Although she does not enjoy sexual relationships very much, she uses sex to manipulate other men into satisfying her need for attention. Actually, she feels inferior, even about the way she looks, in spite of her beauty. Through her sexual prowess and attention-getting ability she tries to prove to herself that she is not a nobody. If, in a depressed mood, she takes an overdose of a few aspirin or Valium, she does not take enough pills to kill herself; she takes just enough to manipulate her guilt-ridden husband. She has many dependency needs and intensely fears rejection.

Marilyn sometimes undervalues and at other times overvalues the opposite sex. Many of her conflicts with her own immature father were never resolved. She learned in childhood that she could control her father by her manipulative actions, but she also felt rejected by him. Left with a fear of being rejected by other men, she developed an ambivalence toward them. A strong pent-up anger toward her father and men in general has made her sexually frigid with her husband, although to some extent she may enjoy sex with other men.

From childhood Marilyn developed her hostile need to compete with men and her desire to achieve power over men through sexual conquest. Through sex, she can attract and control men, choosing men who are all-powerful father figures. Such men see her as a status symbol because of her looks and also as somewhat of a mother figure to satisfy their dependency needs. Marilyn's fantasies tend to center around love and attention.

Marilyn's life is relatively unstable because of an overemphasis on feelings. Since feelings change, Marilyn is unpredictable. Actually she represses many of her deep emotions. Her apparent openness makes new acquaintances feel they have known her for a long time, yet she has difficulty establishing more than a surface relationship with anyone. People actually know her no better after several months than after one hour. She habitually arrives late, an unconscious punishment of her punctual husband. Her husband looks at life objectively and plans ahead carefully, but Marilyn impulsively relies on impressions and hunches. Her vivid imagination enables her to be creative in art and music, but her boredom makes her extravagant and unreliable about money.

As a child, she learned that she could receive increased attention by being sick and that dramatic scenes helped her to get her way. Excessive dependence on her mother made it difficult for Marilyn to mature. Recognizing that special privileges were accorded to males, she reacted with competitive envy. Having been very close to her father when she was very young, when conflicts developed at the time of puberty, she felt an extreme sense of rejection. By her teenage years, Marilyn had become preoccupied with obtaining the approval of others but had poor relationships with most other women out of competition for male attention.

Sociopathic behavior

Antisocial personality—A behavior pattern characterized by actions that violate the rights of others, beginning before age fifteen and continuing until at least age eighteen.

The antisocial or *sociopathic personality* repeatedly has conflicts with other members of society. Basically unsocialized, sociopaths are unwilling to be loyal to individuals, groups, or social values. Selfish, callous, irresponsible, and impulsive, they are unwilling and relatively unable to feel guilt or to learn from experience, including punishment. Their failure to follow rules, however, is not a result of ignorance or an intellectual disorder. Sociopaths have a tendency to blame others, thus rationalizing their antisocial behavior.

The sociopathic personality is charming and often highly intelligent. Under that facade, however, such individuals are unreliable, untruthful, unpredictable, and insincere. After appearing dependable for a time, as soon as they are trusted they may fall back into manipulating others, sometimes skillfully talking their way out of punishment. Highly narcissistic, sociopaths are also very hedonistic, ruling their lives by the pleasure principle. Without apparent motivation for many of their antisocial actions, they appear to have no particular life plan.

The sociopathic personality disorder is a lifelong process, producing behavior problems at home, at school, and in other contacts with society. Antisocial individuals usually engage in a variety of socially unaccepted activities—for example, truancy, drug abuse, burglary—in contrast to a single recurring type of criminal action. Sociopaths often abuse alcohol and drugs because they seek immediate gratification. For the same reason they may engage in all kinds of sexual behavior with little emotional involvement. They lack close interpersonal relationships because the give-and-take of a close relationship often requires deferring satisfaction or tolerating frustration. Normally, fear of punishment will cause individuals to modify their behavior, but neither intelligence nor past consequences deter sociopaths from satisfying their immediate impulses. They tend to have poor school and work records.

Perhaps the predominant characteristic of the antisocial personality is the relative absence of anxiety and guilt feelings. The Bible says that people harden their hearts (Prov. 28:14); hence not feeling guilty means that one has chosen not to feel that way. God's Spirit will continue to strive to convict such people and impress them with a need for salvation, but if individuals continually reject God's call for salvation, they will eventually reach a point where they will feel relatively free of guilt and will have become sociopathic. Some antisocial personalities do come to know Christ as Savior, however, and become progressively less sociopathic as they mature in Christ.

Causes of antisocial personality

Failure to develop a conscience, coupled with failure of the socialization process, produces the sociopathic personality disorder. Some association often can be made between delinquent behavior and loss of a significant love object. As a result of such emotional deprivation, continual angry search for the lost object by a child experiencing grief and depression produces narcissistic and delinquent behavior. Also, lack of an object for identification may make it hard to incorporate a set of standards into a sociopath's own personality. Children repeatedly moved from one foster home to another or from one servant or private boarding school to another may have formed no close relationships with a parent or parent substitute.

In addition to separation from parents, parental inconsistency and hypocrisy can lead to sociopathic behavior. If parents constantly change rules or verbally express one set and then act according to another, children learn not to believe in any rules at all. Such children cannot establish their own range of skills because their parents have not set limits for them. Equally detrimental to normal development are parents whose unreasonable standards and demands impose a value system inconsistent with a child's social environment or institutional standards. Confusion and hostility result. About two-thirds of sociopaths come from homes without discipline. The other one-third come from homes where the child was physically abused, or disciplined to the extreme.

Another factor leading to sociopathic behavior is parental or community rejection. Sociopaths often were unwanted children. Antisocial behavior in a child may be encouraged unconsciously by one or both parents, who vicariously gain pleasure from the child's deeds and subtly carry out their own unconscious hostile and destructive feelings toward the child.

Some evidence exists that sociopathic personality disorders, to some extent, may be biological. Criminals and antisocials seem to have more frequent electroencephalogram (EEG) abnormalities than the general population, suggesting delayed brain maturation. That could account for such antisocial characteristics as difficulty in gaining impulse control and in developing social maturity. Such individuals react to stress with less anxiety and recover from stress more readily than do most others. Other evidence indicates that the sociopathic personality does not learn conditioned fear responses as readily as others do. Even where biological factors play a partial role in the development of personality disorders, precipitating factors never totally excuse a person from responsibility for antisocial behavior.

A great many with antisocial personalities have religious interests. Regrettably, some become pastors or evangelists who use their positions of prestige and power to manipulate and control people. Many who use people "in the name of the Lord" to accomplish their own selfish goals are self-righteous and have very little insight into their own disordered personality. They have superficial relationships with their mates and children; the children usually rebel and the wives remain silent for fear of rejection. Sexual affairs, both heterosexual and homosexual, are common. Yet we must recognize the fact that everybody has some antisocial personality traits, such as selfishness and impulsiveness.

Schizoid personality

> *Schizoid personality*—Personality characterized by indifference to relationships and an ability to show only limited emotions.

Persons with *schizoid personalities* lack in their ability to form close relationships or to express anger appropriately. They daydream excessively. Such individuals tend to be shy and withdrawn, frequently living alone and having few or no close friends. Sometimes they are eccentric. A poorly integrated personality keeps them from expressing normal angry feelings. They withdraw emotionally from their environment and appear detached and unemotional in the face of stress. Particularly in children, fantasy is a common refuge. Attempts to cope with the ordinary problems of childhood evoke feelings of frustration which give rise to poorly handled hostility. The schizoid person is a loner who avoids close or competitive relationships.

Causes of schizoid personality

A strong possibility exists that inheritance influences the introverted personality. Almost without exception, however, the parents of such individuals did not have a close relationship with each other, although appearing sociable on the surface. Hence environmental factors seem to considerably outweigh genetic factors. The parents may have attached great importance to physical care but been unwilling or afraid to impart emotional warmth and acceptance to the child. A schizoid's regression seems to be reactive in nature, an attempt to avoid something threatening from within. Overprotective anticipation of their needs as infants may not have allowed distress, anger, confusion, and rage to surface. More commonly, however, inadequate stimulation and mothering may have caused such infants to give up on having their emotional needs met, thus leading to withdrawal into a schizoid personality pattern. Lack of stimulation in infancy and early childhood (including much hugging, warmth, touching, and laughing) nearly always results in more introverted tendencies as an adult.

A girl who is shy and fears intimacy spends much time in schizoid fantasy about the perfect romance, but refuses to date the boys who ask her out because they do not measure up to the perfect man of her dreams. She may develop anger toward God for not providing her with a mate, when in reality she unconsciously rejects all men.

Paranoia

> *Paranoid personality*—Pattern in which other people's actions are interpreted as threatening or demeaning.

Suspicious, hypersensitive, argumentative, and jealous—the *paranoid* person often blames others for shortcomings and hostilities. The personality disorder is distinguished from paranoid schizophrenia, and the delusional disorder by its nonpsychotic nature and a lack of delusional misinterpretation of reality.

An intense desire to prove their superior worth motivates much of what paranoid personality types undertake. Unconsciously they feel deeply inferior and insecure. Although they may be highly efficient, they are too rigid to accept innovations and react with hostility to suggestions and criticism. They belittle others to avoid being attacked themselves, yet their actions bring about what they try to avoid—further rejection and damage to their self-worth. The paranoid person seldom has close friends and often does not marry. Those who do marry try to control their mates. If their inferiority feelings become too severe, they may gradually lose contact with reality. The basic types of paranoid thinking are *jealousy, eroticism,* and *persecution.*

Jealousy

Paranoid jealousy becomes more profound and relentless than that found under normal circumstances. The individual usually misinterprets what is said or done by others because of feelings of inadequacy, low self-esteem, and ambivalence. Such an individual is constantly watching for confirmation of his jealous suspicions. Paranoids base beliefs on their own wishes and desires, which they project onto others and deny as their own.

Eroticism

Paranoid eroticism denies and projects one's own erotic desires. For example, individuals may have unconscious sexual desires for someone they know, but project their sexual desire onto that person and convince themselves that they are being seduced. A man in this state may get angry at a woman for being seductive when she isn't being seductive at all. He thus can be angry at her for his sin and feel flattered at the same time.

Persecution

The most frequent and severe type of paranoia centers in feelings of persecution. A deep mistrust of others joins an unusually strong tendency to deny and project one's own hostility. This type of paranoid thinking typically occurs during stresses in which previously adequate adaptive and defensive systems suddenly break down.

Paranoid personality results from life-long exposure to stressful conditions (real or imagined) or discrimination. When met with frustration, threat, rebuff, loss, or temptation, and having no one to trust or confide in, individuals with this personality type regress or withdraw from their situation. They reconstruct reality to confirm their suspicions, projecting the increased anxiety so it appears to become a growing danger from their surroundings. The true origin of that anxiety lies within themselves. They become uneasy and suspicious, examining their environment distrustfully. They may feel they are being subjected to all kinds of tests or that they are victims of expressions of contempt. They often feel that others are bent on destroying their reputations or even their lives. Paranoids likely project their irrepressible hostility on authority figures or competitors. The greater their suspicions and misgivings, the less they can depend on anyone but themselves to investigate the situation. They may remain aloof from others and express distrust and resentment, or they may show outbursts of anger and bitterness. Both reactions cause others to avoid them, increasing their loneliness.

Common characteristics in paranoid personality disorders include:

1. *Unwarranted suspicion*, revealing itself in extreme jealousy and envy of others. Saul (1 Samuel 18–31) exhibited many paranoid tendencies toward David.

2. *Hypersensitivity* (1 Cor. 13:5). Although basically a psychological weakness, hypersensitivity can often be transformed into a strength after working out hostile feelings through counseling and maturity.

3. *Excessive self-importance.* This begins as an act put on to compensate for lack of self-worth, but paranoid individuals sometimes convince themselves that they know all the answers.

4. *Supercritical attitude.* Matthew 7:1–5 warns Christians not to be overly critical of others.

5. *Projection and denial.* These primary defense mechanisms of the paranoid personality, are also described in Matthew 7:1–5. Paranoid people often hate their mates for having faults which are really their own. It is less painful to reject one's mate for being selfish than to recognize one's own selfishness and suffer the severe pain of low self-esteem.

Causes of paranoid personality

Extremely harsh or indulgent treatment is also associated with the development of this disorder. Basic trust in parents or parent substitutes is essential in early childhood. Without such trust, frustration, disappointment, and humiliation produce in children a feeling of betrayal and a sense that their environment is hostile. To protect themselves from harm children develop a secretive, critical, insensitive, and hostile personality. Having never felt trust, they cannot trust others. Frequently individuals with a paranoid personality have had an opposite-sex parent who was submissive, passive, and relatively unavailable to the child. Paranoia may also develop if the parent of the same sex instills feelings of inadequacy through intimidation, hostility, and rigid control. Aggressive, hostile feelings toward the feared and rejecting parent may be repressed but often manifest themselves in a continuing battle with siblings, peers, and the world at large. Biological inheritance appears to play a negligible role. Although certain types of brain damage make a person more aggressive, no neurological basis is known for paranoid personality disorders.

Case history

A woman from an ultra-conservative church background married an elderly widower about fifty years her senior. She said she felt "safe" with him. Within a short time the woman cut off all communication between her husband and his now grown children because she suspected that they might take away her home after her husband died, although this was unlikely. Those around her began to realize she was becoming more and more suspicious of them. Overtures of friendship repeatedly made by her husband's family were interpreted as sinister ways of undermining the marriage or trying to possess the house.

All legal documents were transferred to her name, including the house, yet she remained suspicious. She began to intercept all telephone calls and letters to her husband, apparently believing communications with him indicated a threat. By this point even offers of help to care for her dying husband from neighbors were construed as threatening. Everywhere she went, she constantly tried to find evidence of harm to her, and usually she found something that would confirm her assumption, at least in her mind.

Avoidant personality

> *Avoidant personality*—Individuals characterized by being timid, uncomfortable with others, and fearful that others will not like them.

Those with an *avoidant personality* disorder are characterized by hypersensitivity to rejection, often with an unwillingness to enter into relationships because of fear of rejection. Social withdrawal may be present. Such individuals have an intense desire for affection and acceptance, but very low self-esteem. They devalue self-achievements and are dismayed by personal short-comings.

The avoidant personality is sometimes confused with the schizoid personality, since they both involve withdrawal from others. The key difference is that the avoidant personality *desires* social relationships but refuses to attempt a relationship unless he or she receives strong guarantees of uncritical acceptance. The schizoid personality, on the other hand, does not desire social relationships; he or she is a loner who does not want to be with people. Within a relationship, the avoidant personality is devastated by the slightest disapproval.

Causes of avoidant personality

As in the case of the schizoid personality, the source of the avoidant personality's problem probably goes back to early childhood, even infancy, when the capacity to trust and to mistrust is learned. The *DSM* states that physically disfigured people are more likely to develop an avoidant personality.

The evidence for a biological factor in the avoidant personality is very slight. Parental and peer rejection seem to be key factors. When the parents depreciate and reject the child, peer acceptance may still promote a healthy self-esteem. When peers also reject the child, the avoidant personality becomes much more likely.

Dependent personality

> *Dependent personality*—Individual characterized primarily by submissive and dependent behavior.

Individuals with a *dependent personality* get others to assume responsibility for decisions in their lives. They lack self-confidence and feel stupid and helpless. They subordinate their needs to those of supporting persons to avoid their own responsibility. Dependent individuals often feel intense discomfort when alone. The disorder is most commonly found in women.

Usually passive people, dependent personalities make few demands of others. For example, a woman who has such a disorder may live with an abusive husband, yet reporting the abuse or making him stop is unthinkable because "he might leave me." They usually see themselves as stupid and may regularly remind people of that impression. They usually do not want to be alone.

Causes of dependent personality

This disorder may be related to early separation anxiety when the mother leaves the child. Chronic physical illness in children and teenagers may contribute to the need for dependence.

Some babies seem to be born more withdrawn and sad, and parents may encourage more dependent behavior as the child matures. Parental overprotection shelters a child unrealistically. Toddlers want autonomy (self-direction), but if parents discourage such independence and try to perpetuate the strong attachment of infancy, overprotection results.

Such individuals often have suffered repeated failures when they compete with others; thus they learn to submit rather than compete. It may be that more women have this disorder because society has traditionally encouraged women to take a more passive role.

Schizotypal disorder

Schizotypal personality—Problems in relationships combined with strange thinking and behavior.

Various oddities of thinking, perception, communication, and behavior that are not severe enough to meet the criteria of schizophrenia can be brought together under the *schizotypal disorder*. The oddities may include "magical thinking" (superstition, clairvoyance), social isolation, odd communication (tangential or vague speech), or a facial expression devoid of emotion. Suspicion and paranoid fears may be prominent.

The *DSM* (p. 342) notes that schizotypal personalities often have unusual beliefs. A Christian with such a disorder, for example, may engage in magical thinking, believing he or she can open the Bible at random and always get a message from God from whatever passage his or her eyes happen to land upon. Schizotypal persons are likely to have fringe religious convictions and be bigoted (*DSM*, 1980 ed., p. 312).

Schizotypal personalities often have "ideas of reference," the belief that objects and events have unique meanings for them. A man watching a television program about nature might believe that the program contains a special message that he personally should plant trees in his yard. Schizotypal personalities often sense a force or person that is not present, such as believing a dead grandmother haunts the room.

Some secularists suggest that certain Christian beliefs are somewhat schizotypal since Christians sense the presence of the Holy Spirit. The belief that God leads and directs the Christian might be considered an "idea of reference." Affirmation of the reality of miracles could be construed as magical thinking. The doctrines of evil and Satan might be considered paranoid, while theological terms and the "King James English" some use in prayers might be odd communication. Certainly such conclusions would be far from factual, but they should make us wary of those theories that might turn belief in the supernatural into a disorder. Some fringe religious groups may attract more than their share of schizotypal persons, but that does not rule out the reality of the supernatural.

Causes of schizotypal personality

Severe environmental turmoil, persisting over time, often runs through the backgrounds of schizotypal disordered persons. They may have brain deficits. Neglect or indifference during childhood produces a hunger for stimulation. Poor communication patterns in the family result in fragmented thought patterns in children. Parents often deride children who later become schizotypal, while brothers, sisters, and peers humiliate them. The child retreats to fantasy to compensate for poor self-esteem and "stimulation hunger."

For example, an immature Christian seeks God's will about whether to marry the non-Christian girl he has "fallen in love" with. Rather than seeking out mature counselors and the advice of God's Word, he uses "magical thinking" by opening up the Bible at random, looking at the first verse he comes to, reads, "Go and do likewise," and concludes that his marriage definitely is God's will.

An eight-year-old girl becomes angry at her father and has a fleeting wish that he would die. That night she has a nightmare about her father dying. The next day her father really does die in an automobile accident. She naively believes that her anger actually caused her father's death and becomes overwhelmed with guilt and depression. Magical thinking, to a mild degree, is present in nearly all persons. It is present to a greater degree in schizotypal personality and in psychotic proportions in individuals suffering from schizophrenia.

Narcissistic personality

Narcissistic personality—Greatly overestimated view of one's importance, knowledge, power, or worth, with little feeling for others, yet very sensitive to others' evaluations.

The term *narcissistic* is taken from an ancient Greek myth that describes how the young Narcissus fell in love with his reflection in a pool of water. Perhaps, as Christopher Lasch (1979) has stated, ours is a culture of narcissists. We may not all have the disorder, but many of us have some of the traits.

William K. Kilpatrick (1983, 57–89) sees the modern person as basically trying to be God, the original temptation to which Adam and Eve yielded. The person tends to lose any sense of responsibility to others as the self becomes enthroned. Kilpatrick links this problem with the "self-help" movement and an excessive emphasis on self-esteem in modern psychology. While many psychologists have, indeed, enthroned people to look out for themselves and seek only personal gain, it is equally false to assert that all psychologists have done so. The Christian must resist the temptation to become narcissistic, even though everywhere our society seems to emphasize "looking out for number-one."

Causes of narcissistic personality

Three factors are predominant in the development of narcissistic personality: (1) the parents usually indulged and overvalued the child; (2) the person was likely an only child, and (3) the person learned to exploit others. Children who are pampered and who can do no wrong in the parents' eyes come to believe they are special and superior to others and thus expect the world to revolve around their desires and ideas. When the world outside the home does not indulge them as did their parents, they tend to become demanding and exploitative, much like the antisocial personality, who may also have been "spoiled" as a child. Peers and others are seen as inferior, while their own special status means they supposedly deserve more than others. As the only child in the family, the person is often considered a special gift of high value, thus they tend not to have as many restrictions as do other children. As a result they fail to learn a sense of social responsibility. The overvaluing by parents tends to communicate feelings of omnipotence to the child.

Borderline personality

Borderline personality—Behavior characterized by a pattern of unstable relationships and moods.

The characteristic feature of a *borderline personality* disorder is instability in a variety of behaviors, moods, and relationships, and in self-image. The self-damaging behavior may include sex, over-spending, drugs, alcohol, gambling, shoplifting, overeating, or self-mutilating acts, such as suicide attempts or fighting. Such individuals may very quickly go from a normal mood to depression and irritability, or lose their tempers and be angry much of the time. They often feel lonely or bored. Their interpersonal relationships are unstable and intense, with marked shifts of attitude from ideal-ization to devaluation. Their self-image may suffer in career choice, values, goals, or gender identity.

Drastic shifts in attitude can occur within hours; the individual may hate someone one day and be completely infatuated with him or her the next. The borderline personality alternates between extreme dependency and extreme self-assertion. More women than men have this disorder.

Causes of borderline personality

Some forms of the borderline personality come from homes in which relatives are bland and lack energy. As children they are over-protected and excessively attached to one particular adult. Others are rebuffed by their caretakers, upon whom they are very depen-dent, producing trauma and intense separation anxiety.

The person sometimes seems to need an excessive amount of stimulation throughout childhood, constantly seeking approval and recognition from others. Perhaps most important, the person's par-ents often acted inconsistently, alternating abuse with extreme affec-tion. Erratic parenting tends to produce the erratic, constantly shift-ing behavior of the offspring, eventually producing the borderline personality.

Other personality disorders

Personality disorder not otherwise specified—the person has characteristics of several personality disorders but does not meet
the criteria for any single disorder. This category also includes
several proposed personality disorders.

The *DSM* lists two possible personality disorders that have not
been investigated as much as those described thus far, but which may
prove to be genuine with further study. M. Scott Peck suggests a
third.

First, The *DSM* (pp. 369–71) considers that there may be a *sadistic personality* disorder. Here the individual is cruel and demeans
other people. The description rules out this disorder if the sadism is
related to sexual behavior (which makes it a paraphilia). The *DSM*
emphasizes that the sadism must be directed to more than one person,
most likely subordinates at work or in other social situations. Some
with this disorder resort to violence in dominating others, while others portray a fascination with violent behavior or objects associated
with violence (such as weapons, or magazines about torture). The
person with this personality disorder humiliates others and may harshly
punish or restrict a spouse or children or enjoy abusing animals.

Also a proposed personality disorder in the *DSM* (pp. 371–74)
is the *self-defeating personality* disorder. The person avoids situations
that may produce pleasure and enters relationships and contexts that
produce suffering, even when pleasurable alternatives exist. By definition this occurs in situations other than just sexual (which would
make it another paraphilia) and not just when the person is
depressed. Some in the past have called this the "masochistic personality," but the *DSM* states that this term is misleading because
many associate masochism with sexual behavior alone.

Usually those with this disorder refuse help from others. When
something good happens to them, the person with the self-defeating
personality disorder usually becomes depressed or feels a lot of guilt.
They do things to get others to reject them, while people who treat
them well are usually considered boring. They may do things for
others requiring great self-sacrifice, yet fail to complete tasks they
are required to do.

M. Scott Peck (1983) has proposed a personality disorder he has observed in his psychiatric practice. He defines the *evil personality* disorder as a variation of the narcissistic personality. The person scapegoats, blaming anyone else for personal problems. He or she cannot tolerate criticism and is overly concerned about public image. Devious, such people occasionally have a mild disturbance in their thinking, slightly like schizophrenia. Peck notes the sense of revulsion he has when he works with these people in his counseling. All of us can and do sin. However, those with the evil personality make devious behavior and scapegoating a way of life, yet at the same time attempt to give an outward appearance that nothing is wrong. They are "people of the lie," who cover their sinful behavior with misleading and overtly untrue statements, and project their own evil upon others.

Causes of personality disorders

While the sadistic personality disorder has not been researched enough to consider its causes, the *DSM* states that people who have been abused psychologically, sexually, or physically are more likely to have this problem. They may have witnessed spouse abuse between their parents as well. The disorder is more frequently found among men.

The self-defeating personality disorder also arises from uncertain causes, although the *DSM* states that the person more likely comes from an abusive family and perhaps observed one or both parents being abused. Women are more likely to have this disorder. As with any disorder, several factors may be involved, including early environment, and physiological factors. Still, the most important is choice. People do choose chronic maladaptive behavior patterns. Satan loves that choice.

Treatment for personality disorders

Personality disorders so completely influence the person's life that treatment is difficult. Dealing with a few symptoms (as in most disorders) is far different from attempting to restructure an entire personality. In addition, many with personality problems fail to realize they have problems or do things to keep therapy from succeeding. As a result, the effectiveness of various counseling approaches tends to be rather low and success often temporary. Only if the individual is highly motivated to change, or has a major life-transforming event (such as becoming a Christian) is he or she likely to overcome a personality disorder.

We will examine some of the techniques used with a sampling of the personality disorders. While they are listed by specific disorder, many of them could be used with other personality disorders. It is also worthwhile to refer to the guidelines for mental health in chapter 3.

Passive-aggressive personality

Many passive-aggressive individuals first seek help as a result of anxiety. Their behavior invites stress. Obvious anxiety, together with a history of stress, may lead to incorrect diagnoses. Counseling begins by helping these individuals see their maladaptive behavior patterns, the consequences of those patterns, and the need for change. They need to be encouraged to find more workable ways of resolving their dependency conflicts, and to learn new measures to cope with frustration.

A problem inherent in treatment of this personality type is that the client's behavior may antagonize the counselor. Passive-aggressive personalities do not like open confrontation. They tend to show up late for appointments and frequently miss counseling sessions. Out of stubbornness and habitual noncompliance, they often disregard advice. After communicating a problem, they may ask for a solution. The counselor can outline positive steps for solving the problem but such clients may deliberately sabotage the solution or procrastinate and not attempt the solution at all. Subconsciously they want to prove a therapist is powerless by showing the solutions unworkable. Therefore, it is unwise to be directive with passive-aggressives. All responsibility for a solution to a problem must be reached in an indirect or nondirective manner, allowing the counselees full responsibility for their own actions. People do not have to be passive-aggressive to resist recognizing unpleasant truths about themselves, but passive-aggressives are likely to react to suggestions by pouting or covertly expressed anger. Counselors must be extremely careful not to react to an individual's indirect aggression with their own direct or indirect aggression.

Group therapy may help with the passive-aggressive personality. Often, in group therapy, clients themselves discover what they may have denied or rationalized previously. Group members will confront them when they behave too passively and will encourage them to vent their true feelings and to become more outgoing and spontaneous. Usually a group reacts with hostility to nonverbal expressions of anger from passive-aggressive behavior on others, but care must be taken that the group is helpful and not rejecting.

Medications do not help in treating the passive-aggressive personality disorder itself, although tranquilizers may treat superimposed anxiety. Such potentially addicting drugs as Librium and diazepam Valium should be avoided. With passive-aggressive personalities it is best to avoid all drugs. Hospitalization should be a last resort, since it fosters dependency. Long-term psychotherapy is usually required (often for a year or longer). A reality-therapy approach is recommended for this personality type. Even after therapy, 90 percent do not improve significantly because of their strong unconscious need to fail. The only ultimate answers for passive-aggressive personality disorders are that the person must really want to change and be willing to genuinely commit his or her motives to Christ.

Obsessive-compulsive personality

Obsessive-compulsive personalities seldom seek treatment, since their disability is usually slight. Those who do seek treatment may have a vague sense that life is passing them by since they derive little pleasure from relationships and activities. Depression often stimulates a compulsive person to seek help following a real or symbolic loss such as divorce, death of a spouse or parent, retirement, or loss of a child. With typical indecisiveness, compulsives may seek treatment as a way to avoid making an important decision. Or pressure from other people close to them may cause obsessive-compulsives to seek treatment. Whatever the reasons, psychotherapy usually benefits compulsive individuals who can inspect their way of life and reevaluate their goals, so that they can modify their compulsive characteristics without losing the useful components.

The principal strategy of counseling should be, gradually and tactfully, to help such clients recognize their self-defeating behavior. Therapy is often slow and difficult because chronic patterns of behavior are hard to correct. To be effective, a change in the pattern of living must be developed. Insight given the individual provides the tools for altering living patterns.

Typically, obsessive-compulsives are neatly dressed and groomed. Reserved and formal in manner, they may show little emotion in gestures or facial expressions. Stilted posture and controlled body movements accompany highly intellectual talk about simple matters. Obsessive-compulsive clients may use a written or memorized agenda to control a counseling session, to guarantee that nothing is omitted, and to avoid unplanned, spontaneous reactions. The person may resist the counselor's attempt to change the pace or direction of the session or to promote emotion. Compulsive individuals usually maintain formality and distance, so a warm, meaningful relationship develops slowly with this type of personality, if at all.

The prevailing atmosphere in the counseling session should be one of freedom. Clients should be able to say aloud whatever comes to their minds. Competition, authority conflict, rules, and rituals should be minimized in the interest of maximum exchange in which the rights and limits of both parties are clearly understood.

The personality of the counselor is crucial to success in treatment of this disorder. Counselors must not be overly compulsive themselves. They should be active, directive, and closely tuned to irrelevant communications—to avert them as quickly as possible. Counselors must be continually cognizant of obsessive-compulsives' skill in deceiving themselves and others, since such clients' desire for perfection, omniscience, and omnipotence will surface in therapy. The way the therapist reacts to a compulsive's personality will greatly influence the outcome of treatment. Therapists can use their own reactions to initiate insights, pointing out how behavior patterns seem phony, hypocritical, or grandiose. Such a direct approach can be very beneficial.

Generally a therapist will be viewed as an authority figure who expects and demands perfect behavior. Because of that, care should be taken to avoid being cast in an adversary role. Participation must be demanded without challenging or arousing opposition from compulsive clients. Because of their need to control, and because of the nature of the therapy relationship, such individuals resent being placed in a dependent role. The therapist must acknowledge compulsives' defiance and discomfort as an outcome of their very nature. Clients resist perceived pressure to conform or to meet demands. At times they may appear to deliberately confuse the situation by introducing some new idea, but actually they are trying to be precise to avoid making errors, as is consistent with their nature.

In the "tug-of-war" of therapy, obsessive-compulsives may try to gain control by raising doubts about the validity of the process or the capabilities of the therapist. Because therapy is a learning situation, and because of an intense desire to be perfect, compulsives avoid admitting any deficiencies. The ambivalence compulsives feel between their dependent and independent needs aggravates the situation. Obsessive-compulsives expect magical leaps and bounds in therapy and become frustrated if the process moves too slowly to suit them. Their expectations that psychotherapy will make them perfect and invulnerable often overshadow the valid goals of therapy. Anger may arise from the realization that, instead of making one superhuman, therapy attempts to strengthen one's humanness and to allow one to accept imperfections.

Obsessive-compulsive individuals need to gain the insight that they cannot by conscious intent overcome behavior arising from unconscious sources. They should abandon all resolutions, conscious and unconscious, thus letting go and allowing an experience to happen rather than trying to make it happen. They should be encouraged to channel some of their expenditures of effort into more recreation and pleasure. Care should be taken in pressuring such individuals into recreation, however. If they do as they are told out of compliance and obedience, without enjoying it, the purpose has been defeated.

A therapist needs discernment to determine when an individual's therapy should be terminated. The first indication would be a reduction of tension in living. Other clues would be a greater emotional depth in relationships or less ritualistic behavior. Most important, the individual should have an increased capacity to enjoy life without having to fulfill certain demands all the time.

Histrionic personality

Psychotherapy is the best treatment for the histrionic personality disorder. The therapist needs to be somewhat warm and friendly but also to remember that a patient's seductive behavior can cause problems. The histrionic's manipulative skills must be confronted with an adult-to-adult, matter-of-fact approach, particularly when suicide attempts occur or are threatened. A dramatic reaction only rewards such individuals for their threats and keeps them from learning more responsible ways to express anger. Since histrionic individuals tend to concentrate on feelings and neglect logic, a reality-oriented approach is helpful. People with histrionic disorders need to be encouraged to think about what they are doing. They should be confronted with their irresponsible behavior and helped to plan more appropriate behavior and better methods of dealing with specific problems. A therapist should avoid being overly directive. Attention should be given to uncovering significant ego defense mechanisms, investigating childhood experiences leading to conflict, and other repressed material. The primary emphasis, however, should focus on more responsible behavior here and now.

No medicine cures immaturity, but histrionics sometimes become very depressed or anxious. If depression is extreme and accompanied by the risk of suicide, antidepressants should be considered. Very few antidepressant capsules should be given at a time, however, since some histrionic patients overdose on their medications. Significant risk of suicide calls for psychiatric hospitalization. Intensive therapy should take place daily in the hospital so the patient can be discharged as soon as possible, preferably within four to six weeks. Extended hospitalization fosters dependency in histrionics, who love "being taken care of" in a hospital atmosphere. Some will do whatever they can to prolong or repeat stays in a hospital, which tends to remind them unconsciously of the attention and pampering they received as young children. A hospital can become a substitute mother.

One danger to again stress is that of accidental death by histrionics who intend only to feign a suicide attempt. A histrionic woman angry at her husband may overdose on sleeping pills at 5 p.m., expecting him to be home promptly at 5:30 to rush her to the hospital emergency room. If the husband has a flat tire he may get home at 6:30 to find her dead. All suicide threats should be taken seriously, even from histrionic patients because of the potential for accidental death.

Antisocial personality

Antisocial individuals do not view themselves as sick, so they seldom voluntarily seek treatment. Sociopaths often go to psychiatrists to avoid suffering certain consequences of their behavior. A court may rule that they seek psychiatric help for a certain number of weeks or go to jail. Sociopaths need to learn to suffer the consequences of their antisocial actions. The purpose of treatment should be acquisition of a value system or conscience that will allow the development of internal controls for behavior. The personality of the therapist chosen becomes extremely important because identification with the therapist may occur. Since sociopaths live by the pleasure principle, therapists who enjoy life will be better equipped to identify with their feelings. An effective therapist will not be hypocritical or overly rigid, although therapists must have working consciences. Therapists should not allow themselves to be "conned" by antisocial patents; therapists must demand respect while maintaining a good working relationship. Using a matter-of-fact or confrontational approach works best with antisocial personality types.

Psychotropic drugs are rarely used in treatment because of the tendency toward abuse. Group therapy is not recommended because sociopaths are incapable of loyalty and unable to constructively assimilate suggestions for behavior change made by a group. Their unwillingness to adhere to group standards causes problems in maintaining confidentiality.

Sociopaths can become Christians by understanding the gospel and putting their faith in Christ. There is hope because God can change anyone. Many converted sociopaths eventually mature spiritually and make important contributions to the cause of Christ. Apart from conversion to Christ, however, less than 5 percent of sociopaths ever show any significant improvement, even after prolonged psychotherapy.

Schizoid and avoidant personalities

Individuals with these disorders fear intimacy because of experiences in early childhood. They assume friends will reject them if they "see through them," just as their parents did. The cure comes, therefore, when they force themselves to take a chance on loving other persons and accepting love. Fellowship groups in healthy churches can provide a healing environment of Christian love. Dramatic changes can be seen in introverted persons who open up with their feelings and "come out of their shells." Formal group therapy or long-term individual therapy are also good alternatives for treatment.

Paranoid personality

Paranoid personalities are best treated with long-term outpatient psychotherapy by a loving, patient, and well-trained professional. The professional counselor or psychiatrist must win their friendship and trust, which requires working through all the hostility and criticism one receives from paranoid counselees. At the point when a therapist confronts paranoid individuals with the truth about the sin in their lives and their tendency to project it onto others, such individuals have a tendency to reject therapy and to try to get the therapist to reject them through criticism. Therapists must rely on God's love to help them put up with hostility from paranoid counselees and to work through that stage of therapy.

Severe paranoia is nearly impossible to cure because paranoids are extremely defensive and determined to deceive themselves. Intense hostility causes them to misinterpret any loving attempts to help. Treatment of a paranoid patient should have two aims: to reduce anxiety and to reestablish communication on a realistic level. One means of lessening anxiety is through use of major tranquilizers (see appendix B), which can also be used as antipsychotic drugs. After such drugs bring the brain back to its normal level, reality is properly perceived again.

Unless patients are serious threats to themselves or others, it is more effective therapeutically to treat them as outpatients than to hospitalize them. Restriction of freedom often produces increased anger and heightened paranoia. In psychotherapy the therapist should be firm, consistent, and honest. It is essential that therapists obtain the confidence and trust of such patients, thereby encouraging them to communicate more freely about their frightening experiences. Since paranoids often threaten, therapists uncomfortable with their own aggressive feelings should not try to treat them.

Paranoids need to view a therapist as a neutral person who tries not to reject or condemn their ideas. The temptation either to take the patient's side or to oppose it can strengthen a paranoid's defenses of denial and projection. Therapists must be lovingly honest with such patients, all the while showing them respect and acceptance. Building trust and confidence is a slow process, and paranoid patients require much patience and love. The source of the hostility must be explored and such patients must choose not to hold grudges in obedience to Ephesians 4:26. Repenting of hypocrisy and accepting themselves, they can learn to accept others and even God. They need to realize that God is not like the hostile parents who helped produce their paranoia. By meditating daily on Scripture, paranoids can understand their importance to God. They can come to accept the fact that God is loving and not hostile. It is also essential that paranoid patients learn to trust others so their isolation can be broken.

12

Healing
and Preventing
Problems

We have examined the counseling techniques most effective for each kind of
problem discussed. In this chapter we will define the various kinds of
counselors and their specialties, underscore the spiritual basis of
emotional problems, and look at some things that can help prevent
psychological problems.

Christian counseling may be broadly defined as *a relationship in
which one individual, by virtue of both spiritual and psychological
insights, seeks to help another individual recognize, understand, and
solve his or her own problems in accordance with the Word of God.*

The purpose of the entire process was well described by the apostle Paul when he told the Christians at Ephesus that their fellowship
should nurture them out of spiritual infancy, "tossed back and forth

by the waves, and blown here and there by every wind of teaching and by the cunning and craftiness of men in their deceitful scheming. Instead, speaking the truth in love, we will in all things grow up into him who is the Head, that is, Christ. From him the whole body, joined and held together by every supporting ligament, grows and builds itself up in love, as each part does its work" (Eph. 4:14–16).

Believers are encouraged to build up other members of the body by "speaking the truth in love," thus bringing those individuals to maturity in Christ. Of course, as individual believers mature they also strengthen and build the whole body to a healthy functioning maturity. The Christian counselor therefore has the glorious but awesome responsibility of both aiding the individual believer and building the body of Christ. Although the emphasis in Christian counseling is on the relationship between two individuals, the counselor and counselee, a large fellowship stands in the background. Christian counselors generally find in the local church a tremendous resource of fellowship and encouragement to help alleviate a counselee's problems.

Kinds of counselors

In any given community you are likely to find several different kinds of counselors: *pastoral counselors, marriage and family counselors, psychologists, school psychologists,* and *psychiatrists.* Counseling by these individuals varies in setting. Pastoral counselors are likely to work in a church context, psychologists and marriage and family counselors in a clinic or private practice, school psychologists in a public school, and psychiatrists in a clinic or hospital. There are exceptions; some psychologists work in hospitals, churches or colleges, some psychiatrists have a private practice.

A pastoral counselor should have seminary training that includes a strong emphasis in the Bible, theology, and counseling. Most states, however, do not require this because of concern for the separation of church and state. Licensure is not required, although some pastoral counselors are licensed as marriage and family counselors. Generally the only requirement is that the person do counseling under the auspices of a church or interchurch agency. Thus some who describe themselves as pastoral counselors may have only a bachelor's degree or less, and others may have seminary training but little or no background in counseling methods. If you go to a pastoral counselor it is not a bad idea to check his or her credentials or only use counselors at reputable counseling centers. Also ask what counseling approaches are generally used when contacting any counselor.

Marriage and family counselors usually must be licensed by the state. At a minimum they must have a master's degree in counseling, although many today have doctoral degrees. Since their training is often received outside of a department of psychology (perhaps in education or a family department of the university), they are less oriented toward expertise in such severe problems as psychosis. Instead, they are trained to help people with more normal marriage difficulties, child-rearing problems, helping people cope with stress, and similar kinds of problems.

Psychologists are licensed by the state and must have a doctoral degree in psychology, followed by an internship. While a few older psychologists may lack the doctorate, nearly everyone who does psychological counseling either has a doctorate or is working toward one. Those who counsel but have not completed their doctoral work are usually called *psychology assistants* or *psychology associates*, rather than psychologists, and they must regularly consult on cases with a supervising clinical psychologist. Psychological counselors generally have training that equips them to counsel all of the problems described in this book, although they may become specialized in one or more areas. They may not prescribe medications, although they may work with a doctor or psychiatrist who does the prescribing.

School psychologists generally have training beyond a master's degree and often possess a doctorate in their area. They work within the public school system to help children who have learning or behavior problems. School psychologists often give intelligence tests and other kinds of tests, write reports on children referred to them, advise teachers, and sometimes consult with parents.

Psychiatrists are medical doctors who, after completing their medical training, go on for several additional years of psychiatric training. Psychiatry is a blend of psychological theory and counseling techniques, generally with a strong emphasis upon the use of medications for helping psychological problems. Psychiatrists have completed an internship in a mental hospital or similar facility.

A person should see the best Christian counselor available. Problems relating to psychotic disorders, severe depression, and obvious physical matters should be referred to a psychiatrist or a psychologist who works closely with a medical doctor. Psychologists or psychiatrists also handle the other disorders listed in this book, although if the problem is not too severe a marriage and family counselor or pastoral counselor may be of help. Marriage and child-rearing difficulties can usually be helped by Christian marriage and family or pastoral counselors. School-related problems are the domain of school psychologists. These guidelines assume that the counselor is adequately trained for a given problem. A reputable Christian counselor will always refer people they are not equipped to help.

Hospitalization

Psychiatric hospitalization is a useful tool for psychotherapy under certain circumstances. Suppose a clinically depressed patient cannot sleep and has suicidal thoughts. If a psychiatrist sees the person in weekly therapy with no medications, they may be free of clinical depression within six to twelve months (unless the client commits suicide during the first two months while suffering from insomnia and severe emotional pain). Weekly psychotherapy with antidepressant medication probably can relieve the depression in three to six months. Since they sleep well and feel some improvement after the first ten days on antidepressants, suicide is less of a risk. Or such patients can check themselves into the psychiatry ward of a general hospital, get daily psychotherapy and medication, feel better within a week, and be totally over their depression within three to six weeks, requiring only a month or two of follow-up outpatient psychotherapy. Hospitalization is preferred if the individual has children at home who have been hurting for months because of the depression, or if suicide is a real possibility.

For a depressed individual close to suicide or a psychotic break with reality, hospitalization may be vital. For less severely depressed individuals, outpatient psychotherapy with medication will suffice. For mild depressions, medications should be avoided because they are expensive and have some temporary side-effects, such as dryness of the mouth and a slower reaction time when one is driving.

The advantages of hospitalization include:

1. The individuals receive intensive psychotherapy.
2. Medications can be adjusted rapidly.
3. Individuals find a safe retreat from a stressful environment.
4. Individuals are protected by hospital precautions from suicide attempts.
5. There is a friendly, helpful, supportive atmosphere.
6. Meeting other depressed people who are getting better provides encouragement.
7. The symptoms and emotional pain of depression are more rapidly cured.
8. Trained psychiatric nurses and other staff members assist psychiatric physicians in counseling and helping people gain insights.
9. Nurses observe the daily behavior patterns of residents and relay information psychiatrists can use to gain insights.
10. Hospitalization is usually less expensive (in the long run) to the individual than is prolonged outpatient psychotherapy, since it is generally covered by insurance.
11. People frequently return to full employment more rapidly.

The disadvantages of hospitalization are:

1. Some dependent individuals try to escape responsibility through admission to a hospital, even feigning symptoms of depression when the psychiatrist is around.
2. Some social stigma results from psychiatric hospitalization, especially in some socioeconomic classes. It could hinder some job opportunities or promotions.
3. When people are discharged three to six weeks after being admitted, they are happy, enthusiastic, and over the bulk of the problem but some feel rejected if their friends hesitate to ask questions about hospitalization for fear of hurting their feelings.

4. Total costs average several thousand dollars per week. Even with insurance, it is not ethical to run up high hospital bills unless absolutely necessary.

The spiritual basis of emotional problems

Secular psychology emphasizes the close relationship between a person's physical and emotional aspects but ignores the spiritual dimension. Bible-based psychology sees spiritual health as a prerequisite to mental health. Three major sources of emotional pain may be approached from a biblical perspective: (1) A lack of self-worth encompasses feelings of inferiority, inadequacy, self-hatred, and self-criticism. (2) A lack of intimacy with others produces loneliness and other emotional problems. (3) A lack of intimacy with God stifles a mature and growing relationship with the Lord that overcomes emotional pain.

Self-worth

We all need an appropriate self-worth—not pride but a realistic sense of the talents and abilities God has given us to be used for Christ. Alfred Adler (1927) and his followers coined the phrase *inferiority complex*, believing that nearly all emotional conflicts stem from inferiority feelings. Today many psychologists place great emphasis on *self-image*.

The Bible illustrates certain characteristics of insecurity and poor self-image. That an insecure person turns criticism onto others is illustrated in 2 Samuel 12:5–6, in which David overreacts to Nathan's story because of his own faults—and as a result is very critical. An insecure person fears what others think: "Fear of man will prove to be a snare, but whoever trusts in the Lord is kept safe" (Prov. 29:25). Insecure persons may boast of their own ability: "Let another praise you, and not your own mouth; someone else, and not your own lips" (Prov. 27:2). Often people who appear conceited are covering up deep feelings of inferiority or a lack of confidence; people nonetheless need confidence in themselves and their abilities. Finally, self-conscious, insecure individuals cannot accept constructive criticism or admit they are wrong. Saul continually exhibited that characteristic of insecurity in his relationship to David (1 Sam. 18–28).

Every human being has some feelings of inferiority and insecurity. Through the defense mechanism called *reaction formation* some people lie to themselves and others to prove that they are somebody. People want to feel comfortable and loved, two needs evident even from birth. People tend to feel loved when someone cares enough about their feelings to take the initiative to make them feel comfortable, unless the comfort is administered in an unwilling or superficial manner. We need to sense that we are lovable without having to qualify for acceptance. Children deprived of a loving relationship in the home grow up feeling undeserving or inferior. They attempt to prove that they are somebody by emphasizing their appearance, their accomplishments, or the status derived from their social position. Self-image based on those areas is fickle, so people get caught up in self-verification or in constantly proving to themselves that they are not a nobody.

According to Scripture, we try to establish our sense of worth in false ways. "Do not love the world or anything in the world. If anyone loves the world, the love of the Father is not in him. For everything in the world—the cravings of sinful man, the lust of his eyes and the boasting of what he has and does—comes not from the Father but from the world" (1 John 2:15–16). The Greek text lists these problems as the "lust of the flesh," "lust of the eyes," and the "pride of life."

Lust of the flesh desires sensual pleasure. Many people try to prove that they are somebody by their physical appearance or sexual prowess. Sensual pleasure is a natural desire as long as it is satisfied in appropriate ways, but many people have sexual affairs to compensate for inferiority feelings. Sexual prowess or a self-image based on physical appearance is transitory, however, so the basic insecurity will persist.

Lust of the eyes seeks materialism. Many people base their self-worth on their possessions and acquisitions. Financial blessings add to life unless the acquisition of possessions becomes a goal. Those who base their self-image on wealth must always protect themselves from losing what they own, thus increasing the anxiety reflected in their inadequate self-concept.

The pride of life desires importance and admiration from others. The desire for social status, power, and prestige is subtle and directly related to a defense against inferiority. Again, the status must continually be maintained or surpassed, so that greater insecurities and anxieties often develop in its pursuit. People who feel most insecure are usually the most perfectionistic.

Self-verification stems from three basic desires: being wanted, being good, and being adequate. To have a healthy self-image, people must have a sense of belongingness, worthiness, and competence. If they experience empathy, identification, and love, their inner security grows. On the other hand, hostility, guilt, and fear make people feel emotionally insecure. Their sense of being somebody is threatened.

Intimacy with others

People really *need* other people. We were not made to live alone, but building intimate friendship is not always easy. Even intimate friends offend from time to time, but the pain of conflict with friends, however, is far better than the pain of loneliness. Many people allow a fear of intimacy to dominate their will, not wanting to become aware of their own irresponsibility in personal relationships.

Ideally, a married person's mate should be that person's best friend of the opposite sex. In addition, everyone needs at least two close friends of the same sex. We all need someone with whom we can share our innermost feelings and frustrations in confidence. Christ exemplified such friendship in his close relationship with Peter, James, and John.

Much of our self-concept develops from our relationships with others. Harry Stack Sullivan and his followers in what is called the interpersonal school of psychoanalysis believed that most inner conflicts come from poor personal relationships. Parents' attitudes play a large role in the formation of a child's healthy self-image. If parents are overly strict, children blame themselves for not being perfect and not meeting their parents' expectations. False guilt can develop, especially in a first child, of whom parents tend to be more demanding.

A child needs to feel respected when corrected. Parental anger in discipline increases a child's sense of separation and loss of belongingness. Children who feel threatened by their environment and their relationship to others react in defiance, compliance, or withdrawal.

We need to feel special to the one we love or who loves us. When children try to control their parents' love and fail, yet continue to be impressed that their parents sincerely love them, they learn their own uniqueness. They do not have to maintain a special, exclusive relationship to verify their own sense of being somebody. They do not have to control their love objects. In fact they learn that they lose the love they desire by attempting to control, because they rob the lover of being voluntary in expressing love. When children who feel rejected by their parents begin to feel like a nobody, feelings of rejection can be overt or covert. *Overt rejection* conveys openly and obviously that a person is unwanted or unloved. *Covert rejection* is inferred. It is more subtle and many times unintended. A third form of rejection, *overprotection*, prevents people from developing normally, producing feelings of inadequacy which color their self-image.

Rejection is a prime cause of psychological disturbances. Those who have been severely rejected do not learn how to handle love. Their ability to give and receive love has been impaired. A rejection syndrome develops in which individuals feel that those who do accept them must somehow be "turned off" to finally reject them, fitting the pattern with which they can cope. As a result they are programmed to see rejection in everyone and everything, so they reject others in anticipation of rejection.

Need for another's love is emphasized throughout Scripture. Believers are encouraged to "consider how we may spur one another on toward love and good deeds. Let us not give up meeting together, as some are in the habit of doing, but let us encourage one another—and all the more as you see the Day approaching" (Heb. 10:24–25).

Intimacy with God

The only complete answer to the problem of alienation from the love of God can be found in reconciliation with God and restoration. God loves people unconditionally, and through a relationship with God they develop a true sense of identity as God's somebody. We feel a sense of belonging because God accepts us unconditionally (Eph. 2:8–9) after we have confessed our sins and admitted our inability to go it alone (1 John 1:9). We know we are not inferior or inadequate because God is with us at all times (Heb. 13:5) and we are adopted sons and daughters of the Creator (Eph. 1:5), heir to all his riches (Rom. 8:17). Thus to be complete persons we must know ourselves and then commit ourselves as we are to God. Emotional pain can be conquered through a reciprocal love relationship with God, loving him with all of our heart, soul, and mind (Matt. 22:37) and his loving us in such great measure (John 3:16; Eph. 2:4, and 1 John 4:10).

The three sources of emotional pain—lack of self-worth, lack of intimacy with others, and lack of intimacy with God—are interrelated. In general, emotional pain can be relieved by avoiding sin, by maintaining a clear conscience, and by keeping priorities straight.

To gain self-acceptance, we must realize that God accepts us unconditionally, "to the praise of his glorious grace, which he has freely given us in the One he loves" (Eph. 1:6). God prescribed us before we were born: "Your eyes saw my unformed body. All the days ordained for me were written in your book before one of them came to be" (Ps. 139:16). Even when we do not understand the trials that beset us, God has a purpose in them for us: "And we know that in all things God works for the good of those who love him, who have been called according to his purpose" (Rom. 8:28).

God looks more closely at internal qualities than at outward beauty: "Therefore we do not lose heart. Though outwardly we are wasting away, yet inwardly we are being renewed day by day" (2 Cor. 4:16). If we are wise we will not compare ourselves with others, as that can produce feelings of either pride or inferiority (2 Cor. 10:12). We gain self-acceptance by detecting ungratefulness in our attitude and evaluating what the Lord wants us to do. Christ himself says, "My grace is sufficient for you, for my power is made perfect in weakness" (2 Cor. 12:9). We need to correct any correctable defects (Col. 3:8–10) but glory in our unchangeable defects, thanking God for the way we are made (Psalm 139). We must realize that all our problems can be overcome because each of us "can do everything through him who gives me strength" (Phil. 4:13). Perhaps the best way for us to gain self-acceptance and a healthy self-image is to reprogram our lives with the Word of God: "Do not let this Book of the Law depart from your mouth; meditate on it day and night, so that you may be careful to do everything written in it. Then you will be prosperous and successful" (Josh. 1:8).

Solving spiritual problems

Some troubled individuals seek counsel from a Christian because they recognize the spiritual foundation of their problems. Others come because of emotional problems, not realizing that their unhealthy emotional life signals an unhealthy spiritual life. Spiritual birth and growth overcome spiritual problems.

The need to know Christ

Although Christians have problems like everyone else, they possess in Christ a superior resource to draw on. To employ Christ as a resource, though, individuals first must accept him as their Savior. To do this, certain facts must be known. For example, one must know that Christ is more than just a good man. He is also the Son of God who died on a cross to satisfy the punishment due for the sins of the world. He became guilty so that a holy God might justly forgive the sins of whomever turns to him. He not only died on the cross so that anyone who asks might be forgiven; he also rose from the dead to give victory over death to those who trust him. Those are the basic facts about Christ that must be known. Merely knowing those facts is not enough, however. Individuals must also develop personal relationships with Christ. They must take the step of declaring their guilt and put aside their own control of their lives. That step of personal trust in Christ takes different forms in different individuals, for God perfectly understands and reaches into each inner self. Whether the experience comes as a sudden insight or slowly growing realization in prayer, the relationship with Christ must be personal.

Trusting in Christ demands a choice of the will. The degree of emotion accompanying that choice differs from individual to individual. Some seem forever unsure that they have trusted enough, for they confuse belief with full emotional persuasion. Emotions are sometimes evasive and hard to change if set in psychological roots of many years past. For example, a woman who could never trust or depend on her parents may have trouble feeling that she can always depend on God. Belief for her initially involves the will; later, as she spends time growing in Christ and in his Word, her emotions will also change and she will become more fully convinced.

If a person's response to the Holy Spirit's call did not involve the will, we would not be able to know how much belief—that is, of emotional conviction—to feel before we could know we are in Christ. Where would the line be drawn in determining whether belief is strong enough or still too weak? Mark 9:17–27 records the story of a father who brought his son, who was probably suffering from epilepsy, to see Jesus. Jesus told the father that all things were possible if he believed. That man told Jesus that he did believe, but then asked Jesus to help his unbelief. In other words, some aspects of his emotions were not fully convinced, although with his will he was choosing to believe. *Belief*, or some such equivalent term, is listed in the New Testament 115 times as the condition for salvation. Many such passages are very familiar to Christians: "Jesus said to the woman, "Your faith has saved you; go in peace" (Luke 7:50; see John 1:12). "For God so loved the world that he gave his one and only Son, that whoever believes in him shall not perish but have eternal life" (John 3:16). "For it is by grace you have been saved, through faith—and this not from yourselves, it is the gift of God—not by works, so that no one can boast" (Eph. 2:8–9).

To believe is to realize what Christ has done for us and to accept his death on the cross in our place for the punishment of our sins. Belief is *not* a public acknowledgment of Christ, although the two can occur at the same time. It is not prayer, although one can express belief in prayer. It is not repentance, although repentance does occur simultaneously with belief. It is not confession of sin, although as individuals realize their sin and the atonement only available in Christ, they want to talk to the Lord about their sin. Belief is not a change in lifestyle, although it definitely produces a change in lifestyle.

In summary, the belief that the Bible calls *faith* simply trusts Christ to save us, an act of our wills. God does all the work through Christ's atonement and the Holy Spirit's conviction. We humans merely choose to accept salvation or we choose to reject it. According to John 3:16–18 and many other passages, the punishment due sin before a holy God awaits those who actively or passively reject Jesus Christ as Savior. But those who accept Christ have available a tremendous resource that they did not have before, since God becomes their personal father. Most earthly fathers want to help their children. Far more deeply, God wants to help his children when they suffer in any way.

The need to grow in Christ

Just as some people lack emotional maturity, others are spiritually immature. In fact, we all fit somewhere on the spectrum from spiritual immaturity to spiritual maturity. A number of factors help people move toward spiritual maturity.

Daily quiet time

Probably the first step in helping individuals grow in Christ is to help them develop a daily quiet time set aside each day for deepening one's relationship with Christ. In any relationship the way to become close to someone is to spend time together. There is no short cut, as Christ himself demonstrated: "Very early in the morning, while it was still dark, Jesus got up, left the house and went off to a solitary place, where he prayed" (Mark 1:35). Young Christians often benefit from scheduling a specific time, a specific place, a specific passage of the Bible to read, a certain amount of time allotted for Bible reading and a certain amount for prayer.

A daily quiet time helps Christians avoid the criticism leveled in Hebrews 5:12–14: "Though by this time you ought to be teachers, you need someone to teach you the elementary truths of God's word all over again. You need milk, not solid food! Anyone who lives on milk, being still an infant, is not acquainted with the teaching about righteousness. But solid food is for the mature, who by constant use have trained themselves to distinguish good from evil."

In the quiet time, one is in pursuit of God. It was said that King Hezekiah "held fast to the Lord and did not cease to follow him; he kept the commands the Lord had given Moses" (2 Kings 18:6). To pursue God goes beyond simply exercising self-control or knowing the Bible. It is the element of holding fast to the Lord. The Hebrew word for "held fast" in 2 Kings 18:6 is used in Genesis 2:24 for a man and woman "uniting" to become one flesh, translated "to cleave" in the King James Version. To "cleave to God" means that we desire to spend time with him, to walk and talk with him, to know him as we would any other friend, and to be close to him.

Scripture provides a worthy model in Hezekiah's pursuit of God. In 2 Chronicles 29:11, Hezekiah urged the Levites to spend time with the Lord. In 2 Chronicles 29:20, Hezekiah "gathered the city officials together and went up to the temple of the Lord." It takes time to develop a close friendship with God. "King Hezekiah and his officials ordered the Levites to praise the Lord with the words of David and of Asaph the seer. So they sang praises with gladness and bowed their heads and worshiped" (2 Chron. 29:30). Time spent in singing songs to the Lord about himself can aid us in knowing the Lord. It is real worship to sing praises with gladness as did the Levites.

King Hezekiah exercised self-control to assure that nothing would keep him from the pursuit of God. In 2 Chronicles 30:8 Hezekiah urged his people to yield themselves to God and serve him. "In everything that he undertook in the service of God's temple and in obedience to the law and the commands, he sought his God and worked wholeheartedly. And so he prospered" (2 Chron. 31:21). He sought God with all his heart. We need to seek God with all our heart, determine that we are going to build a relationship with him, that we are going to know him intimately, and that we are going to know him better than we know any friend here on earth.

Some people may imagine that God picks certain individuals to whom he reveals himself intimately—men and women with whom he walks and to whom he is very close. But as the years pass, it becomes clear that God does not work that way. God already pursues us, looking for those who will pursue him. "For the eyes of the Lord range throughout the earth to strengthen those whose hearts are fully committed to him" (2 Chron. 16:9). To such persons he reveals himself, cultivating an intimate relationship with them.

An intimate relationship with God maintained through a daily quiet time can do more to help a Christian overcome mental problems than any other single factor. In some situations where counseling shows little progress, dramatic results follow when the individual agrees to begin a daily quiet time. One woman in therapy for approximately two years had remained hostile, depressed, and defensive. Suddenly her anger seemed to leave, her mood became positive, and she was no longer defensive. Asked why she had improved, she explained that she had begun to spend a couple of hours each day with the Lord. Christians caught up in extramarital affairs have had a change of heart after agreeing to try a daily quiet time for a two-week period. Realizing how selfish they have been, they begin to think less of their own needs and more of the spiritual condition of those with whom they are involved. A man who was "impossible to live with" (according to his wife—who was not perfect either), agreed to have a daily quiet time for two weeks. After two weeks his wife commented, "He is like a different person."

Scripture

When enjoying and memorizing Scripture becomes part of a quiet time, one is already practicing a second way to grow in Christ. Jeremiah said, "When your words came, I ate them; they were my joy and my heart's delight" (Jer. 15:16). The apostle Paul referred to "the word of his grace, which can build you up" (Acts 20:32). Jesus Christ called the words that he spoke "spirit" and "life" (John 6:63). The Bible is more than a document to be studied; it is "living and active. Sharper than any double-edged sword" (Heb. 4:12).

The Word of God instructs us, corrects us, reproves us, and nourishes us. By memorizing specific verses that meet our needs, by praying God's Word back to him, and by enjoying it with others, we find the Scriptures coming alive. We need both their nourishment and their protection in an age of spiritual and mental confusion. In psychology some concepts run contrary to what the Bible teaches; but others are helpful and do not disagree with Scripture. The best way to critique psychological concepts is to evaluate them according to the Word of God. Christians who memorize the Word of God are no longer open prey to confusion.

An important aspect of evaluation, of course, has to do with thoughts and inner conflicts. Are they merely of ourselves, or of God? The Word of God "penetrates even to dividing soul and spirit, joints and marrow; it judges the thoughts and attitudes of the heart" (Heb. 4:12). It is now known that the unconscious mind plays an important role in conscious behavior. Since significant events recorded by the brain affect present behavior, it is important to saturate our minds with the Word of God, by enjoying it and memorizing it. In our subconscious it can significantly determine behavior for years to come. As David said, "How can a young man keep his way pure? By living according to your word. . . . I have hidden your word in my heart that I might not sin against you" (Ps. 119:9, 11).

When an individual becomes a Christian, it is the spirit that becomes new (John 3:6) and not necessarily the mind, emotions, or will. In Romans 12:2, the apostle Paul stated that we should not be conformed to this world but be transformed by renewing our minds. Such renewal is a gradual process, not a once-for-all phenomenon. It begins at the time of the new birth and continues throughout life. If the mind has had a lot of bad programming in earlier years, many years may be required to reprogram it in a more healthy direction.

According to Isaiah 55:11, God's Word will accomplish the purpose that he desires, and his Word can reprogram our minds. Joshua understood that process: "Do not let this Book of the Law depart from your mouth; meditate on it day and night, so that you may be careful to do everything written in it. Then you will be prosperous and successful" (Josh. 1:8). So did the Psalmist: "But his delight is in the law of the Lord, and on his law he meditates day and night. He is like a tree planted by streams of water, which yields its fruit in season and whose leaf does not wither. Whatever he does prospers" (Ps. 1:2–3). Jesus Christ said: "If you remain in me and my words remain in you, ask whatever you wish, and it will be given you" (John 15:7). In Colossians 3:16 the apostle Paul encouraged the church to let the Word of God dwell in them richly. In 1 John 2:14 the apostle noted that he was writing to young men who were strong and in whom the Word of God was "living." Having reprogramed their computer according to the Word of God, they were emotionally strong and stable.

Prayer

A third way to grow in Christ is through prayer. Prayer is more than the power of suggestion or "magical thinking," as some psychiatrists describe it. Prayer calls on the power of God himself, who is available to his children. "This is the assurance we have in approaching God: that if we ask anything according to his will, he hears us. And if we know that he hears us—whatever we ask—we know that we have what we asked of him" (1 John 5:14, 15). James said that we have not because we ask not. As he did for Elijah (James

5:17, 18), God will honor our prayers today and help us to over-come our problems. In Ephesians 6 the apostle Paul spoke of spiritual warfare and encouraged Christians to pray. Through mental problems Satan can render Christians as ineffective as if they had committed some gross sin. Prayer can overcome many psychological problems.

Perhaps the most important advice concerning prayer is simply to exercise ourselves to do it, so God can gradually teach us its applications and wonders. According to the Bible, Moses talked with God as friend to friend. Such a deep relationship could develop because of the amount of time Moses spent talking with God. God longs for us to consider him a friend, and to talk with him and call on him.

Fellowship

A fourth way to grow in Christ is through fellowship. Many mentally disturbed people feel they do not have a friend with whom they can talk or just be themselves. Simply developing a friendship can greatly help them overcome mental problems. The Bible says many wise things about friendship. "He who walks with the wise grows wise" (Prov. 13:20). "As iron sharpens iron, so one man sharpens another" (Prov. 27:17). "Two are better than one, because they have a good return for their work: If one falls down, his friend can help him up. But pity the man who falls and has no one to help him up" (Eccles. 4:9–10). The anguish of loneliness was expressed by the psalmist: "Look to my right and see; no one is concerned for me. I have no refuge; no one cares for my life" (Ps. 142:4). Good friends watch over our souls. We can bare our hearts to them and know that we will be accepted.

Solitary confinement has been used to break prisoners of war. After a few days in solitary confinement, some prisoners will tell their captors all they want to know. Prisoners without enough water may hallucinate about water, but prisoners kept in solitary confinement tend to hallucinate about people. People *need* people. "See to it, brothers, that none of you has a sinful, unbelieving heart that turns away from the living God. But encourage one another daily, as long as it is called today, so that none of you may be hardened by sin's deceitfulness" (Heb. 3:12–13).

True warm, caring, and open friends share problems and help one another overcome difficulties. They accept each other and are willing to give of themselves. As the apostle Paul said to one group of Christians, "We loved you so much that we were delighted to share with you not only the gospel of God but our lives as well, because you had become so dear to us" (1 Thess. 2:8). He called another group "my dear children, for whom I am again in the pains of childbirth until Christ is formed in you" (Gal. 4:19). Paul really cared as a good friend when others hurt.

Many people experience great relief from mental stress when a friend sits down to listen to them and gives them support and guidance. Individuals with mental problems often have difficulty developing friendships because they cannot understand how anyone could care for them. But as they overcome their fear of rejection and begin to develop friendships, they discover that such thinking was inaccurate. Their mental problems are on their way to being solved, because a friend is willing to help.

"He who walks with the wise grows wise, but a companion of fools suffers harm" (Prov. 13:20). People tend to become like their friends whether or not they intend to. Committed Christians should of course have non-Christian friends, but their most intimate friends will probably also be committed Christians. Do not overestimate your own spiritual strength. Although Christians can be a strong witness, influence goes in both directions. Christians subject to depression or other mental problems should be especially careful to cultivate friendships with mature Christians who are enjoying the fruits of Christian life. After all, "a cheerful heart is good medicine, but a crushed spirit dries up the bones" (Prov. 17:22).

Witnessing

Fifth, Christians can grow in Christ by sharing with others what Christ has done for them. Individuals who spend time with Christ find it quite natural to talk about him to others. The apostles Peter and John said they could not help "speaking about what we have seen and heard" (Acts 4:20). The apostle Paul said that "Christ's love compels us" and that he was one of "Christ's ambassadors, as though God were making his appeal through us" (2 Cor. 5:14–20). Witnessing is both an encouragement to those who hear (and receive) and an encouragement to those who share. It helps us to grow in Christ.

Spiritual growth takes place as one grows in prayer, Bible study, fellowship, and witnessing, as one seeks balanced growth. One area should not be emphasized to the exclusion of the others. Spiritual balance indicates a mentally healthy Christian.

Preventing psychological problems

These guidelines can help a Christian flourish spiritually and avoid psychological problems. Yet throughout this book we have noted that the home plays an important part in influencing a person towards difficulties. Families can do much to minimize the likelihood that children and spouse eventually will develop psychological problems. While there cannot be an absolute guarantee of mental health from any list of suggestions because of the distinctive influences of heredity, personality of the individual, and so on, five characteristics generally can be found among healthy families that produce emotionally healthy children and spouses. Emphasizing these five qualities should go a long way to prevent many psychological problems: love; discipline; consistency; example, and authority.

Love

Love is more than an emotion, though it has a large emotional component. Love affects an individual's entire being. God has designed human beings to share love on spiritual, emotional, and physical planes. The complete absence of love (rejection) can destroy a person emotionally and in some cases physically. In the thirteenth century the Emperor Frederick I conducted an experiment with fifty infants to see what language the children would speak if never spoken to. Some thought that Hebrew was man's innate and natural language and that these children would begin to speak Hebrew if they did not hear another language spoken. After assigning foster mothers to bathe and suckle the children, he forbade them to pet, cuddle, or talk to their charges. As a result of not being loved and caressed, all fifty infants died.

Many studies (such as Spitz 1945, Beres and Obers, 1950, and Provence and Lipton 1962) have shown that an absence of love can completely destroy a person. Ideally, love should be as the apostle Paul stated:

> If I speak in the tongues of men and of angels, but have not love, I am only a resounding gong or a clanging cymbal. If I have the gift of prophecy and can fathom all mysteries and all knowledge, and if I have faith that can move mountains, but have not love, I am nothing. If I give all I possess to the poor and surrender my body to the flames, but have not love, I gain nothing. Love is patient, love is kind. It does not envy, it does not boast, it is not proud. It is not rude, it is not self-seeking, it is not easily angered, it keeps no record of wrongs. Love does not delight in evil but rejoices with the truth. It always protects, always trusts, always hopes, always perseveres. Love never fails. But where there are prophecies, they will cease; where there are tongues, they will be stilled; where there is knowledge, it will pass away. For we know in part and we prophesy in part, but when perfection comes, the imperfect disappears. When I was a child, I talked like a child, I thought like a child, I reasoned like a child. When I became a man, I put my childish ways behind me. Now we see but a poor reflection as in a mirror; then we shall see face to face. Now I know in part; then I shall know fully, even as I am fully known. And now these three remain: faith, hope and love. But the greatest of these is love. [1 Corinthians 13]

That type of love, termed *agapē* in Greek, does not seek anything in return, not even acceptance of itself; its first concern is for the other. As self-sacrificing love, *agapē* in its absolute form denotes God's love—not human affection. Christians regard Christ's crucifixion as the supreme manifestation of God's love, since Christ died for helpless, sinful, unworthy human beings (Rom. 5:5–8).

In contrast to *agapē* is *eros*, self-centered love, wanting something in return for what it gives. Seeking self-gratification, erotic love tends to exploit and take advantage of someone for personal ends. It is also known as conditional love.

A third type of love is denoted by the Greek verb *phileō*. *Phileō* is based on an inner communication and mutual attraction between the person loving and the person loved. That kind of friendship feeling is commonly called brotherly love.

Genuine parental love

Healthy genuine love is essential for a good home environment. Possessive, excessive, or "super love" can cause neurotic development. It may be that overprotective mothers who never discipline their children may actually repress feelings of rejection toward the child. Awareness of such feelings produces an uncomfortable guilt. As a result the mother who excessively cuddles tries to convince herself that she loves her child. In fact she is causing the child to be immature and overly dependent.

Some overprotective parents have a neurotic need for their children to like them. Such parents will not discipline a child when that child needs it for a fear of the child's anger. A mother may ignore or complain about her child's disobedience or threaten to tell the father when he gets home, thus transferring the discipline task to another person. Her lack of discipline is a defense mechanism (called *reaction formation*) to hide underlying feelings of hatred toward herself and others. Although parents may genuinely believe they are doing what is best for the child, in reality they may be fostering attitudes of hostility and dependence.

Psychiatrists are not the only ones concerned about the genuineness of parental love for children. According to the Bible, God showed the same concern nearly three thousand years ago. "He who spares the rod hates his son, but he who loves him is careful to discipline him" (Prov. 13:24). One way to show genuine love for our children is to discipline them when they need it. We will return shortly to the subject of discipline.

Positive reinforcement also shows genuine love for a child. Some children misbehave because only in that way can they get attention from their parents. Children need positive attention and stimulation. If they cannot get it by good behavior, they will at least get some form of attention by bad behavior. Parents who often praise their children for their good behavior positively reinforce continued good behavior. Being praised makes children feel good and helps them like themselves. The biblical injunction to "make every effort to do what leads to peace and to mutual edification" (Rom. 14:19) applies to children as well as to adults. It is extremely important that each child be considered a significant person and encouraged to feel important. Really listening to a child is a good way to show that child love and respect.

Loving God

Love of God is a vital foundation for a healthy family. The Bible commands us to love God with all our heart, soul, and strength (Deut. 6:5). Loving God prepares one to love others. Jesus said, "A new commandment I give you: Love one another. As I have loved you, so you must love one another. All men will know that you are my disciples if you love one another" (John 13:34–35). The apostle John wrote, "And this is his command: to believe in the name of his Son, Jesus Christ, and to love one another as he commanded us" (1 John 3:23). God promises to reward men and women for having enough love in their hearts to live by his principles. Jesus said, "Whoever has my commands and obeys them, he is the one who loves me. He who loves me will be loved by my Father, and I too will love him and show myself to him" (John 14:21).

Husband-wife love

Love between husband and wife must be genuine for a home to be healthy. Most neurotic mother-child relationships occur at least partly because the mother needs emotional and physical love from her husband. The apostle Paul wrote:

> Husbands, love your wives, just as Christ loved the church and gave himself up for her to make her holy, cleansing her by the washing with water through the word, and to present her to himself as a radiant church, without stain or wrinkle or any other blemish, but holy and blameless. In this same way, husbands ought to love their wives as their own bodies. He who loves his wife loves himself. After all, no one ever hated his own body, but he feeds and cares for it, just as Christ does the church—for we are members of his body. [Eph. 5:25–30]

Note that "he who loves his wife loves himself" (v. 28). Loving oneself in a healthy manner is essential for developing intimate love with a mate. To love God, to love oneself in a scriptural way, and to love one's mate and children enables the person to reach out and share love with others. Many people reverse the proper order, trying to be self-sacrificing humanitarians while ignoring their children, mates, themselves, and God. It is certainly not good to put oneself self-ishly above others. Yet we cannot genuinely love others until we love ourselves in a healthy manner. God commands people to love their neighbors as much as they love themselves (Mark 12:31).

God's Word also admonishes, "Husbands, love your wives and do not be harsh with them" (Col. 3:19). Anger is not wrong; it is what we do with our anger that can be harmful. Pent-up hostility can be expressed in unconscious ways that affect one's entire family. The Bible says, "'In your anger do not sin: Do not let the sun go down while you are still angry" (Eph. 4:26). When angry with another person it is best to talk it out and then forgive one another. It is not always a sin to be angry, but it is a sin to go to bed without dealing with our anger.

Love encompasses many aspects. Love in the home implies self-worth, intimacy with one's mate, intimacy with one's children, and intimacy with God. The kind of love found in mentally healthy families provides emotional, social, and physical security.

Discipline

"Train up a child in the way he should go and when he is old he will not turn from it" (Prov. 22:6). Discipline is necessary for a child's good. Solomon warned, "Do not withhold discipline from a child; if you punish him with the rod, he will not die. Punish him with the rod and save his soul from death" (Prov. 23:13–14). "The rod of correction imparts wisdom, but a child left to himself disgraces his mother" (Prov. 29:15). Undisciplined children grow up to be imma-ture and emotionally stunted. According to Scripture, a child should be disciplined to give wisdom (Prov. 29:15 and Eph. 6:4), to avoid shaming the parents (Prov. 29:15), to keep the child from hell (Prov. 23:13–14), and to avoid ruining his or her life (Prov. 19:18).

A classic example of the result of discipline is found in 1 Samuel. Samuel's mother Hannah vowed that if she should be blessed to bear a son, she would dedicate him to the Lord (1 Sam. 1:11). Samuel grew to manhood as a very disciplined child. When the Lord called to him three times, Samuel responded without hesitation, "Here I am" (1 Sam. 3:1–10). Yet in the same household in which Samuel was raised, the priest Eli's sons were "wicked men; they had no regard for the Lord" (1 Sam. 2:12). In the end the sons of Eli the priest were slain (1 Sam. 4:10–12) and Samuel lives to be a revered and respected leader.

In the Old Testament the concept of discipline is expressed by several Hebrew words, each with a different connotation. One word, *ḥănāk*, means to train, correct, discipline, or set restrictions (Prov. 22:6). Another word for correction, *mûsār*, refers to securing obedience by physical force (Prov. 23:13). "Stern discipline awaits him who leaves the path; he who hates correction will die" (Prov. 15:10). The Hebrew *yāsēr* implies correction with both the rod and the tongue: "Discipline your son, and he will give you peace; he will bring delight to your soul" (Prov. 29:17). Taking time to talk with or train a child results in more than just blind obedience. The Hebrew *yôkyaḥ* expresses both the way God disciplines or reasons with his children, and correction imposed by parents: "My son, do not despise the Lord's discipline and do not resent his rebuke, because the Lord disciplines those he loves, as a father the son he delights in" (Prov. 3:11–12). *Yôkyaḥ* is translated "reason together" in Isaiah 1:18: "'Come now, let us reason together,' says the Lord. 'Though your sins are like scarlet, they shall be as white as snow; though they are red as crimson, they shall be like wool.'" The word *reason* implies listening, pointing out error, and directing. Thus, *yôkyaḥ* deals with the whole personality.

Discipline takes many forms. One of the best is communication. A child who understands the advantages and disadvantages of a proposed action is more willing to make the proper choice to gain the respect of parents. Another excellent method is positive reinforcement. To reward or praise a child for good deeds strengthens desirable behavior. The opposite of reinforcement is called extinction. A child who misbehaves is not rewarded, and thus undesirable behavior is weakened. The story of the prodigal son (Luke 15:11–24) is a classic example of another form of discipline: following natural consequences or trial and error. Allowing nature to take its course avoids a power struggle. Neither parent nor child becomes angry because there is no conflict. In such situations children change their behavior simply because they realize what is best for them. Rational thinking or logical consequences demonstrate another mode of discipline. Wrong is avoided because undesirable consequences may be imposed. The Bible clearly speaks of reproof and spanking as appropriate discipline for young children. Spanking occurs immediately after the offense and then discipline is over. That way a young child knows exactly why he or she is being punished. The same principle is affirmed in Scripture: "When the sentence for a crime is not quickly carried out, the hearts of the people are filled with schemes to do wrong" (Eccles. 8:11). Another method of discipline is imitation, requiring the continuous setting of a good example by the parents. Withdrawing privileges effectively disciplines older children.

Discipline sets limits as a demonstration of love. The fact that someone is in charge, just as God is ultimately in charge, produces a sense of security. Although discipline can be defined in many ways and takes many forms, it is essential. It results in peace and happiness for parents and feelings of being loved and protected for a child.

Consistency

Parental consistency is essential for healthy development of children. To feel secure, children must know their limits. When limits are not predetermined and consistently enforced, confusion arises. A child harshly treated suffers the humiliation of total domination and may live in constant fear of parental authority. Because of such oppression a child may become dependent and hostile. On the other hand, inconsistent permissiveness is equally tragic. The child may become totally self-centered, developing contempt and disrespect for those closest to him or her.

Husbands and wives must provide a united front so they can be consistent with each other in the home. Research has shown that emotional illness is not as closely related to the degree of discipline— the severity or leniency—as to inconsistency of its application. Parents should agree in order to prevent confusion, so one parent cannot be played against the other, and so the child knows what to expect. Children need to expect the same consequences every time they break a certain rule. If parents disagree on discipline, their disagreement should not be communicated in front of the children. Some Christian parents pray until they come to agreement; others assume that biblical passages referring to the husband as head of the household imply that his opinion on discipline should prevail. Jesus accepted everyone, without always accepting their behavior. Christian parents should follow his example, but their acceptance must be consistent. It is hard for children to feel accepted if they get favorable treatment at one time and unfavorable treatment another. Even when children are being disciplined, parents can show that they accept and love them in spite of their undesirable behavior.

King David once asked, "Lord, who may dwell in your sanctuary? Who may live on your holy hill?" (Ps. 15:1). David answered that question by saying that anyone who wants to live with God or have fellowship with God must be the kind of person who "honors those who fear the Lord" and "keeps his oath even when it hurts" (Ps. 15:4). David was talking about being consistent. The apostle Peter said, "Finally, all of you, live in harmony with one another; be sympathetic, love as brothers, be compassionate and humble. Do not repay evil with evil or insult with insult, but with blessing, because to this you were called so that you may inherit a blessing" (1 Pet. 3:8–9). Harmony and consistency build relationships with spouses and children.

Example

Children learn much of their behavior from their parents. They do what their parents *do* more often than what parents *say* they should do. The apostle Paul told his converts to follow his example—to do as he did. God said, "Oh that their hearts would be inclined to fear me and keep all my commands always, so that it might go well with them and their children forever" (Deut. 5:29). God shows his tremendous love for people by voicing his desire that they live by his principles so that things will go well for them and for their children, and their children's children. If people live by God's principles, later generations will follow their example.

Good example should extend beyond family into the community. God warns that any "overseer" in a church (pastor, deacon, elder) "must manage his own family well and see that his children obey him with proper respect. (If anyone does not know how to manage his own family, how can he take care of God's church?)" (1 Tim. 3:4–5). Fathers who fail to manage their own family well do not set a good example and hence should probably not be a church leader.

Authority

For various reasons more children are growing up in one-parent families. Through the grace of God it is possible for a widowed mother or a young father whose wife has deserted him and their children to "go it alone" in child-raising. The poignant difficulties experienced in such situations, however, demonstrate that families are healthiest when a father and mother cooperate in the task of parenting. Struggle for leadership between father and mother can produce neurotic children, as can the absence of a parent.

The father's role in the family is extremely important, though often neglected. Many men, their energies exhausted by their role as sole breadwinner, come home from work with little desire to play a leadership role at home. In families in which the husband alone has an outside job, his wife may envy his supposedly more satisfying place in the world. Having no other sphere in which to exercise authority, such women sometimes dominate the family. The vast majority of emotionally disturbed adults grew up in a home governed by a strong, smothering mother and a weak father who neglected his parenting and leadership responsibilities. A child's "life script" is determined by his or her identity with the parent of the same sex as well as by the interaction of the parents.

The biblical concept of headship is now a popular subject of debate. It is clear that Jesus Christ should ultimately head every Christian home, as he is head of the church. Husband and wife are equal in importance but have different biblical roles in the home. One problem is that many Christians interpret Ephesians 5:23 to mean that the man should have his way in all disagreements, in spite of the model of humble servant-leadership presented by Jesus Christ in his own teachings (Mark 10:45) and his own example (Matt. 11:29; Phil. 2:5–8). If the husband is the president, the wife should be the vice-president. In some families, however, the husband (as president) treats his wife like the secretary, filing clerk, and janitor all put together. This is neither healthy nor biblical. From the beginning God said, "It is not good for the man to be alone. I will make a helper suitable for him" (Gen. 2:18). Yet that same Hebrew word for *helper* is used most often to refer to God himself in his role of helping his people (as in Exod. 18:4; Deut. 33:7; Ps. 70:5; Hos. 13:9). It is not a master/slave relationship.

God's words to Eve after her sin were "Your desire will be for your husband, and he will rule over you" (Gen. 3:16). God intended harmony, not conflict, between the sexes. However, passages such as

Colossians 3:18 ("Wives, submit to your husbands, as is fitting in the Lord"), which speak of the subjection or submission of women have long been misused by men to justify prideful dictatorship. God desires for the husband to be the final authority in the home, but husbands should be reminded also that Ephesians 5:21 tells all Christians and family members in particular, to "submit to one another out of reverence for Christ."

The world pressures women to recognize their basic equality with men, an equality the Bible long age emphasized in its statement that God created both male and female human beings in his own image (Gen. 1:27). Many couples have come to develop a biblical leadership style as a partnership of equals—under Christ as head of the church and head of the family. God commands husbands to "be considerate as you live with your wives, and treat them with respect as the weaker partner and as heirs with you of the gracious gift of life, so that nothing will hinder your prayers" (1 Pet. 3:7). Men and women are *equal in importance in the eyes of God* even though God gave husbands and wives different leadership responsibilities within the family partnership.

Clearly, the biblical pattern of male leadership in the home is challenged today by Christians as well as non-Christians. Unfortunately, this debate extends beyond legitimate issues about how to interpret traditional husband-wife roles to condemning or subverting the institution of marriage itself. Some feminist complaints are legitimate and should be evaluated, but Christians must not let the world squeeze them into its mold (Rom. 12:2). God's advice to husbands and wives in Scripture will always be the best to follow. The concept of authority is best taught through a father who assumes the leadership role and a coleading mother who shows respect for his authority. The most psychologically healthy family environment surrounds parents who submit to Christ's authority and to each other, respectfully sharing leadership, with the husband serving as a humble, loving leader and his wife submitting in a self-assertive way.

Appendix A
Personality Types in Marriage

A vast difference exists between a personality type and a personality disorder. But each personality type combines strengths, weaknesses, and some degree of tendency toward the psychological problems of a bruised and broken world. Within a marriage each personality tendency potentially stirs up conflict—especially when combined with certain other personality inclinations in a mate. Some personalities who mix with greatest difficulty attract one another most readily. Thus, it may be helpful to consider the special needs of some more frequent personality pairings, even though neither partner may experience the extreme *disorders* found in most of our discussion.

Compulsive husband—histrionic wife

Most American marriages pair a compulsive male and a histrionic female. The husband is dutiful, conscientious, and concerned about doing everything the right way. One of the things he does correctly in Western culture is to marry a passive-dependent or histrionic wife. They complement each other. Because he infrequently feels or expresses strong emotions, he enjoys the emotional response she arouses in him. She, on the other hand, being less stable emotionally, is attracted to his apparent stability and nonemotional nature.

227

Initially such couples, through their opposite natures, attract and fulfill one another, but problems usually arise after a time. That "He can't feel!" and "She can't think!" annoys each. She seems too emotional and impulsive. He is too disciplined and rigid.

The husband's need to control himself and others becomes tiresome when he also tries to control his wife. Although passive-dependent, she may actually feel competitive within and desire to achieve power over men. The husband's emotional distance does not alleviate her intense fear of rejection. A power struggle can arise over expectations. Because his fantasies center on receiving power and hers on receiving love and attention, they have difficulty understanding each other and meeting one another's needs

He has trouble with commitment since he fears any loss of control. Commitment to marriage sacrifices a degree of control, which can frighten a compulsive individual. His stubborn frugality may be matched by her extravagance. She may tire of his constant focus on the future; he may dislike her constant emphasis on present problems. He is orderly; she tends to be disorderly. He is punctual; she doesn't care about punctuality. He is good at details; she finds it hard to plan in detail. She dislikes routine work and may be bored as a housewife, which may annoy and frustrate him. Critical by nature and logical in outlook, he gets upset with what he considers her naive actions. Although she gives an outward impression of being a poised and self-confident extrovert, she is insecure and has difficulty getting close to people on a deep level. Actually both compulsive and histrionic personalities have trouble relating to others in an intimate manner, although she conveys more warmth on the surface.

Both probably have disturbed sexual functioning. She seems frigid to him but his fear of closeness causes him to be very unspontaneous and routine in his approach to their sexual relationship. Because she is probably charming and vivacious, she may represent something of a status symbol to him. Often she grows to resent that, and she also may tire of representing a mother figure to satisfy her husband's dependency needs.

The wife may grow to feel that her husband has an overdeveloped conscience, while he may feel that hers is underdeveloped. His insistence on ultimate truth in all matters of their marriage may lead him to tell his wife things that produce hurt. She may respond in kind.

Although these two personality types can complement each other, they can also compete intensely and destroy the relationship. If the mates are willing to overlook or accept each other's basic personality traits, the husband can add stability to the marriage while the wife supplies the feelings. Christian psychotherapy or astute pastoral counseling can help such a couple to make a truly complementary relationship out of a chaotic marriage.

Histrionic husband—compulsive wife

In other marriages the wife may be perfectionistic, dutiful, and conscientious, the husband emotional on the surface and possessing a winning personality and charm. He may be a salesman. Troubles often develop because of his basic immaturity or because his surface emotions lead to extramarital affairs. The wife's rigidity and inflexibility may add to the conflicts. Their problems are reversals of the combination discussed above.

Compulsive husband and wife

When both parties stress dutiful, perfectionistic, conscientious, and orderly living, a highly competitive relationship occurs, in which each individual usually pursues his or her own interests. With unrealistic expectations for themselves and each other, both mates tend to be overly critical. Insecurity arises because both feel an intense need to depend on another individual, yet both fear that dependency and the mutual commitment that means loss of control.

Since both husband and wife have trouble relaxing and lack feelings, this is a cold marriage. Both "keep score" on themselves and their mate. Their sexual intimacy is routine and unspontaneous. The husband may have trouble with premature ejaculation and the wife with frigidity. Both problems can be traced to anxiety and a fear of losing control.

Both husband and wife may live for a future that never comes, minimizing most present pleasures. Compulsives characteristically are angry individuals, although anger is not always evident because of their defense mechanisms. Hidden anger leads to problems in this type of marriage, even when both deny being angry. Repressed anger buried in their unconscious often leads to feelings of depression.

Histrionic husband and wife

Both individuals in some marriages are likable and charming, their marriages emotional, excitable, and unstable. Because of immaturity and self-centeredness, each has trouble giving to the other. Surface emotions are emphasized because both fear deeper emotions. Neither partner is able to build deep relationships or develop intimacy.

An intense need for affection often leads to sexual conflicts to which each is prone. Her need to achieve power over men may lead to seductive conquest; so may his need to achieve power over women. Feelings rule in the marriage, and anger may be expressed continually. Each tries to manipulate the other, deeply fearing rejection. Boredom is a problem for them individually and for their marriage. Being impulsive, they have trouble planning and managing, so they may overextend themselves financially, for example.

Passive-aggressive husband and wife

In some marriages both partners are dependent, clinging, and tend to feel helpless. Each looks to the other for direction and therefore both have trouble making decisions. Stubborn and uncooperative, they both tend to put things off. Their immaturity causes trouble because each wants to receive more than he or she is willing to give. Neither understands the needs of the other because both are selfish. A low self-image is common, with neither able to build up the other. They make childish demands, both pouting at times and nagging at other times. Neither feels fairly treated by the other. Aggression, anger, and hostility are usually taken out in a passive way, but occasionally they may become more aggressive and attack each other's character.

Passive-aggressive husband—compulsive wife

In this type of marriage a passive husband needs someone to lead, control, and dominate him. All goes well until he tires of his wife's domination or she becomes frustrated, since she has none to depend on but herself, and her dependency needs remain unmet. Most male alcoholics are passive-aggressive personalities married to a compulsive, mothering type of wife. In such a case both have problems to overcome.

Sociopathic husband—histrionic wife

Histrionic women often marry sociopathic (antisocial personality) men, foolishly looking for a good-looking, sexy, and "ultra-masculine" man. Both partners are immature, self-centered, impulsive, and irresponsible. With a low frustration tolerance, both tend to blame others for their problems. Neither can accept his or her share of responsibility, and both have trouble deferring pleasure. The husband may have a poor work history, and the wife may be unstable as will. Sometimes both have been promiscuous prior to marriage. Extramarital affairs on both sides are common.

Both husband and wife manipulate, seeing their mate as someone through whom they can accomplish their own desires. Chronically feeling rejected and misunderstood, they both have trouble satisfying an inner emptiness. Such marriages usually do not last very long. Multiple marriages are common for these types of self-centered individuals.

Paranoid and/or sadistic husband—self-defeating wife

A paranoid husband is angry, hostile, jealous, and sadistic. A sadistic husband sometimes has a need to hurt others. A depressed wife with a low self-image willingly accepts blame for everything, feeling that she deserves what is imposed on her. Her masochistic need to be hurt may have prompted her to marry him because she felt she could do no better anyway. His major defense is *projection*, blaming others for his own shortcomings. Her main defense mechanism is *interjection*, accepting blame for events over which she has no control. Often a wife who is masochistic had very critical and demanding parents so she unconsciously sought a husband with the same qualities. We estimate that at least three-fourths of us tend to marry someone very similar to our parents of the opposite sex, no matter how terrible a person that parent may have been.

Self-defeating husband—paranoid and/or sadistic wife

In the opposite relationship the wife is paranoid, angry, hostile, and jealous. She projects blame onto others. If she has a depressed husband with a low self-image, he readily accepts blame and feels that he deserves what he gets. A sadistic wife has a need to hurt oth-

ers and he has a need to be hurt. She reinforces his tendency to
worry, feel blue, and be pessimistic. Guilt permeates his thoughts,
and she adds to this guilt by blaming him for everything. Craving
love, he nevertheless expects rejection. He may seek such a painful
experience in marriage because he has many times before accepted
guilt or blame for situations be did not create. The suffering also
may ease his self-critical ego. "How can I be a nobody," he reasons,
"if I am continually called an awful somebody?"

Compulsive husband—dependent wife

In this type of marriage the husband needs to feel omnipotent.
The wife needs someone to take care of her because she feels inadequate. Her attitudes, weaknesses, and illnesses make him feel more
secure because he is responsible for someone weaker than himself.
The arrangement is mutually satisfying until one or the other begins
to feel frustrated in it. The husband may grow to resent her strong
dependency and her continuing sicknesses. The wife may resent her
total dependence on someone else, although it is basically self-
imposed, since it undermines her feelings of self-worth.

Explosive husband—passive-aggressive wife

The intense outbursts of the explosive husband reveal his impaired
self-control. The passive-aggressive wife is dependent and clinging,
sometimes pouting, sometimes nagging in her behavior. Passive in
response to his authority yet stubborn and uncooperative, her half-
hearted compliance infuriates him. She may not recognize that passive-aggressive behavior has a part in triggering her husband's explosive episodes by her passive-aggressive behavior. Because of her
immaturity, she usually waits for him to apologize first. Wife-beating
occurs frequently in this type of marriage.

Schizoid or avoidant husband—histrionic wife

In this type of marriage the husband is shy and aloof, avoiding
close relationships. In contrast, the wife is emotional and intensely
needs superficial interaction on an emotional level. Both have many
dependency needs and a low self-concept, so both have a fear of
true closeness. He is afraid of people and very suspicious. She is

incapable of developing strong relationships, although to others she seems emotionally warm and extroverted.

Schizoid or avoidant husband and wife

In some relationships both partners are introverts. They are both shy, aloof, withdrawn, over-sensitive, and suspicious. Neither can lead because each is overdependent on the other. Both hunger for emotional relations, but fear the warmth and closeness of other people. Both have low self-concepts, which can produce much trouble in their marriage and also cause their children to be schizoid or avoidant. Group therapy or small-group interaction in a healthy local church frequently brings such couples "out of their shell."

Making a go of marriage

Any two personalities can develop a happy, healthy marriage if they are mutually committed to the lordship of Jesus Christ and deeply committed to each other. Rarely are personality types totally incompatible. Any two personality types can make marriage work if they grow in Christian maturity. Divorce is not necessary if both marriage partners will seriously work on their own problems.

Appendix B

Medications Used in Therapy

Although *psychoanalysis* (Freudian therapy) was once the major thrust in psychiatry, today *psychopharmacology* is at the forefront. In the past twenty years the proper use of drugs in psychiatry has completely changed the prognosis for patients. Since many psychological problems have obvious biological components, and since the Lord usually works by natural means, a Christian can accept as God's healing gift what drugs can contribute to psychiatric therapy. Because the field of psychopharmacology is broad and rapidly developing, not every physician is closely acquainted with the effects and side-effects of every drug available. Counselors and most physicians have to trust the judgment of those psychiatrists who have specialized in the field. The following discussion, adapted from chapter 10 of Frank B. Minirth's *Christian Psychiatry* (1977), focuses on four problems often seen in psychiatry or general practice.

Schizophrenia

Today a group of drugs known as the major tranquilizers has revamped the therapy of schizophrenia. The introduction of Thorazine and reserpine in 1954 stimulated the modern upsurge of interest in psychopharmacology. On these or other major tranquilizers, most schizophrenics will improve, some dramatically. For example, a woman on the verge of a break with reality, who had disturbing nightmares or could not sleep at all, showed by her speech that distorted thinking was beginning. After a few weeks of medication with a major tranquilizer, she was sleeping well with no nightmares and her disturbance in cognition had cleared up. It is impressive to see severe symptoms, such as hallucinations, delusions, and rambling speech patterns improve or disappear entirely.

Because these drugs have a wide range of biochemical reactions in the body, the specific reaction responsible for their beneficial effects remains obscured, but they have generally been proven safe and are not addicting

Depression

Because depression is so rampant in America, the introduction of antidepressive medication in 1954 has been of immeasurable value. Perhaps 70 percent of the depressed population are helped by antidepressive medication. Many patients respond with happier expressions, better moods, improved sleep, improved appetite, and increased ability to deal with their problems.

Biochemically, these drugs stimulate the brain's limbic system, improving mood, sleep, and libido. They inhibit the reticular activitating system, which also encourages sleep, and stimulate the hypothalamus, which improves appetite. Finally, they increase neurohumoral deposits, which are deficient in depressive disorders. Treating depression as a biochemical problem should be as acceptable to Christians as treating diabetics with insulin.

Anxiety

In the past few decades many minor tranquilizers have been developed to treat anxiety. Unlike the major tranquilizers and antidepressants, most of these drugs can produce physical tolerance and be addicting. Although certain intrinsic qualities have made these drugs very popular, they are potentially hazardous and should always be administered carefully. One exception seems to be Vistaril, which in the author's experience has not proven addicting.

Hyperactive children

Many children have suffered from secondary emotional and educational problems resulting from a neurologically based hyperactivity and short attention span, and learning disability. Most of these problems can now be prevented by appropriate medications that slow the hyperactivity and increase the attention span. In the author's experience, improvement is seen in perhaps 90 percent of the children.

Pharmaceutical Terms Key

One goal in this book is to describe abnormal mental conditions and their treatments as simply as possible. A stumbling block along that road is the nomenclature used for pharmaceutical drugs. Throughout the text we have opted to identify these drugs by the brand name under which most people buy and use them.

Listed below are brand names referred to in text and the generic names under which these medications are formulated. Where drugs are manufactured under more than one brand name, one name has been used throughout.

brand names	generic names
Antabuse	disulfiram
Aventyl	nortriptyline
Tagamet	cimetidine
Clozaril	clozapine
Cytomel	liothyronine sodium
Elavil	amitriptyline
Eutonyl	pargyline
Haldol	haloperidol
Librium	chlordiazepoxide
Marplan	isocarboxazid
Mellaril	thioridazine
Nardil	phenelzine
Navane	thiothixene
Parnate	tranylcypromine
Prolixin	fluphenazine

Reserpine	reserpine
Ritalin	methylphenidate
Sinequan	doxepin
Stelazine	trifluoperazine
Thorazine	chlorpromazine
Tofranil	imiprimine
Valium	diazepam
Vistaril	hydroxyzine
Vivactil	protriptyline

Summary

The following charts, which summarize several authors' experience with drugs used in psychiatry, are intended for academic use only. They are not intended to direct the use of any particular brand-named drug or treatment program.

Information presented in the following charts was compiled from several sources, including:

Blaylock, Jerry. "Psychopharmacology." Unpub. diss., University of Arkansas Medical Center, 1972.

Carson, Robert C.; James N. Butcher, and James C. Coleman. *Abnormal Psychology and Modern Life*, 9th ed. New York: Harper Collins, 1992.

Central NP Research Laboratory, Veterans Administration Hospital. *Drug Treatment in Psychiatry*. Washington: Veterans Administration, n.d.

Krupp, Marcus A., and Milton J. Chatton, eds. *Current Medical Diagnosis and Treatment*. Los Altos, Calif.: Lange, 1973.

Shannon, Robert. "Psychodynamics." Unpub. lecture, University of Arkansas Medical Center, 1972.

Smythies, J. R., et. al. *Biological Psychiatry: A Review of Recent Advances*. New York: Springer-Verlag, 1968.

Solomon, Philip, and Vernon D. Patch. *Handbook of Psychiatry*, 3d ed. Los Altos, Calif.: Lange, 1974.

Psychiatric diagnosis: # Depression

Symptoms: Sad facial expression, feelings of hopelessness and helplessness, problem with sleep, feelings of guilt, decreased appetite, anxiety.

Drug therapy indicated: antidepressant

History of drug: The prototype tricyclic was Tofranil. It was synthesized in 1954 and tested as a tranquilizer. It was accidentally found to have antidepressive activities. The first MAOI was Iproniazid. It was used to treat tuberculosis and accidentally found to have antidepressive properties.

Drugs	Side-effects	Approximate Dosage* (mg./day)
tricyclics—		
imipramine (Tofranil, SK-Pramine)	Autonomic effects, such as dry mouth and difficulty in urination.	Starting dose of tricyclics often 25–50 (3x/day).
amitriptyline (Elavil)	Cardiovascular effects, such as hypotension, tachycardia, and heart tracing changes.	Tricyclics can be given at bedtime; typical bedtime dose is 150.
doxepin (Sinequan)	Endocrine effects, such as impotence, amenorrhea, decreased sex drive, increased weight.	Maximum dose 250–300.
nortriptyline (Aventil)	Central nervous system effects, such as drowsiness, ataxia, and tremor	
protriptyline (Vivactil)		
Monoamine oxidase inhibitors (MAOI)—		
tranylcypromine (Parnate)	Similar to above.	
phenelzine (Nardil)	Hypertensive crisis.	
isocarboxazid (Marplan)		
Norepinephrine/serotonin reuptake inhibitor—		
fluoxetine (Prozak)	Nausia, sleeplessness, possible suicidal tendencies.	

*Dosages on all charts are not exact. Doctors needing details should refer to the *Physician's Desk Reference*.

Mode of Action of Antidepressants:

Some known affects are:

limbic system—stimulated, improving mood.

hypothalamus—stimulated, improving biologic functions (sleep, appetite, libido).

reticular activating system—inhibited, improving sleep.

neurohumoral deposits (deficient in depressive disorders)—increased.

Other Comments on Antidepressants:

Approximately 70 percent of depressed population can be helped by antidepressants. They do not produce tolerance and are not addicting. One to two weeks needed for antidepressants to take effect.

Tricyclics are as effective if given in a single dose at bedtime.

Therapy should usually be maintained for six months.

Tofranil, Elavil most often prescribed among antidepressant drugs. Tofranil will help in phobic reactions and is most often prescribed for bedwetting (enuresis). Usually given by mouth but also may be given intramuscularly. Elavil has sedative effects and helps induce sleep; Tofranil best for those who need to remain alert.

If a patient on MAOI has hypertrensive crisis he could be treated with Regitine (5 mg. intraveneously; repeat as needed).

Psychiatric diagnosis: # Anxiety
Drug therapy indicated: minor tranquilizer
History of drug: A large number of minor tranquilizers introduced in the last few decades.

Drugs	Side-effects	Approximate Dosage* (mg./day)
benzodiazepines—		
chlordiazepoxide (Librium)	Drowsiness. Vertigo.	15–100
diazepam (Valium)	Increased appetite. Headache.	5–60
propanediols—		
meprobamate (Miltown, Equanil)	Muscular weakness. Impaired judgment. Poor coordination. Hypotension. Bizarre behavior. Menstrual irregularities.	800–2400

*Dosages on all charts are not exact. Doctors needing details should refer to the *Physician's Desk Reference*.

Mode of Action of Minor Tranquilizers:

Antianxiety effects probably caused by depressant influence on limbic structures. They have a polysynaptic depressive effect that releases muscular spasms and muscular tension.

Other Comments on Minor Tranquilizers:

They can produce tolerance and can be addicting. If stopped abruptly, withdrawal symptoms may occur.

They produce an immediate lift.

They should not be taken with alcohol.

Most minor tranquilizers can be given by mouth, intramuscularly, or intravenously.

Psychiatric diagnosis: **Schizophrenia**
Drug therapy indicated: major tranquilizer
History of drug: Chlorpromazine and reserpine were introduced as tranquilizers in 1954.

Drugs	Side-effects	Approximate Dosage* (mg./day)	
phenothiazines—		outpatient	inpatient
chlorpromazine (Thorazine)	drowsiness, allergic skin reactions.	30–400	400–1600
thioridazine (Mellaril)	parkinsons syndrome. Mellaril may delay ejaculation.	50–400	75–800
trifluoperazine (Stelazine)	Allergic skin reactions.	4–10	6–30
fluphenazine (Prolixin)	hemotologic disorders.	1–3	2–20
perphenazine (Trilafon)	Metabolic effects (such as menstrual irregularities).	8–24	12–65
thioxanthenes—			
thiothixine (Navane)	Restlessness.	6–15	10–60
butyrophenone—			
haloperidol (Haldol)	Jaundice.	2–6	4–15
dibenzodiazepine—			
clozapine (Clozaril)	Possible immune deficiency, death.		

*Dosages on all charts are not exact. Doctors needing details should refer to the *Physician's Desk Reference.*

Mode of Action of Major Tranquilizers:

Phenothiazines are extremely active and have a wide range of biochemical reactions. Thus, it is difficult to know which reactions account for desired effects. Some known effects on the brain are:

hypothalamus—inhibited.
limbic system—unknown.
thalamus—affects neurotransmitters as dopamine.
neurohumoral deposits—inhibited.

Other Comments on Major Tranquilizers:

They decrease anxiety.
They have antiemetic, antipuritic, and analgesic effects.
They do not produce tolerance.
They have beneficial effects on cognitive disturbances and perceptual changes characteristic of schizophrenia.

When sedation is desired, Thorazine is appropriate; when sedation should be minimized, Stelazine is indicated.

In some conditions one major tranquilizer may be recommended over others. If depression is also present in schizophrenia, some therapists use Mellaril. If agitation is prominent in schizophrenia, many therapists use Haldol. For obsessive-compulsive neurosis, some therapists try Haldol.

Phenothiazines may produce depression.

Phenothiazines are more effective than electroconvulsive therapy or psychotherapy in the treatment of schizophrenia.

Most patients improve, although amount of improvement varies.

The treatment of extrapyramidal side-effects is with anticholinergics, such as Artane (2 mg. 3x/day).

Most phenothiazines can be given by mouth or intramuscularly.

Psychiatric diagnosis: # Bipolar Disorder
Drug therapy indicated: lithium carbonate
History of drug: Cade first reported beneficial effects in the manic phase of this disorder in 1949.

Drugs	Side-effects	Approximate Dosage* (mg./day)
lithium carbonate (Eskalith, Lithane, Lithonate, Lithōtabs, Phi-Lithium)	drugged feeling, drowsiness. Fine tremor. Muscular twitch. Slurred speech. Nausea, vomiting, diarrhea. Central nervous system effects.	Starting dosage, lithium carbonate, 300. A therapeutic level is a blood serum level of 1.0–1.5 mg./liter.
carbamazepine (Tegretol)	Restlessness, tremor, unsteadiness.	

*Dosages on all charts are not exact. Doctors needing details should refer to the *Physician's Desk Reference.*

Comments on Lithium:

Initially, serum levels should be monitored daily. Later they can be monitored every one to three months.

Mania breaks in five to 10 days on lithium. Contraindications to lithium therapy are brain and renal damage. Caution should be used if patient has heart damage.

Psychiatric diagnosis: # Attention-Deficit Hyperactivity Disorder
Drug therapy indicated: psychomotor stimulant

Drugs	Side-effects	Approximate Dosage* (mg./day)
methylphenidate: (Ritalin) dextroamphetamine (Dexedrene) amphetamine (Benzedrine)	Possible slowing of growth.	5–60

*Dosages on all charts are not exact. Doctors needing details should refer to the *Physician's Desk Reference.*

Bibliography

Adler, A. 1927. *The Theory and Practice of Individual Psychology*. New York: Harcourt, Brace, and World.

Atkins, J. 1991. "The State's Bad Bet." *Christianity Today* (Nov. 25): 16–21.

Bagley, C. 1973. "Occupational Class and Symptoms of Depression." *Social Science and Medicine* 7(5):327–40.

Beres, D., and S. Obers. 1945. "The Effects of Extreme Deprivation in Infancy." In vol. 1, R. Eissler, et al., eds. *The Psychoanalytic Study of the Child*, 19 vols. New York: International Universities.

Brown, B. 1974. "Depression Roundup." *Behavior Today* 5(17):117.

Brushaer, G. 1989. "Editorial." *Christianity Today* (Sept. 8).

Carson, R.; J. Butcher, and J. Coleman. 1992. *Abnormal Psychology and Modern Life*. New York: Harper Collins.

Carter, A. 1949. "The Prognosis of Certain Hysterical Symptons." *British Medical Journal* 1:1076–80.

Cole, C. 1983. "Is Gambling Sin? Christian Perspectives on the News." Radio transcript 453. Chicago: Moody Bible Institute.

Collins, G. 1972. *Fractured personalities*. Carol Stream, Ill.: Creation House.

_____. 1969. *Search for Reality*. Santa Ana, Calif.: Vision House.

Eaton, M., and M. Peterson. 1969. *Psychiatry*, 2d ed. New York: Medical Examination.

Foreyt, J. 1986. "Treating the Diseases of the 1980s." *Contemporary Psychology* 31:658–60.

Franz, W., and O. Gans. 1987. "Post-Abortion Syndrome: What We Know." In D. Andrusko, ed. *Window on the Future*. Washington, D.C.: National Right to Life Committee.

_____. 1988. "New Breakthroughs Heighten Interest in Post-Abortion Syndrome." In D. Andrusko, ed. *A Passion for Justice*. Washington, D.C.: National Right to Life Committee.

Freedman, A., and H. Kaplan, eds. 1975. *Comprehensive Textbook of Psychiatry*. Baltimore: Williams and Wilkins.

Friesen, J. 1991. *Uncovering the Mystery of MPD*. San Bernardino: Here's Life.

Gottesman, I., and J. Shields. 1972. *Schizophrenia and Genetics*. New York: Academic.

Grazier, J. 1989. *The Power Beyond*. New York: Macmillan.

Hemfelt, R.; F. Minirth, and P. Meier. 1989. *Love Is a Choice*. Nashville: Nelson.

_____. 1990. *We Are Driven*. Nashville: Nelson.

Karno, M., et al. 1988. "The Epidemiology of Obsessive-Compulsive Disorders in Five U.S. Communities." In *Archives of General Psychiatry* 45:1094–99.

Kallmann, F. 1958. "The Use of Genetics in Psychiatry." *Journal of Mental Science* 104:542–49.

Kilpatrick, W. 1983. *Psychological Seduction*. Nashville: Nelson.

Kolb, L. 1973. *Modern Clinical Psychiatry*, 8th ed. Philadelphia: Saunders.

Kringlen, E. 1978. "Adult Offspring of Two Psychotic Parents." In L. Wynne, et al., eds. *The Nature of Schizophrenia*. New York: Wiley.

Krupp, M., and M. Chatton, eds. 1973. *Current Medical Diagnosis and Treatment*. Los Altos, Calif.: Lange.

Langer, E., and R. Abelson. 1974. "A Patient by Any Other Name." *Journal of Consulting and Clinical Psychology* 42:4–9.

Lasch, C. 1979. *The Culture of Narcissism*. New York: Warner.

Locke, B., and D. Regier. 1985. "Prevalence of Selected Mental Disorders." In *Mental Health, United States, 1985*. Washington, D.C.: U.S. Government Printing Office.

Masserman, J. 1961. *Principles of Dynamic Psychiatry*, 2d ed. Philadelphia: Saunders.

McKenna, D. 1978. *Contemporary Issues for Evangelical Christians*. Grand Rapids: Baker.

_____. 1977. *The Jesus Model*. Waco, Tex.: Word.

Mehr, J. 1983. *Abnormal Psychology*. New York: Holt, Rinehart and Winston.

Meier, P. 1977. *Christian Child-Rearing and Personality Development*. Grand Rapids: Baker.

Meier, P., et al. 1991. *Introduction to Psychology and Counseling*, 2d ed. Grand Rapids: Baker.

Meier, R., et. al. 1988. *Sex in the Christian Marriage*, 2d ed. Grand Rapids: Baker.

Meyer, R., and P. Salman. 1984. *Abnormal Psychology*, 2d ed. Needham Heights, Mass.: Allyn and Bacon.

Millon, T., and G. Everly, Jr. 1985. *Personality and Its Disorders*. New York: Wiley.

Minirth, F. 1977. *Christian Psychiatry.* Old Tappan, N.J.: Revell.

Minirth, F., and P. Meier. 1978. *Happiness Is a Choice.* Grand Rapids: Baker.

Minirth, F., et. al. 1988. *Taking Control: New Hope for Substance Abusers.* Grand Rapids: Baker.

Minirth, F., et al. 1989. *Worry-Free Living.* Nashville: Nelson.

Nolan, W. 1974. *Healing: Doctor in Search of a Miracle.* New York: Random.

Owens, C. 1982. *A Promise of Sanity.* Wheaton: Tyndale.

Peck, M. 1983. *People of the Lie: The Hope for Healing Human Evil.* New York: Touchstone.

Provence, S., and R. Lipton. 1962. *Infants in Institutions.* New York: International Universities.

Ratcliff, D. 1985. "Ministering to the Retarded." *Christian Education Journal* 6:24–30.

Reardon, D. 1988. *Aborted Women: Silent No More.* Westchester, Ill.: Crossway.

Regier, D., et al. 1988. "One Month Prevalence of Mental Disorders in the United States." *Archives of General Psychiatry* 45:877–986.

Reisser, T. 1987. "Counselor Outlines the Stages of Post-Abortion Grieving." *Focus on the Family* (July).

Rogers, J.; J. Nelson, and J. Phifer. 1987. "Validity of Existing Controlled Studies Examining the Psychological Effects of Abortion." *Perspectives on Science and Christian Faith* 39:20–30.

Rosenhan, D., and M. Seligman. 1984. *Abnormal Psychology.* New York: Norton.

Rue, V. 1986. *Mourning Responses, Reconciliation, and Abortion.* Washington, D.C.: Family Research Council.

Slater, E. 1944. "Genetics in Psychiatry." *Journal of Mental Science* 90:17–35.

Smith, N. 1977. *Winter Past.* Downers Grove, Ill.: Inter-Varsity.

Smythies, J., et. al. 1968. *Biological Psychiatry: A Review of Recent Advances.* New York: Springer-Verlag.

Solomon, P., and V. Patch. 1974. *Handbook of Psychiatry,* 3d ed. Los Altos, Calif.: Lange.

Spitz, R. 1945. "Hospitalization: An Inquiry into the Genesis of Psychiatric Conditions of Early Childhood. In vol. 1, R. Eissler, et al., eds. *The Psychoanalytic Study of the Child,* 19 vols. New York: International Universities.

Spitzer, R., ed. 1987. *Diagnostic and Statistical Manual of Mental Disorders,* 3d. ed., rev. Washington, D.C.: American Psychiatric Association. Referred to in this book as *DSM.*

Szmukler, G., and G. Russell. 1986. "Outcome and Prognosis of Anorexia Nervosa," in K. Brownell and J. Foreyt, eds. *Handbook of Eating Disorders.* New York: Basic.

Watson, J., and R. Rayner. 1920. "Conditioned Emotional Reactions." *Journal of Experimental Psychology* 3 (1920): 1–14.

Wender, P., et al. 1986. "Psychiatric Disorders in the Biological and Adoptive Families of Adopted Individuals with Affective Disorders." *Archives of General Psychiatry* 43: 923–29.

Wheat, E., and G. Wheat. 1977. *Intended for Pleasure*. Old Tappan, N.J.: Revell.

Index

A Promise of Sanity, 96
Aaron, 90
Abnormal culture, 28
Abnormality, 11–20
Abortion. *See* Grief; Post-abortion syndrome.
Abusive, behavior, 25, 43, 120, 126, 150. *See also* Child abuse; Sexual abuse; Spouse abuse.
Acceptance, by God, 28, 44, 207–8; in family, 45, 51, 161–62;
Accident as stress, 25, 64
Achievement problems, 121, 144, 162
Acid secretions, 113
Acrophobia, 76
Acute diagnosis, 31
Adam, 186
Adaptive behavior, 144–45
Addiction, 8, 15, 57, 117–31, 120–23, 129, 161, 172, 187, 236, 240
Addisons disease. *See* Adrenal cortex insufficiency.
Adjustment disorders, 40–41, 67–71
Adjustment reaction. *See* Adjustment disorders.
Adler, Alfred, 204
Adolescent, depression, 38; disorders, 94, 123, 143–57; stresses, 154, 155
Adrenal cortex insufficiency, 112
Adrenal gland, 111–12

Adrenal medulla, 111
Adrenaline, 57
Aggression, 54, 56, 89, 115, 118, 121, 126, 150, 190, 196, 230. *See also* Passive-aggressive.
Agoraphobia, 75, 76
Alcohol, abuse, 38, 39, 54–55, 109, 118; dependency, 22, 39, 59–60, 110, 118, 161, 121–23, 125, 128, 129; intoxication, 118, 187; withdrawal, 119–20. *See also* Addiction; Alcohol amnestic syndrome; Alcohol withdrawal syndrome; Impulse control disorders.
Alcohol amnestic syndrome, 110, 118
Alcohol withdrawal syndrome, 108
Alcoholics Anonymous, 128, 130
Alzheimer's disease, 110
American Association for Mental Deficiency (AAMD), 145
American Psychiatric Association, 12, 140
Amitriptyline. *See* Elavil.
Ammonium chloride, 58
Amnesia, 85, 87; continuous, 85; fugue, 86, 87; general, 85; intoxication induced, 118; localized, 85; syndrome, 85

Amnestic disorder, 85, 108, 110, 115
Amphetamines, dependency, 118, 119, 121; intoxication, 120; therapy, 57, 58, 242; withdrawal, 120
Analgesics, 114
Anger, adolescent, 38; aggressive, 54; at God, 50, 169; alcoholism, 39; cyclothymia, 62; explosive, 43, 54, 125–26, 130–31, 176, 177, 180, 187, 231, 232; expressing, 110, 126, 148, 160, 161–62, 190–91, 196, 230; following abortion, 66; in organic disorders, 115; inappropriate, 22, 49–50, 51; psychosomatic illness and, 107; repressed, 36, 42, 165, 166, 174, 178, 194, 229; stage of grief, 40; verbalizing, 50
Animal abuse, 188
Anorexia nervosa, 34, 105–7, 114–15
Antabuse (disulfiram), 128, 237
Anti-hypertensive drugs, 114
Anticonvulsant medication, 130
Antidepressant medication, 115, 154, 194, 202, 236, 239
Antipsychotic medication, 115, 196
Antisocial personality, 18, 175–77, 186, 195. *See also* Sociopathic personality.

247

Anxiety, adjustment disorders, 67–68; after trauma, 64; attachment disorders, 152–55; childhood, 14, 146, 156; disorders, 13, 14–15, 73–92, 152, 159; during depression, 35, 36; generalized, 74–75, 110, 153; in marriage, 229, 232; in physical problems, 110–12, 113–14; in war, 66; incidence of, 74; intoxication, 119, 121, 123, 128; lack of, 176, 177; paranoid, 180, 196–97; persistent, 74; realistic concern, 73; treatment of, 8, 57, 61–62, 130, 191, 236, 239, 240, 241
Apathy, 110, 111, 112, 118
Apostle Paul, 41, 48–49, 51, 69, 71, 82, 148, 164, 199–200, 214, 215
Arteries, 113, 114
Asaph, 41–42, 212
Assertiveness, 50, 54, 113, 156
Assessment, 29
Association, 138
Asthma, 105–6, 114
Astraphobia, 76
Asylums, development of, 19
Attention-deficit hyperactivity disorder, 144, 146, 242
Atypical depression, 57. See also Depression.
Auditory hallucinations, 36. See also Hallucination.
Authority in families, 224–26
Autistic disorders, 146, 148–49, 156
Aventyl (nortriptyline), 57, 237, 239
Aversion therapy, 127, 128, 130
Avoidance, 16, 77, 91, 134
Avoidant personality, 152–53, 155, 182–84, 195–96

Barbiturates, dependency, 121; intoxication, 118; therapy, 58; withdrawal, 119
Behavior, disorders, 149–50; patterns, 203; abnormal 118; bizarre, 94, 95–96; in children, 146–56, 157; intoxicated, 117, 119; modification, 130, 156; self-destructive, 42; unpredictable, 21; violent, 120. See also Personality disorders.

Behavioral psychology, 20, 140, 156. See also Rewards and punishments.
Benzedrine, 242
Benzodiazepines, 240
Bible, in counseling, 199; reprogramming lives with, 208; study, 27, 52, 53, 54, 71, 77, 211, 213–14, 216
Biblical teaching, on alcohol abuse, 122–23; on antisocial personality, 176; on faith, 210; on friendship, 215–16; on gambling, 125; on homosexuality, 138–39; on love, 17–21; on obsessive-compulsive attitudes, 164–65; on passive-aggressive attitudes, 162; on self-image, 204–8; on sex, 135
Biochemical imbalance, 90, 96
Biofeedback, 102, 113–14, 116, 128
Biological factors, 39–40, 183
Bipolar disorder, 45, 47, 242
Birth control pills, 59
Blood and urine tests, 108, 109
Blood pressure, 15, 106, 107, 109, 111, 112, 118; See also Hypertension.
Body chemistry and depression, 40. See also Biochemical imbalance; Biological factors.
Body dysmorphic disorder, 80, 83
Borderline personality, 187
Brain, 15, 116; chemical interactions in, 57–58, 60, 90, 108; deterioration, 38, 102, 108, 109; dysfunction, 149; fluid pressure on, 115; surgery, 115; tumors, trauma, 28, 29, 60, 108, 112–13, 181
Brain wave changes, 152
Brief reactive psychosis, 100–1
Briquets syndrome, 81
Bronchitis, 122
Bulimia, 105–7, 114–15
Butcher, James N., 69
Butyrophenone, 241

Cabamazepine, 242
Caffeine, 118, 119
Cain, 18, 34
Cancer, 109, 113
Cannabis. See Marijuana.
Cardiopulmonary symptoms, 81

Carson, Robert C., 69
CAT scans. See Computerized scanning
Catatonic behavior, 95, 100, 102
Causes, of antisocial personality, 176–78; of anxiety disorders, 154–55; of autism, 149; of avoidant personality, 183; of behavior disorders, 150; of borderline personality, 187; of dependent personality, 183–84; of emotional problems, 204, 207, 208; of histrionic personality, 170–71; of mental retardation and learning disabilities; of narcissistic personality, 186–87; of obsessive-compulsive personality, 165–68; of paranoid personality, 181; of paraphilias; of passive-aggressive behavior, 161–62; of personality disorders, 189; of post-traumatic stress, 65–67; of psychological problems, 12, 13, 18, 21–32; of schizoid personality, 178–79; of schizotypal personality, 185; of sexual dysfunction, 139; of speech disorders, 148–49; of substance abuse, 123; of tic disorders, 151–52
Center for Pathological Gambling, 124
Central nervous system, 117
Cerebral cortex, 241
Certainty in diagnosis, 30–31
Charisma of histrionic, 168, 173–74, 229, 230
Chemical changes in brain, 57, 58, 60, 108, 117
Child abuse, 24, 126, 139, 155, 177, 187, 188, 189. See also Early environmental factors; Pedophilia; Psychological abuse; Sexual abuse.
Child and adolescent disorders, 16, 116, 143–57
Chlordiazepoxide. See Librium.
Chlorpromazine. See Thorazine.
Christ, accepting, 48, 129, 176, 195, 209–17; as counselor, 18; as leader model, 225–26; death of, 209, 218; example of, 16; growth in, 211–17; model for friendship, 206;

need to know, 209–11; resource of, 209; self-worth in, 204; sufficiency of, 42; victory in, 48, 104, 129, 176, 191, 195, 204, 207–8

Christian, beliefs, 185; counselors, 17, 20, 55, 56, 82, 172, 200, 202, fellowship, 199–200, 215–16; problems, 11, 26–29

Chromosome changes, 60

Cimetidine. See Tagamet.

Cirrhosis, 121

Classification, mental disorder, 12–17, 25

Classifying mental disorders, 12–17

Claustrophobia, 76

Cleanliness compulsion, 167

Clinical depression. See Depression.

Clinical psychologists, 56

Clozapine. See Clozaril.

Clozaril (clozapine), 102, 237, 241

Cluttering, 147

Cocaine, 118, 119, 121

Cognitive, disturbances, 241; retraining, 103

Cole, C. Donald, 125

Colitis, 106

Collins, Gary, 13, 16–17, 26–29, 65–66, 77, 123, 129

Commitment to marriage, 228

Communication, 140, 224; disorders, 156

Community mental health clinics, 20

Compulsions, 12, 15, 38, 76–80. See also Obsessive-compulsive.

Compulsive. See also Obsessive-compulsive.

Computerized scanning, 112–13

Concentrate, ability to, 119, 146, 156, 237

Conditional love, 165, 166

Conduct disorder, 68, 149, 157, 162

Confession. See Sinful behavior.

Conscience, 24, 37, 41, 176, 195, 228. See also Guilt.

Consciousness, change in. See Dissociative disorders.

Continuous amnesia, 85

Conversion disorder, 80, 82–83, 84, 91

Coronary artery disease, 122

Counseling, children, 151, 153, 157; Christian, 17, 55, 56, 82, 90, 209; definition of, 25, 199; effectiveness of, 20, 89, 212; in organic problems, 113–16; in personality disorders, 189–90; inpatient, 203; methods, 113, 114; need for, 8, 12, 16, 17, 64, 181; of obsessive-compulsives, 90–91; of psychotics, 102, 103; post-abortion, 71–72; post-rape, 71; specialties, 199, 200–202; techniques, 29–31, 128, 139, 196

Crisis telephone services, 71

Cultural factors, 13, 40, 106, 107, 123

Cure. See Recovery.

Cushings syndrome, 110. See also Hyperactive adrenal cortex.

Cycle, of depression, 37; of inhibition and rejection, 162; sexual response, 133, 134, 139

Cyclothymia, 45, 46, 47, 61–62

Cytomel (liothyronine sodium), 59, 237

David, 26, 34, 41, 100, 180, 204, 212, 213–14, 224

Death, 14, 127, 171, 152, 153, 155, 185, 191

Defense mechanisms, 37, 54, 167, 180, 181, 194, 197, 205, 219, 229, 231

Deficiency diseases, 109, 112

Deficient receptive language problems, 146–47

Deinstitutionalization movement, 20.

Delayed language acquisition, 146

Delinquency, 24, 123, 150, 176

Delirium tremens, 108

Delirium, 107, 108, 111, 118

Delusional disorder, 100, 103. See also Delusions.

Delusions, depressive, 36; of reference, 94; organic, 108, 109, 112, 118; psychotic, 15, 93, 94, 95; schizoaffective, 101, 179; treatment of, 236. See also Paranoid; Schizophrenia.

Dementia, 107, 109–10, 115, 118, 145

Demon possession, 19, 86–87

Denial, 40, 181, 197

Dependency, 16, 42, 51, 54–55, 73, 130, 160–62, 173, 183, 187, 190, 191, 192–93, 194, 219, 227, 229, 230, 232

Dependent personality, 183–84. See also Dependency; Histrionic personality.

Depersonalization disorder, 85, 87, 119

Depression, 33–62; adult, 38, adolescent, 38; alcoholic, 121; atypical, 57; causes of, 7–8, 13, 24, 36–37, 126; clinical, 14, 34–45, 202; post-abortion, 66; from dementia, 115; from medication, 114; from stress, 26; genetic factors in, 22, 23–24; in antisocial, 176; in children, 153–54; in personality disorders, 159, 163, 168, 173, 185, 187, 188, 191, 194, 231; in war, 66; incidence of, 17, 34; organic causes for, 109–13, 115; schizoaffective, 100; substance abuse related, 118, 119; symptoms of, 35–36; treatment for, 202, 212, 236, 239. See also Moods, extreme.

Desensitization, 89–90, 156

Development, 154; arithmetic disorder, 144, 146; articulation disorder, 144, 146; disorders, 146; expressive writing disorder, 144; language disorder, 144, 146–47; reading disorder, 144, 146

Dexedrene, 242

Dextroamphetamine, 242

Diabetic delirium, 108

Diagnosis, 29–32;, 112–13, 190

Diagnostic and Statistical Manual of Mental Disorders. See DSM.

Diagnostic labels, 30–32

Diazepam. See Valium.

Dibenzodiazepine, 241

Diet, 58, 115. See also Eating disorders.

Directive therapy, 20

250 Index

Discipline, parental, 24, 42,–45, 97, 126, 152, 156, 177, 205, 219, 221–23
Disorganized schizophrenia, 95
Disorientation, 107, 108, 109, 111, 115
Dissociative disorders, 85–92; treatment of, 91–92
Disulfiram. See Antabuse.
Divorce, 25, 38, 41, 67, 127, 153, 191
Dopa, 57
Dopamine, 57, 103, 241
Dosage levels, 57, 58–59
Double bind hypothesis, 97
Downs syndrome, 147
Doxepin. See Sinequan.
Dream anxiety disorder, 47
Dreams, 120, 153
Drug dependency. See Addiction; Impulse control disorders.
Drug therapy. See Medications.
DSM, 12, 14, 16, 33, 81, 87, 93, 95, 96, 106, 108, 118, 120, 134, 138, 140, 143, 183, 184, 188, 189
Dysfunctions, sexual. See Sexual disorders.
Dyspareunia, 134, 135
Dysthymia, 33

Early childhood. See Early environmental factors.
Early environmental factors, 24–25, 26, 27; anxiety, 75, 89; depression. 36, 42–45; family, 28, 97, 127, 156, 205, 219, 221–23; impulse control disorders, 123, 126, 129; personality disorders, 165, 170–71, 176–77, 181, 183, 185–87, 189, 195; phobias, 77–79; psychosis, 101; retardation, 147; schizophrenia, 96–97; sexual dysfunction, 135, 137, 138, 139, 141; somatoform disorders, 83; stresses, 13, 22, 113; trauma, 91–92.
Early treatment of mental illness, 18
Eating disorders, 35, 54, 105–7, 114–15
Eccentric thought, 94, 95–96, 184
Echolalia, 149

ECT. See Electroconvulsive treatment.
EEG. See Electroencephalography.
Ego dystonic homosexuality, 140–41
Ego gratification, 160
Elation. See Manic episode.
Elavil (amitriptyline), 57, 115, 237, 239
Elderly, depression in, 38; medication for, 59
Elective mutism, 147, 148
Electroconvulsive treatment (ECT), 60–61, 102, 104, 241
Electroencephalography (EEG), 109, 112, 126, 130, 177
Electrolytes, 58
Electrostimulation, 130
Eli's sons, 221–22
Elijah, 40, 214–15
Elimination disorders, 150–52, 156
Emotions, 68, 109, 191; changes in, 49, 110, 111; handling responsibly, 22; of histrionic, 168, 173; of schizophrenia, 94, 95–96; reserves, 55; self-destructive, 42
Emphysema, 122
Encephalitis, 149
End around, 103–4
Endocrine system, 40, 110, 112
Environmental factors, 13, 178. See also Early Environmental factors.
Envy, 180
Epileptoid personality, 126
Episodic diagnosis, 31, 100
Equanil, 240
Eroticism, 179, 180. See also Sexuality.
Eskalith, 242
Estrogen replacement therapy, 59
Etiology, 12
Euphoria, 60, 118, 119
Euthanasia movement, 19
Eutonyl (pargyline), 57, 237
Eve, 186, 225
Evil personality disorder, 189
Evil spirits, 18
Exercise, 92, 114
Exhibitionism, 136, 137
Exodus, Book of, 90
Expectorants, 58

Explosive, disorders, 43, 124, 125–26, 130–31; personality, 231. 232. See also Anger.
Eyes, 82, 118, 120

Facial expression, 120, 184, 191, 239
Factitious disorder, 81
Faith, 28, 68
Fall of humankind, 26
False guilt, 49, 165, 206
Family, 28, 30, 42, 51; communication, 96–97, 101; dysfunctions, 28, 155–56; healthy, 217–26; help from, 130
Fantasy, 178–79, 185
Fatigue, 110, 111, 120, 121; and depression, 34, 40; in war, 66
Fearful thoughts, 17, 38, 73, 87, 107, 111, 119, 152–53, 165, 166, 167, 177, 182, 184, 196, 206, 230, 232
Feedback, 37
Fellowship groups. See Group therapy.
Female sexual arousal disorder, 133, 135
Fetal alcohol syndrome, 147
Fetishism, 136, 137–38
Flagellant movement, 19
Flashback hallucinations, 119. See also Reexperiencing an event
Flooding, 90
Fluoxetine, 239
Fluphenazine. See Prolixin.
Folie a deux. See Induced psychotic disorder.
Foreplay, 135, 139–40
Forgiveness, 19, 41, 50, 51, 61, 66, 71, 141, 165, 209
Fragmented thought, 185
Free association, 89, 91–92
Friendship, 51, 54, 69, 92, 157, 206–7, 215–16
Friesen, James, 86–87
Fromm, Erich, 28
Frotteurism, 136
Fugue state, 86
Functional, encopresis, 150–52; enuresis, 150–52

Gambling, 123, 124, 127, 187
Gastrointestinal problems, 81

Gender identification disorders, 136, 137, 152, 154, 155, 187

General amnesia, 85, 88, 89–92

Generalized anxiety, 74–75, 110, 153

Genetic factors, 22–24, 25, 26, 27, 39, 46, 75, 96, 120, 123, 147, 178, 181

Genius, 17

German measles, 149

Gheel colony, 18–19.

God, alienation from, 13; correction from, 26–27; grace of, 44, 49, 108, 165; help from, 128; law of, 165; love of, 218; pursuit of, 211–12; reconciliation with, 207; sovereignty of, 23, 29, 65; ability to restore, 65; will of, 185

Grand mal seizures, 119

Grandeur, delusion of, 36, 94

Grief, 13, 14, 25, 38, 40, 67, 69; post-abortion, 66–67, 71; somatoform disorders and, 83

Group therapy, 20, 90, 114, 129, 130, 156, 191, 195, 196, 233

Growth, physical, 110

Guidelines for mental health, 48–62, 190

Guilt, feelings of, 53, 66, 71, 84, 167, 188, 206, 209, 219, 232, 239; as stage of grief, 40; false, 13, 41, 49, 185; inability to feel, 175–77; irresponsible handling of, 22, 77, 169; true, 35, 41, 49, 209

Haldol (haloperidol), 102, 115, 237, 241

Halfway houses, 103

Hallucinations, 15, 93, 94, 95, 100, 101, 103, 108, 109, 110, 111, 112, 119, 120, 121, 215, 236

Hallucinogen intoxication, 118, 119, 121

Hallucinosis, 118

Haloperidol. See Haldol.

Hand washing compulsion, 76–77

Hannah, 221

Head trauma, 108, 110, 113, 115, 144, 147

Headaches, 106, 107, 120. See also Migraines.

Headship. See Authority in families.

Healing, emotional, 7–9; spiritual, 18

Heart, problems, 59, 102; pulse, 105–6, 107, 118, 119, 120

Heat/cold intolerance, 110, 111

Heights, fear of, 78

Helping others as therapy, 67

Hepatitis, 121

Heredity. See Genetic factors.

Heroin. See Opioids.

Hezekiah, King, 212

High blood pressure. See Hypertension.

High, drug, 118, 121

Hippocrates, 18

History of treatment, 17, 18–20

Histrionic personality, 24, 168–75, 193–94, 227–30, 232–33; seductive, 169–70, 172, 173, 230, manipulation, 171, 172, 174, 175, 230, 231, impulsiveness, 168, 175, 194, 230, 231

Hitler, Adolph, 19

Holy Spirit, 42, 48, 185, 210, 214

Homeless, 20

Homosexuality, 22, 39, 126, 136, 138–39, 140–41, 178

Hope, 55–56, 164

Hormones, 40, 107, 110–13

Hospitalization, 12, 16, 17, 61, 102, 109, 129, advantages of, 203; disadvantages of, 203–4. See also Inpatient treatment.

Hostility, 35, 38, 42, 43, 46, 51, 100, 125–26, 178, 179, 180, 181, 206, 212, 219, 230, 231

Humor in counseling, 104

Hydrocephalis, 115

Hydrophobia, 76

Hydroxyzine. See Vistaril.

Hyperactive adrenal cortex (cushings syndrome), 111–12

Hyperactivity, 16, 110–11, 146, 156, 237

Hyperkinetic reaction of childhood. See Hyperactivity.

Hyperparathyroidism, 111

Hypersensitivity, 179, 181, 182

Hypersomnia, 47

Hypertension, 57, 59, 113, 114

Hyperthyroidism, 106, 110–11

Hypoactive sexual desire, 133, 134

Hypochondriasis, 35–36, 73, 80, 81–82, 84

Hypocrisy, 192, 197

Hypoglycemia (low blood sugar), 112

Hypomanic episodes, 45–46, 61–62

Hypoparathyroidism, 111

Hypothalamus, 236, 239, 241

Hypothyroidism, 110, 111

Hysteria, 18, 57

Ideas of reference, 184

Identity disorder, 152, 154, 155. See Dissociative disorders.

Illnesses, imagined, 36, 37, 38. See also Hypochondria; Masked depression.

Illogical fear. See Phobias.

Illusions, 119

Imiprimine. See Tofranil.

Imitation, 113

Immaturity, 123, 229, 230, 231, 232

Immune system, 118

Implosion, 90

Impotence, 126, 135

Impulse control disorders, 15, 117–31, 123–31

Impulsive tendencies, 121, 146, 230; of histrionic, 168, 175, 194, 230, 231; of hypomanic, 46; of antisocial, 175–78

Incidence, of abnormality, 17; of depression, 39; of manic depression, 46

Incoherence, speech, 94, 95, 100; thoughts, 93, 95

Induced psychotic disorder, 100, 101

Inferiority, complex, 204, 205; feelings of, 101, 163–64, 204

Influences on behavior, 21–32

Inhalants, 58, 60, 118, 120, 121–22, 123, 127–28, 161

Inhibited orgasm, 133–34

Inpatient treatment, 169, 202–4. See also Hospitalization.

Insecurity, 13, 24, 161, 165, 167, 204–8

Insight, 55, 199, 203, 209
Insomnia, 34, 47, 119, 120,
    121, 152, 202. *See also* Sleep
    deprivation.
Insulin coma therapy, 61
Intelligence quotient (I.Q.),
    143, 144, 146, 149, 172
Intermittent explosive disorder.
    See Anger; Explosive disor-
    ders.
Intern's syndrome, 31
Internalizing feelings, 54
Interpersonal school of psycho-
    analysis, 206
Interview, counseling 30
Intestinal problems, 119
Intimacy, feelings of, 48, 51,
    167, 179, 204, 206–7; with
    God, 204, 207–8
Intoxication, 108, 117, 118–19,
    120. *See also by type.*
Introspection, 28–29, 34–35,
    49, 55
Introverted personality, 178–79
Iproniazid, 239
Irrational beliefs, 94, 141
Irresponsible behavior, 22–23,
    37, 39, 121, 175, 206
Irritability, 36, 45, 73, 118, 121
Isocarboxazid. *See* Marplan.

Jealousy, 94, 100, 179–80, 231
Jerusalem, Jeremiah's lament
    for, 64–65
Job, 40
Jones, Jim, 28

Kegel muscle, 140
Kidneys, 109, 111
Kilpatrick, William K., 186
Kleptomania, 123, 125, 130
Korsakoff syndrome. *See* Alco-
    hol amnestic syndrome.

Language, development, 146,
    149; repetitious, 7; use, 115
Larynx, 110
Lasch, Christopher, 186
Laughter in mental health, 56
Learning disorders, 143–44,
    146–49, 155, 157, 237, 242
Learning theory of phobias, 75,
    77, 80
Left-right discrimination, 146
Legalism. *See* Perfectionism.
Lesbianism. *See* Homosexuality.
Lethargy in depression, 14, 94,
    95, 119

Librium (chlordiazepoxide), 89,
    191, 237, 240
Licensure, counselor, 201
Limbic system, 236, 239, 240,
    241
Liothyronine sodium. *See*
    Cytomel.
Lipid tissues, 58
Lithane, 242
Lithium, 47, 57–58, 242
Lithonate, 242
Lithotabs, 242
Liver disease, 109
Living one day at a time, 92
Localized amnesia, 85
Loneliness, 38, 51, 178, 183,
    187, 204, 206–7
Lot, 122
Love, for others, 52; for God,
    77, 220; for self, 56; in fam-
    ily, 24, 150, 217–21,
    223–24, need for, 205,
    217–21, 232; worldly, 205
LSD, 110. *See also* Hallucino-
    gens.
Lust, 54, 87, 136, 205

McKenna, David, 125
Madonna-prostitute complex,
    126
"Magical thinking," 84, 184,
    185
Major depression, 33, 45, 100
Major tranquilizers, 58, 59,
    115, 196, 236, 241
Maladjustment. *See* Stress.
Male erection disorder, 133
Manic, depression, 23–24,
    45–47, 57–58, 111;
    episodes, 33, 45, 100, 101.
    See also Hypomanic episodes.
Manipulating, environment, 56;
    others, 37, 51, 55, 84, 160,
    168, 171, 172, 173–75,
    194, 230, 231
MAOI inhibitors. *See*
    Monoamine oxidase
    inhibitors.
Marijuana, 60, 119; depen-
    dency, 121
Marplan (isocarboxazid), 57,
    237, 239
Marriage and family counselors,
    200, 201, 202
Marriage relationships, 14, 39,
    43, 52, 67; avoidant person-
    ality, 231, 232–33; obses-
    sive-compulsive personality,

163–64, 166–68, 227–29,
    230, 232; dependent person-
    ality, 183, 232; explosive
    personality, 232; histrionic
    personality, 227–230, 231,
    232; incompatibility, 173;
    paranoid personality, 182,
    231; passive-aggressive per-
    sonality, 162, 230–31, 232,
    232; sadistic personality,
    231–32; schizoid personality,
    232–33; self-defeating per-
    sonality, 231–32; sociopathic
    personality, 231
Masked depression, 37
Masochism, 37, 136, 137, 138.
    See also Masochistic personal-
    ity.
Masochistic personality, 188,
    231
Masserman, Jules H., 88
Maturity, 199–200, 211
Medical doctors, 57, 201, 202
Medication, prescribing, 201;
    abuse, 195; antidepressant,
    39, 40, 47, 57–60; antipsy-
    chotic, 101–2, 103; anxiety,
    71, 89; for children, 156; for
    obsessive-compulsive disor-
    ders, 90; for organic disor-
    ders, 115; for passive-aggres-
    sive disorders, 191; for
    psychosomatic illness, 113;
    in-patient treatment, 203;
    listing, 235–42; need for, 8;
    for sleepwalking, 153; reac-
    tion to, 26, 58; schizophre-
    nia, 235–36, 241; side-
    effects, 59, 128, 202,
    235–42
Meditation to alleviate anxiety,
    92
Megavitamin therapy, 59, 102
Mellaril (thioridazine), 58, 102,
    115, 237, 241
Memory, impairment, 60, 107,
    108, 109, 112, 115, 118;
    healing therapy, 71; suppres-
    sion, 87
Meningitis, 149
Menstrual, cycle in depression,
    35, 40; pain, 106
Mental retardation, 16, 26, 143,
    144–45, 146, 149, 156, 157
Meprobamate, 240
Metabolism, 120
Methadone, 128
Methylphenidate. *See* Ritalin.

Middle-life, changes in, 38
Migraine headaches, 114
Miltown, 240
Minimal brain dysfunction
    (MBD), 146
Minimal cerebral dysfunction,
    146
Minor tranquilizers, 59, 236,
    240
Misconceptions about abnor-
    mality, 16–17
Modeling, 90, 91, 104, 127,
    141, 155
Mongolism. *See* Downs syn-
    drome
Monoamine oxidase inhibitors
    (MAOI), 57, 59, 239
Mood, disorders, 14, 33–62;
    enthusiasm, 7; genetic fac-
    tors in, 23–24; swings, 7,
    23–24, 74, 118, 120, 187;
    treatment of, 48–62. *See also*
    Depression.
Moral treatment movement, 20
Mosaic law, 122, 138
Moses, 90, 148
Motivational disturbances, 60,
    94, 119, 121
MRI scans. *See* Computerized
    scanning.
Multiple personality disorder,
    15, 85, 86–88
Muscle movement, involuntary,
    82, 95, 111, 119. *See also*
    Tic disorders.
Muscular coordination loss, 108
Myxedema madness. *See*
    Hypothyroidism.

Nail biting, 151
Narcissistic personality disorder,
    186–87, 189
Narcissus, 186
Narcolepsy, 47–48
Nardil (phenelzine), 57, 237,
    239
Nasal decongestants, 57
Nathan, 204
National Council on Compul-
    sive Gambling, 124
National Institute of Mental
    Health, 11
Nausea, 106, 112, 118
Navane (thiothixene), 58, 102,
    237, 241
Nebuchadnezzar, 18, 96
Necrophobia, 76

Negative thinking, 48–49, 55,
    103
Neurohumoral deposits, 236,
    239, 241
Neurological, abnormality, 130;
    factors, 181; impairment,
    152; somatoform disorder,
    81
Neuron response, 40, 103, 115
Nicotine. *See* Inhalants.
Night terrors, 47, 153
Nightmares, 153, 236
Noah, 122
Non-rapid-eye-movement
    (NREM) sleep, 48
Nonadrenaline, 57
Nonschizophrenic psychotic dis-
    orders, 100–1
Nonsensical speech, 93, 95
Norepinephrine, 239
Nortriptyline. *See* Aventyl.
Novocaine, 57

Obedience-defiance conflict,
    165
Obesity, 106
Obsessions, 15, 76–80. *See also*
    Obsessive-compulsive.
Obsessive-compulsive, disorder,
    74–75, 76–80, 90; traits, 12,
    160, 163–68, 191, 220–21,
    227–29, 230, 232
Obstructionism, 160, 169
Occupational problems, 14, 19,
    67
Odd communication, 184, 185
On Stage as One, 86
One-parent families, 224–25
Opioids, 118–21, 128
Oppositional defiant disorder,
    150, 157
Organic, anxiety disorder, 108,
    110; brain syndrome, 12–13,
    112; causes, 113, 177, 189,
    235–42; treatment, 113–16;
    delusional disorder, 108; dis-
    orders, 8, 14, 107–13; fac-
    tors, 27, 28; hallucinosis,
    108, 110; mood disorder,
    108, 110, 118; obsessive-
    compulsive disorders, 90;
    personality disorder, 108,
    110. *See also* Physical illness.
Orgasm, 118, 134, 135,
    139–40
Outpatient psychotherapy, 202
Overanxious disorder, 152, 153

Oxygen deprivation, 26, 108,
    109, 115, 147, 149

Pain, somatoform disorder, 81
Painful thinking, 34–35
Pamelor, 40
Panic, attacks, 108, 110, 119;
    disorder, 74–75, 89
Paralysis conversion, 82
Paranoid, personality, 179–82,
    196, 231–32, schizophrenia,
    179; thoughts, 95, 111, 118,
    119, 185. *See also* Delusional
    disorder.
Paraphilias, 15, 133, 136–40,
    188
Parathyroid gland abnormalities,
    111
Parental, control, 181; disci-
    pline, 206; inconsistency,
    187; love, 219–20; neglect,
    185; overprotection, 97,
    184, 187, 207, 219; passiv-
    ity, 24, 97; rejection, 183,
    207; relationships, 14, 52,
    206; separation, 152, 177.
    See also Early Childhood fac-
    tors.
Parents, 150
Pargyline. *See* Eutonyl.
Parnate (tranylcypromine), 57,
    59, 237, 239
Passive-aggressive, behavior,
    150, 169, 173; personality,
    159–63, 181, 190–91, 230
Pastoral counselors, 17, 200–1,
    202
"Patient" vs. "client," 32
PCP, 118
Peck, M. Scott, 188, 189
Pedophilia, 15, 136, 138, 139
"Peeping Tom." *See* Voyeurism.
Peer group, 123, 155, 183
Perception, 119, correcting
    faulty, 91; of schizophrenia,
    94, 95–96; of stressful event,
    68–69
Perfectionism, 24, 41, 43, 44,
    49, 56, 77, 107, 159,
    163–68, 192, 206, 229
Pernicius anemia, 112
Perphenazine, 241
Persecutory delusions, 36, 94,
    179, 180–81
Persistent hypersomnia, 47
Personality, changes, 60, 110,
    112; disorder not otherwise
    specified, 188; disorders, 16,

27, 29–30, 108, 121, 159–97; influence of, 22; traits, 113; types, 38; types and disorder, 227

Pervasive developmental disorder, 149

Pessimism, 34–35, 49, 55

PET scans. *See* Computerized scanning.

Pharaoh, 90

Phenelzine. *See* Nardil.

Phenothiazines, 241

Phenylketonuria, 149

Phi-Lithium, 242

Phobias, 12, 14–15, 21, 57, 74–80, 89–90

Physical, effects of substance abuse, 117–23; coordination, 119; defects, 183; evaluation, 29, 108; hygiene, 115; illness, 15, 67, 103. *See also* Hypochondriasis; Organic; Psychophysiological disorders; Psychosomatic illnesses; Somatoform disorders.

Physician's Desk Reference, 239–42.

Pituitary gland, 112

Plan of action, 52–53

Play therapy, 116, 156

Pontius Pilate, 77

Post-abortion syndrome, 66, 71

Post-traumatic stress disorder, 63–67, 70

Postpartum depression, 38–39, 40

Pramine, 239

Prayer, 18, 27, 52, 70, 92, 211–12, 214–15, 216, 214–15, 216

Precipitating stress, 22, 25–26, 27, 40–42

Predisposition. *See* Genetic factors.

Presenile dementias, 109–10

Preventing problems, 199–226

Pride of life, 205–6, 208

Procrastination, 92, 160, 169

Prodigal son, 222

Prohibition, 129

Projection, 180, 181, 197, 231

Prolixin (fluphenazine), 102, 237, 241

Propanediols, 240

Protriptyline. *See* Vivactil.

Provisional diagnosis, 30

Prozak, 239

Psychiatrists, 12, 14, 56, 57, 84, 200, 201, 202

Psychoactive drugs. *See* Medications.

Psychoanalysis, 235

Psychogenic fugue, 85, 86

Psychological, abuse, 189; effects of substance abuse, 117–23; problems, 11–16

Psychologists, 12, 73, 140, 147, 186, 200, 201, 202

Psychology assistants, 201

Psychology associates, 201

Psychomotor, retardation, 118; stimulation, 242

Psychopharmacology, 235–42

Psychophysiological disorders, 27, 105–16, 110

Psychosis, 15, 27, 93–104, 185, 202; biblical examples of, 1896, 100; during grief, 25; causes, 96–97, 112, 118–19; symptoms, 109, 115; treatment, 58, 60, 61, 101–4, 202, 241

Psychosomatic illness, 8, 15, 68, 105–7, 113–16

Psychosurgery, 104

Psychotherapy, 12, 25, 114, 130, 191–97, 202, 203, 241

Psychotic disorders. *See* Psychosis.

Punishment. *See* Discipline, Rewards.

Pyromania, 124, 125, 127

Quiet time, 211–13

Rape, 64, 71

Rapid-eye-movement (REM) sleep, 48

Rational emotive therapy, 140

Reaction formation, 167, 205, 219

Reactive, attachment disorder, 152, 154; depression, 34

Reality, distorted, 15, 93; therapy, 191

Reconciliation, with self, 66–67

Recovery, 17, 32, 94, 115, 199–226

Recreation, 130

Reexperiencing an event, 63, 64

Regression, 91–92, 178

Reisser, Terri, 66–67

Rejection, fear of 42, 51, 54; feelings of, 35, 42–45, 47, 188; in family, 43, 45, 97,

126, 150, 177, 183, 187, 195, 205; of God, 27; of those with problems, 16; syndrome, 51

Relaxation therapy, 70, 89–90, 91, 104, 113, 114, 156, 193

Religion as factor, 28

Religious tendencies, of antisocial, 177; of histrionic, 169, 172; of obsessive-compulsive, 163–64

Reliving past, as treatment, 91; during grief, 40–41. *See also* Reexperiencing an event.

Remission, 31

Renal dialysis, 102

Repentance. *See* Sinful behavior.

Repression, 39, 78, 79, 181

Reproductive problems, somatoform disorder, 81

Reprogramming thinking, 48, 49, 50

Requirements of counselors, 200–1

Reserpine (reserpine), 59, 236, 238, 241

Residual schizophrenia, 96

Responsibility, 35, 55, 169, 183, 186–87, 190, 194, 203

Responsiveness, 56, 149

Rest, 65, 70, 113, 114, 115

Retardation, levels of, 145. *See also* Mental retardation.

Reticular activating system, 236, 239

Retirement, 67

Retreat at York, 19–20.

Revenge, 50

Rewards and punishment, 114, 116, 126, 127, 138, 155, 156, 157, 171. *See also* Behavioral psychology.

Ritalin (methylphenidate), 58, 59, 156, 238, 242

Rituals, 76–77, 128, 167

Role-playing, 89, 113

Rue, Vincent, 71

Rumination disorder of infancy, 14

Sad affect, 34, 38

Sadistic, personality, 37, 231–32; disorder, 188, 189

Samuel, 221–22

Sanctification, 167

Satiation, 130

Saul, King, 18, 100, 180, 204

Scapegoating, 189

Schizoaffective disorder, 100, 101
Schizoid personality, 178–79, 182, 195–96
Schizophrenia, 7–8, 15, 93–100, 189; causes, 96–97, 112; genetic factors, 24; medications used to treat, 235–36, 241; types of, 96, 184, 185
Schizotypal personality, 184–85
School psychologists, 200, 201, 202
Secondary gain, 84–85
Sedative abuse, 118
Seductive behavior, 168, 169–70, 171, 172, 173, 180, 194, 230
Seed program, 129
seizures, 110
Self, assertiveness, 183, 187; centeredness, 52, 49, 229, 230, 231; concept, 13, 35, 36, 41, 43, 45, 49, 50, 51, 56, 231, 233; control, 232; criticism, 34–35, 55, 165, 204; deceit, 26; defeating personality, 188, 189, 191, 231–32; esteem, 20, 39, 48, 182, 183, 186, 187; gratification, 176; insight, 193; labeling, 128; problems with, 128; talk, 70, 90, 128, 130, 141; punishment, 36, 37; understanding, 167; verification, 206; worth, 181, 204–8, 232
Self-help movement, 186
Selfishness, 163, 164, 175, 178
Sensate focus, 139
Sensory deprivation, 110
Separation anxiety, 183–84, 187, 206; disorder, 152
Seratonin in brain, 90, 239
Servant-leadership, 225
Sexual, abuse, 24, 171, 189; aversion, 133; behavior, 38, 110, 169–70, 171, 177–78, 187, 205, 212–13, 229, 231, 176; desire, 180; development, 106; disorder not otherwise specified, 140–41; disorders, 133–41; during depression, 35; dysfunction, 15, 102; fantasies, 133, 134; feelings, 165, 133, 134, 139–40; from medication, 114; hormonal, 40; inhibi-

tions, 118; paraphilias, 15, 133, 136–40, 188; premature ejaculation, 134, 140; repression, 167; response cycle, 133, 134, 139; sadism, 136, 137, 138, 188 ; somatoform disorder, 81, 84
Shock, after trauma, 64; in war, 65–66
Shock treatment. See Electroconvulsive treatment.
Short-term memory, 110
Shyness. See Avoidant disorder
Side-effects, medication, 59, 128, 202, 235–42
Sinequan (doxepin), 57, 238, 239
Sinful behavior, 16, 18, 26, 41, 49, 56, 136, 138, 141, 150, 189, 197, 207, 208, 209
Sleep, disorders, 33, 35, 65, 47–48, 64; nightmares, 153, 236; paralysis, 48; therapy, 60, 61, 92; terrors, 47, 153, 236; walking, 47, 153
Sleep-wake schedule disorder, 47
Smiling depression, 34
Smoking. See Inhalants.
Snakes, fear of, 21, 76, 78, 89–90
Social, adjustment, 149; isolation, 184; phobia, 76, 90; relationships, 67, 152
Socio-economic factors, 23, 34, 94
Sociopathic behavior. See Antisocial personality.
Sociopathic personality, 231
Solomon, 17, 49, 135
Somatic therapies, 60–61
Somatization disorders, 80, 81, 82, 84–85
Somatoform disorders, 80–85, 91
Song of Solomon, 135
Spanking, 223
Specific developmental disorders, 146
Speech, disorders, 147–49, 157; in schizophrenia, 7, 184–85; 236; problems, 115, 118; therapy, 146–47, 156
Spiritual, factors, 26, 204–17; growth, 27, 73; healing, 82–83, 84
Spouse, abuse, 188, 189, 232; love, 220–21

Stages of trauma recovery, 64–65
Stanford-Binet intelligence test, 144
Stealing, 150, 187
Stelazine (trifluoperazine), 102, 238, 241
Stereotypy/habit disorder, 150–52
Steroid medication, 110
Stigma of abnormality, 16, 17, 203
Stimulation deprivation, 147, 185
Straight drug abuse program, 129
Stress, 22, 146–72, 152, 153, 177, 178, 180, 190, 203, 216; disorder, 75; in organic illness, 113; inoculation therapy, 70; overwhelming, 41; reactions, 107; universality of, 16. See also Precipitating stress.
Stroke, 115
Stuttering, 16, 147–48
Subconscious. See Repression.
Submissive personality, 160, 161, 183
Suggestibility after trauma, 64
Suggestion, 91
Suicide, 8, 24, 26, 28, 35, 44, 53, 60, 61, 80, 121, 124, 162, 163, 164, 168–69, 171, 187, 194, 202, 203
Sullivan, Harry Stack, 206
Supercritical attitude, 181, 204
Superego, 46, 126
Support, 215–16, 233
Suspicion, 50, 94, 110, 159, 179, 180, 181–182, 184, 232, 233. See also Paranoid.
Sybil, 86
Symbolic desires, 167

Tagamet (cimetidine), 113, 237
Talkativeness, 45, 118, 119
Teen Challenge, 129, 157
Tegretol, 242
Temper. See Anger.
Temporary hypersomnia, 47
Temporary insomnia, 47
Temptation, 180
Tension, 73, 74
Tests, intelligence, 144; psychological 29–30
Thalamus, 241
Thiamine deficiency, 110

Thioridazine. *See* Mellaril.
Thiothixene. *See* Navane.
Thioxanthenes, 241
Thorazine (chlorpromazine),
    102, 236, 238, 241
Thought-stopping, 91
Three Faces of Eve, The, 86
Thumb-sucking, 151
Thyroid, extract, 59; gland, 40,
    108, 109, 110–11
Thyroxin, 110
Tic disorders, 150–52, 156–57
Tobacco. *See* Inhalants.
Toccoa Falls College disaster, 67
Tofranil (imiprimine), 40, 57,
    115, 238, 239
Token economy system, 103
Tolerance, medication, 120
Tourettes syndrome, 151, 152
Toxic psychosis, 111
Toxicity, medication, 102
Toxins, 109
Traits, personality, 16, 159. *See
    also by personality type.*
Tranquilizers, 114, 191; major,
    58, 59, 115, 196, 236, 241;
    minor, 59, 236, 240
Transient tic disorder, 151
Transsexualism, 136, 137, 154,
    155
Transvestic fetishism, 136, 137,
    138
Tranylcypromine. *See* Parnate.
Trauma, 28, 87, 109, 110. *See
    also* Post-traumatic stress dis-
    order; Stress.

Treatment, child and adolescent
    disorders, 156; impulse con-
    trol disorders, 127; mood
    disorders, 48—62; personal-
    ity disorders, 189; psychotic
    disorders, 101–4; sexual dys-
    function, 139–41; stress and
    adjustment disorders, 69–72
Trembling, 111, 119, 121
Trichotillomania, 124
Tricyclic antidepressants, 57,
    58, 59, 60, 239
Trifluoperazine, 238, 241
Trifluoperazine. *See* Stelazine.
Trilafon, 241
Tuke, William, 19
Tumors, 111, 112, 113, 115
Twin studies, 23, 24, 39, 96

Ulcers, 15, 106, 107, 111,
    113–14
Undifferentiated schizophrenia,
    96

Vaginismus, 134, 135
Valium (diazepam), 59, 89,
    191, 238, 240
Value system, 24, 130
Vascular, accidents, 110; dis-
    ease, 122
Verbalizing feelings, 61, 70, 91
Viral illness and depression, 40,
    110
Vision, blurred, 119
Vistaril (hydroxyzine), 236, 238
Visual hallucinations, 36

Visualizing therapy, 70
Vitamin, and hormone therapy,
    59; B_6, 59; B_{12} deficiency,
    112 ; C, 58
Vivactil (protriptyline), 57, 238,
    239
Voice and body language, 30
Voyeurism, 15, 136, 138

War, stress of, 14, 64, 65–66
Watson, John, 77
Weakness, physical, 110, 111,
    112
Wechsler adult or child intelli-
    gence test, 144, 145
Weight, body, 110, 111, 120
Western culture, 163
Wheat, Ed and Gayle, 140
Witchcraft, 19.
Withdrawal, 40, 42, 44, 68, 94,
    95, 97, 108, 117, 118,
    119–20, 127–28, 178, 180,
    182, 184, 206
Witnessing, 216–17
Workaholism, 163–68
Worry, 68, 73, 74, 92. *See also*
    Anxiety.
Worship, 77
Worthlessness, feelings of, 14

X-ray photography, 112
Xenophobia, 76

Zoophilia, 136, 137
Zoophobia, 76